The Art of Literary Research

Third Edition

ALSO BY RICHARD D. ALTICK

PREFACE TO CRITICAL READING
THE COWDEN CLARKES
THE SCHOLAR ADVENTURERS
THE ENGLISH COMMON READER
LIVES AND LETTERS
BROWNING'S ROMAN MURDER STORY (*with James F. Loucks II*)
TO BE IN ENGLAND
VICTORIAN STUDIES IN SCARLET
VICTORIAN PEOPLE AND IDEAS
THE SHOWS OF LONDON

Editions

THOMAS CARLYLE: PAST AND PRESENT
ROBERT BROWNING: THE RING AND THE BOOK

ALSO BY JOHN J. FENSTERMAKER

CHARLES DICKENS 1940–1975: AN ANALYTICAL SUBJECT INDEX TO
PERIODICAL CRITICISM OF THE NOVELS AND CHRISTMAS BOOKS

The Art

of

Literary

Research

RICHARD D. ALTICK

Third Edition

Revised by John J. Fenstermaker

W · W · NORTON & COMPANY

New York · London

Copyright © 1981, 1975, 1963 by W. W. Norton & Company, Inc.

Published simultaneously in Canada by
Penguin Books Canada Ltd,
2801 John Street, Markham, Ontario L3R 1B4.

Printed in the United States of America
All Rights Reserved
Third Edition

Library of Congress Cataloging in Publication Data
Altick, Richard Daniel, 1915–
  The art of literary research.
  Bibliography: p.
  Includes index.
  1. Literary research.
2. English literature—
Study and teaching.
3. American literature—
Study and teaching.
I. Fenstermaker, John J.
II. Title.
PR56.A68 1981   807.2
81–11178
AACR2

W. W. Norton & Company
500 Fifth Avenue, New York, N.Y. 10110
W. W. Norton & Company Ltd.
37 Great Russell Street, London, WC1B 3NU

ISBN 0-393-95176-6

3 4 5 6 7 8 9 0

Contents

Preface to the First Edition

This volume is the final one of a totally unpremeditated trilogy which began with *The Scholar Adventurers* (1950) and continued with *Selective Bibliography for the Study of English and American Literature* (edited in collaboration with Andrew Wright, 1960). Like those earlier books, *The Art of Literary Research* is meant for everyone interested in the whys, whats, and hows of literary investigation, from the college undergraduate writing his research paper or honors thesis to the scholar of mature years who doesn't mind reading about things he already knows by heart.

The approach is designedly informal; I have had no intention of composing a systematic treatise on the materials and methods of literary research. Except for Chapter Three, which is made up of brief and simplified descriptions of several important individual branches of inquiry, the book is concerned with the spirit and techniques that are common to all research. Its aim is less to teach the reader how to accomplish specific tasks than to suggest what it is like to be a scholar. There is a real distinction.

Most of my examples and suggestions for further reading are derived from the published scholarship of the past twenty or thirty years. I have thus passed over numerous more or less "classic" illustrations of this or that point, but the loss is at least balanced, I think, by the gain in immediacy. I have tried to show the prospective or newly fledged scholar what kinds of research are now most pursued, and what contributions they make, in their various ways, to our understanding of literature and of literary history. Many better-informed readers doubtless will regret the omission of some of their favorite examples of good or bad, fruitful or futile, scholarship, which may well be as apropos and instructive as those which I cite. To them I can only offer my apologies and confess myself among the number who, in Dr. Johnson's phrase, "are ignorant in spite of experience."

Presiding over the development of the volume have been Professors M. H. Abrams and Stephen M. Parrish, both of Cornell University, to whom I owe a great deal of hardheaded advice. I need hardly add that nothing I say in these pages should be held against them. My research assistant, David Young, has carefully verified the factual material, but for whatever errors may remain I of course assume sole responsibility. I shall be chagrined but grateful if notified of them, although I cannot offer the guinea with which, by tradition, the Oxford University Press used to reward every discoverer of a mistake in its Bibles.

Two enormous debts must be recorded. One is to my colleagues in the Department of English at the Ohio State University, who by their intellectual stimulation and their published research have constantly exemplified to me the full meaning of the phrase "community of scholars." In addition, they have, for the past twenty years, let me teach English 980, a graduate seminar in Bibliography and Methods of Research; this book is in part an extension of remarks made there. The other debt is to the alumni of the course themselves, some of whom, after recuperating from the long days and nights spent "working on 980" in the university library, have admitted to me that the experience, however traumatic, was residually instructive. They will never know how much I learned from having to keep one step ahead of them. In brief, whatever worth the following chapters possess may be taken as proving afresh the old truth that one's post-doctoral education may confidently be entrusted to one's colleagues and students—at least if they are of the kind mine have been.

R. D. A.

Preface to the Third Edition

This freshly revised edition of *The Art of Literary Research* appears at a time when short-term prospects for academic employment in the humanities, including the field of literature, are bleak. We have thought it best, however, not to address this discouraging situation in the text, since every reader will be aware of it without any reminder from us. But we should stress a point which is at least implied in the pages that follow: namely, that the habits of mind congenial to, and nurtured by, literary research are valuable in more than a few occupations outside Academia—in law, for example, in journalism, and in some areas of business and government. Far from equipping young men and women solely for positions in higher education, where research, accomplished or prospective, normally is a condition of employment and advancement, the principles and techniques described here can help qualify them for satisfying occupations wholly removed from the classroom. Hence, the book's practical usefulness is in no way diminished by the current depression of the academic job market; the width of its applicability is simply more demonstrable in these new circumstances.

Various changes have been made to bring the book up to date. In recognition of the increasing importance of electronic aids in humanistic scholarship, the pages on the functions of the computer in specifically literary research have been revised and somewhat expanded. The text, exercises, and reading list contain much new material. In part, the new exercises and illustrative examples have been drawn from recent publications in what might be called "traditional" scholarship in English and American literature, with greater attention than heretofore to research in the work of present-day authors. Others have been chosen to show how readily the principles and procedures of that scholarship can (indeed, if the published results are to carry authority, must) be adopted for research in such recently developed fields of serious literary interest as women's studies, black studies, film, and science fiction. But the new material offered here does not necessarily represent, by any means, the best that might be drawn from the published research of the past five years. It is simply selected from what has chanced to come to our attention for one reason or another.

Although frequent references to doctoral-level graduate study have been retained from earlier editions, we should emphasize that the reported experience of many teachers and students has justified the author's hope that the book would prove equally serviceable to those pursuing literary research in a master's degree program, and even, to a substantial degree, in undergraduate honors work.

We gratefully acknowledge the counsel we have received from teachers of courses in the materials and methods of literary research, as well as, on occasion, their students; their criticisms have been most helpful in our efforts to bring this edition in line with current needs, even though we have been unable to adopt some of their individual suggestions. Our reviewers, Frederick Newberry, University of Oregon, Gertrude Schroeder, Troy State University, and Peter L. Shillingsburg, Mississippi State University, were also extremely helpful. The library staff at Florida State University, where the revision was carried on, remained unflappable despite frequent queries and occasional frantic searches. And our particular thanks go to Dr. Linda A. Dover, who worked long hours, carefully and resourcefully, on the new material and offered many excellent editorial suggestions.

R.D.A.
J.J.F.

* * *

In no other subject [but literature] is the pupil brought more immediately and continuously into contact with original sources, the actual material of his study. In no other subject is he so able and so bound to make his own selection of the material he wishes to discuss, or able so confidently to check the statements of authorities against the documents on which they are based. No other study involves him so necessarily in ancillary disciplines. Most important of all, no other study touches his own life at so many points and more illuminates the world of his own daily experience. I see no reason why we should be afraid to confess that our subject is highly delightful to study and to teach at any and every level.

 —Helen Gardner, "The Academic Study of English Literature," *Critical Quarterly*, I (1959), III.

* * *

A love of precision joined to aspirations toward general ideas; respect for historical facts, and warm appreciation of beautiful writings; minuteness in research, and breadth of view; finesse in analysis; strictness in criticism; penetration in aesthetic judgments; lastly, exacting loyalty toward oneself, toward facts, toward the ideas and the men studied,—these are a few of the valuable qualities that, thoroughly understood and thoroughly carried out, literary studies tend to develop.

 —André Morize, *Problems and Methods of Literary History* (Boston, 1922), p. viii.

* * *

Genuine scholarship is one of the highest successes which our race can achieve. No one is more triumphant than the man who chooses a worthy subject and masters all its facts and the leading facts of the subjects neighbouring.

 —E. M. Forster, *Aspects of the Novel* (New York, 1927), p. 22.

* * *

* * *

Life is a continuous process of finding the holes and plugging them and making as few new ones as possible.

—Sir William Haley, then editor-in-chief of the *Encyclopaedia Britannica,* quoted in the *New York Times,* March 10, 1968.

* * *

Over all [the scholar's work] should rule a searching intelligence, asking that fundamental question of the sceptic: just what do you mean by that? And if that question is asked with a real desire to know and understand, if the imagination is centred upon people —dead people once alive—and sympathy and judgment are controlled by scholarship and by a mind of quality, the work can be done. All the deficiencies of knowledge and writer notwithstanding, the historian can rest assured that he can fulfill his ambition to know and tell about the past. His can never be the last word, an ambition in any case bred out of vanity, but he can establish new footholds in the territory of truth.

—G. R. Elton, *The Practice of History* (New York, 1967), p. 141.

* * *

Le spectacle de la recherche est rarement ennuyeux. C'est le tout fait qui répand la glace et l'ennui.

—Marc Bloch, French historian, quoted in Iris Origo, *Images and Shadows: Part of a Life* (New York, 1970), p. 184.

* * *

Abbreviations of Titles Used in This Book

AL	American Literature
BL	British Library
BNYPL	Bulletin of the New York Public Library
ELN	English Language Notes
JEGP	Journal of English and Germanic Philology
MLN	Modern Language Notes
MLQ	Modern Language Quarterly
MLR	Modern Language Review
MP	Modern Philology
NCBEL	New Cambridge Bibliography of English Literature
NUC	National Union Catalog
PBSA	Papers of the Bibliographical Society of America
PMLA	PMLA: Publications of the Modern Language Association of America *
PQ	Philological Quarterly
RES	Review of English Studies
SB	Studies in Bibliography
SEL	Studies in English Literature
TLS	[London] Times Literary Supplement
UTQ	University of Toronto Quarterly
VS	Victorian Studies

Except in one or two respects, notably the omission of the publisher's name in citations of books, the *form* of documentation throughout has been made to agree with that urged by the *MLA Handbook*. However, rigid consistency in the distribution of references between text and footnotes and in the fullness of citations in the text has not been sought, in order that the various alternatives available to the scholarly writer might be illustrated. Conciseness, clarity, and convenience are more to be desired than absolute standardization of practice.

* The initials are the official title.

The Art of Literary Research

Third Edition

CHAPTER ONE

Vocation

Our business, as I understand it, is to find out in a humble spirit of inquiry what literary masterpieces really say.
—Howard Mumford Jones in *Sewanee Review,* 39 (1931), 76.

All literary students are dedicated to the same task, the discovery of truth. Some prefer to regard themselves primarily as critics, some as scholars; but the dichotomy between the two is far more apparent than real, and every good student of literature is constantly combining the two roles, often without knowing it. The difference is mainly one of emphasis. The critic's business is primarily with the literary work itself—with its structure, style, and content of ideas. The scholar, on the other hand, is more concerned with the facts attending its genesis and subsequent history. Believing that every work of art must be seen from without as well as from within, he seeks to illuminate it from every conceivable angle, to make it as intelligible as possible by the uncovering and application of data residing outside itself. The ultimate beneficiary of his fact-

gathering, therefore, is criticism. While facts have a certain
charm in themselves, as every history-minded person knows,
the scholar values them in direct proportion to the help they
afford—at once or in prospect—in understanding specific pieces
of literature and the interaction of many works that constitutes
what is called literary history.

Neither criticism nor scholarship occupies an exclusive territory, nor does either have a monopoly on certain methods. Both
study the literary text; both bring external information to bear
on it. And both, at their best, observe the same rigorous respect
for facts and logic. The inseparability of the two has been well
stated by the Canadian scholar-critic George Whalley:

> No true scholar can lack critical acumen; and the scholar's eye is
> rather like the poet's—not, to be sure, "in a fine frenzy rolling," but
> at least looking for something as yet unknown which it knows it
> will find, with perceptions heightened and modified by the act of
> looking. For knowing is qualitative and is profoundly affected by
> the reason for wanting to know. Again, it is clear that no critic can
> afford *not* to be a scholar—even a scholar in a pretty impressive
> degree—if his work is to go much beyond delicate impressionism,
> penumbral rhetoric, or marginal schematism. Without scholarship
> every synoptic view will be cursory, every attempt at a synthesis a
> wind-egg; without scholarship the criticism of a poem may easily
> become a free fantasia on a non-existent theme.[1]

This belief, that the scholar and the critic are engaged in a
common pursuit and that each is indispensable to the other,
underlies all the following pages. These will be devoted for the
most part, however, to that portion of the enterprise which
conventionally (however arbitrarily) is supposed to be the
research scholar's province: the quest for truth in places outside
the literary work. Apart from brief discussions of the methods
of establishing a sound text and of dealing with disputed authorship, this book will not touch on questions which presumably
can be decided by a close analysis of the author's words alone.
But it will continually try to show how vital external data are
to the accurate and adequate understanding of the text.

Here is a *Hamlet*, here is a lyric by Shelley, here is a *Huckle-*

---

1. "Scholarship and Criticism," *UTQ*, 29 (1959), 40–41.

berry Finn. Each is intelligible in itself, and any attentive reader can derive immense pleasure from it. But almost every literary work is attended by a host of outside circumstances which, once we expose and explore them, suffuse it with additional meaning.

It is the product of an individual human being's imagination and intellect; therefore, we must know all we can about the author. Sainte-Beuve's critical axiom, *tel arbre, tel fruit,* is a bland oversimplification, to be sure, but the fact remains that behind the book is a man or woman whose character and experience of life cannot be overlooked in any effort to establish what the book really says. The quality of a writer's imagination, the genetic and psychological factors that shaped his personality and determined the atmosphere of his inner being, the occurrences, large and small, that fed the store from which he drew the substance of his art: all these must be sought, examined, and weighed if we are to arrive at a valid understanding of what he intended when he put pen to paper.

But a writer never exists in a vacuum. Whatever private influences are involved, he is also the product of his age and place; however original, even rebellious, his attitude toward his world may be, his mental set is fatefully determined by his social and cultural environment. To understand his book we must also understand the manifold socially-derived attitudes—the morality, the myths, the assumptions, the prejudices —which the writer brought to it. And since, in the overwhelming majority of instances, he wrote not for himself but for a specific audience of his contemporaries, and only incidentally for us, we must try to find out precisely how the mingled ideas of his and their world affected the book's shape and content. Most especially is it necessary to reconstruct the standards of taste, of literary intention and craftsmanship, which prevailed in his time.

Again, a book has both antecedents and a history of its own. Not only can its content be related to more or less immediate models or sources of inspiration; it may belong to a tradition that stretches back for centuries or even millennia and can be traced in the literature of half a dozen countries. "No poet, no artist of any sort," wrote T. S. Eliot in his seminal essay on "Tradition and the Individual Talent," "has his complete meaning alone. His significance, his appreciation is the appreciation of his relation to the dead poets and artists. You cannot value him alone; you must set him, for contrast and comparison, among the dead." But at the same time, he must be set among the poets and artists who were to come. His book has cast its shadow across later ages, perhaps inspiring new fashions and traditions, and in any event affecting other writers and suggesting the form and manner of other works. To read *Gulliver's Travels* or *Erewhon* with ideal perception, we have to know how they fit into man's perennial quest for a happier society, either through satire or through the vision of Utopia; and that means ranging from Plato's *Republic*, Juvenal's satires, and medieval Celtic imprecations to *Candide*, *News from Nowhere*, and *1984*.

Literary research, then, is devoted, for one thing, to the enlightenment of criticism—which may or may not take advantage of the proffered information. It seeks to illuminate the work of art as it really is, and—the difference may be considerable—as it was to its first audience; equally, it tries to see the writer as he really was, his cultural heritage and the people for whom he wrote as they really were. But while this is unquestionably its major *raison d'être*, it has at least one other important function. Literary history constitutes one of the strands of which the history of civilization itself is woven. Like its sister disciplines of musicology and art history, it finds its material in the vast array of records we have inherited of the imaginative side of human experience—in its case, the representation in language of that experience. Literature preserves for us, for example, the poignance of medieval man's aspiration towards Heaven though held down by mortal chains; the excitement of Renaissance man's awareness of the splendors that environ him in the here and now; the cool and candid re-estimate of the world and himself that eighteenth-century man made under the auspices of revolutionary science and skeptical philosophy; and the spiritual chiaroscuro of wasteland and earthly paradise, the bewildering series of shocks and recoveries, to which modern man has been subjected in the past two centuries. Literature, then, is an eloquent artistic document, infinitely varied, of mankind's journey: the autobiography of the race's soul. And whatever the practical "uses" of history may be, one of the marks of civilized man is his absorbed interest in the emotional and intellectual adventures of earlier generations. Looked upon simply as a branch of cultural history, the reconstruction and interpretation of our literary past has its own dignity.

Finally, there are the unmeasurable but intensely real personal satisfactions that literary research affords men and women of a certain temperament: the sheer joy of finding out things that have previously been unknown and thus of increasing, if but by a few grains, the aggregate of human knowledge. I have sought to describe the sources and qualities of this pleasure in an earlier book, and they will occasionally appear again in the following chapters. The genuine scholar is impelled by a deeply ingrained curiosity, an undeniable urge to learn as well as to teach. "And *gladly* wolde he lerne."

Dramatic discoveries do not occur as often now as they did earlier in the century, when a steadily enlarging body of eager scholars first studied great hoards of rare books and manuscripts, in both institutional and private ownership, which had hitherto been inaccessible to inquirers or simply unknown. Still, significant finds do occur from time to time. Not long ago, Charles W. Mignon, a professor at the University of Nebraska, upon being informed that there was "some old book" at Ernie Long's bookstore in Lincoln which might prove interesting, dropped into the shop for a browsing session and found, in a batch of books awaiting assessment, a hitherto unidentified manuscript of thirty-six sermons written in the seventeenth century. These were no ordinary sermons, because they were from the pen of the colonial New England poet Edward Taylor, whose devotional poems themselves had come to light as recently as 1936. This manuscript had been owned by one of the poet's descendants, whose great-grandmother had brought it to Nebraska from North Carolina in 1877. A second-hand bookstore in Lincoln, Nebraska, "right next to Marie's Oasis bar and—on the other side—Dirty Dick's Pawn Shop and not too far from the Adult Bookstore and Cinema X," is not the most likely nor even the most suitable place for the long-lost sermons of a colonial poet and divine to resurface. But, as Mignon says, "Rising up out of this scum I think would somehow have pleased Taylor."

An obviously undeterminable amount of material bearing upon literary history and biography remains in private hands, not only in Britain and America but wherever a writer's descendants or the purchasers or inheritors of his manuscripts may have settled. In the 1760's, Bishop Thomas Percy, an early student of English literature from Chaucer to Dryden and the editor of the first collection of old ballads (*Reliques of Ancient English Poetry*, 1765), wrote in at least two copies he owned of Langbaine's *An Account of the English Dramatic Poets* that a number of manuscript plays by one Cosmo Manuche, who was writing in the 1650's, were in the library of the Earl of Northampton at Castle Ashby. A century and a half later, in 1907, Sir Sidney Lee, gathering material for an article on Manuche in the *Dictionary of National Biography*, came upon Percy's list of those plays in the copy of Langbaine that had been acquired by the British Museum. Inquiries established that the manuscript of one Manuche play was indeed at Castle Ashby, but access to it was not to be had. The possible presence of others prompted Alfred Harbage, when he was writing his *Caroline Drama* (1936) and again when preparing the first edition of his *Annals of English Drama* (1940), to send letters of inquiry to Castle Ashby. They went unanswered.

There matters rested until 1977, when another American scholar, William P. Williams, was editing Manuche's play *The Banished Shepherdess* from the manuscript copy owned by the Huntington Library in California. Another copy of this play was among those which, Percy had recorded, "usually lie on ye shelf over the Door" in the library at Castle Ashby. Now an editor of a literary text must take account of all manuscript copies of the text that he can locate; and so Williams, though he had no expectation of succeeding where Harbage and others had failed, wrote to the ninety-two-year-old Marquess of Northampton. After an interval during which one reply was lost in the mail, the Marquess's son, the Earl Compton, reported to Williams that, quite by accident, he had found the manuscript of *The Banished Shepherdess* at the back of a drawer in an old desk.

Williams flew at once to England and, welcomed by Lord Compton and his household staff, was given the rediscovered manuscript to inspect prior to taking it away to be micro-filmed. "After I had examined the manuscript for about thirty minutes," says Williams, "Lord Compton came back to see how I was getting on, and after a few minutes of conversation I framed the crucial question. 'Have you,' I asked, 'found any other manuscripts along with this one?' He replied that he had found these other 'things'—indicating a pile of manuscript volumes—in the same drawer. 'Why, would they be of interest to you?' I indicated that they would, and we began to work through the pile." One by one, each of the plays in Percy's list turned up in these volumes, some of which also contained plays that were *not* in the list. During that September after-noon in the heart of the Northamptonshire hunt country, no fewer than seventeen old plays came to light. The next year, the entire collection was bought by the British Library.[2]

Episodes like this sometimes occur not only in English country mansions but in modern research libraries, where, efficient though most of them are nowadays, important manu-scripts and individually significant copies of printed books re-main inadequately catalogued or simply overlooked. Another recent discovery suggests that Providence has been looking with special favor upon students of seventeenth-century Eng-lish literature. In 1973, Arthur H. Scouten and Robert D. Hume were the first to recognize and act upon a clue that had been in plain sight for almost a decade, in S. Schoenbaum's revision (1964) of Harbage's *Annals of English Drama*. On pages 166–67 of that standard guide it is noted that a play called *The Country Gentleman*, by Sir Robert Howard and G. Villiers (i.e., the Duke of Buckingham), was projected for production in 1669 but never performed, and that its text was

2. We are grateful to Professor Williams for providing this narrative. For details of his discovery, see his article, "The Castle Ashby Manu-scripts: A Description of the Volumes in Bishop Percy's List," *The Library*, 6th series, 2 (1980), 391–412.

lost. (Contemporary records tell us that it could not be performed for political reasons; its explosive content had, in fact, caused a governmental crisis.) On page 317 of the same work, in a list of extant play manuscripts, occurs the entry: "*The Country Gentleman*. Folger Shakespeare Lib. MS. V. b. 228." Scouten and Hume put two and two together and, merely by visiting the Folger and calling for the manuscript, had their hunch rewarded. Here, in a scribal copy made about 1695, was the very play that had been lost for three centuries (and only the second Restoration play to be recovered during the present century). If clinching proof of its authenticity were needed, it lay in the fact that the manuscript contained a scene described by people who had seen the original, or heard about it, in 1669.[3]

Not many years ago, in the basement of the Archbishop's House, Westminster, an old cobwebbed tea chest proved to contain the voluminous editorial correspondence of the *Dublin Review*, an important nineteenth-century periodical. The two thousand letters to the *Review*'s editor enabled the editors of the *Wellesley Index to Victorian Periodicals* (see below, page 91, note) to identify the authors of 90 percent of the periodical's articles, only 4 percent of which had been signed when printed. At about the same time, the long despaired-of lifting of the legal interdict which had formerly prevented the publication of any part of the rich treasure of Tennyson manuscripts at Trinity College, Cambridge, initiated a whole new era in the study of the poet's texts. As a result, the history of the composition of such poems as *In Memoriam* and *Idylls of the King* is now being rewritten.

Such developments are occurring in almost every field of literary study. Although discoveries may not be as frequent as they used to be, the existing materials make it certain that, given a fair degree of imagination, originality of approach, solidity of learning (to avoid mare's nests), and the wish and the will to see works of literary art and their creators from new perspectives, everyone called to the profession will discover amply rewarding projects.

In America during the last half century or so, most literary research has been done by academic people, and publishing

3. See *TLS*, September 28, 1973, pp. 1105–6.

the results of research has provided the traditional boost up the professional ladder. Unfortunately, the notorious cliché "publish or perish" still describes the attitude of many college and university administrators charged with deciding the fate of young untenured faculty members. The validity of such a criterion for promotion and tenure remains, as it has been for many years, a hotly debated issue. A three-word slogan, of course, grotesquely oversimplifies what is, in truth, a complicated academic situation and an equally complicated relationship between published scholarship and the purposes of higher education. Any external pressure to write scholarly books and articles is pernicious not only because it may well divert a career from its natural course, thus causing a good deal of personal unhappiness, but because scholarship performed under duress is seldom very good scholarship. Indeed, it is to the "publish or perish" mentality that we can attribute the present bloated condition of the annual bibliographies and the appearance, in the proliferating journals, of a lamentable amount of incompetent, pretentious, or trivial writing that should have been intercepted somewhere between the typewriter and the press.[4] Furthermore, and perhaps worst of all, this mentality falsifies the whole rationale of scholarship, placing it on a crass mercenary basis whereas, if it deserves to be supported in a humanistic society, its practice must be motivated by altruism.

Among the wisest words ever uttered on this much-vexed topic are those of the late Morris Bishop, the Cornell specialist in French literature and writer of light verse and detective stories:

. . . I am not against research. I practice it, I honor it, I love it. But a taste for literary research is something special. It is not the same thing as delight in reading, or delight in introducing others to the pleasures of reading or the pleasures of writing. We do well to encourage literary research. We do ill to impose it as a requirement for promotion and status in the teaching profession. Literary research is a privilege, deserving of no reward except

---

4. The *MLA International Bibliography* for 1960 included 13,000 entries from approximately 1000 periodicals; by 1970 the number of serials and journals the bibliographers examined had climbed to 2500 and in that year yielded 36,000 entries; in 1978, 206 bibliographers tabulating the contents of 2877 periodicals listed 46,762 items.

the writer's joy in his article, his book, his public utterance of his precious thought.[5]

It may well be that, as Dr. Johnson held, "no man but a blockhead ever wrote, except for money"; if so, the history of literary scholarship at its best is populated with amiable blockheads. The crucial test of a scholar's devotion is his indifference to the rewards, in rank and salary, that his publications bring him. He may be as attentive to the creature comforts as any man, but it is his itch to learn more, not the prospect of enlarged salary checks, that draws him to the library after his classes are met, his papers graded, and his appointments kept.[6]

Besides the pleasure of learning things, the habit of research, when assiduously cultivated, offers one other undeniable reward —that of doing something well. To anyone whose pretensions

5. *PMLA*, 80 (1965), p. A-6. Similar sentiments have been expressed more recently and perhaps more bitterly by William D. Schaefer, executive director of the Modern Language Association of America, 1971–78: ". . . during that critical period of the 1960's our record was flawless in that, as a profession, we managed to do everything wrong and nothing right. . . . The stupidest thing we did, and this was not forgivable because its implications were and are so ugly, was to perpetuate a rewards system based on publication. . . . Thus for the first-time (or second- or third-time) job seeker, finding a place in the sun meant finding first a place in a scholarly journal. What should have been a natural and healthy act, sharing ideas with colleagues through print, became unnatural, sick. What should have remained student papers or notes for undergraduate lectures became 'articles' in which, in emulation of the sciences, we more often than not pretended to 'solve' literature rather than to interpret, understand, and appreciate it." *Profession 78* (New York, 1978), p. 2.

6. Of course, not all scholars are on academic payrolls, and the very fact that a few business and professional men do literary research in their spare time is the best possible evidence of the pleasure scholarship affords people who have nothing else to gain from it. They are scholars for the same reason that T. S. Eliot, a publisher, Wallace Stevens, an insurance executive, and William Carlos Williams, a pediatrician, were poets. Britain, admittedly, has produced more non-professional scholars than has America. Sir Geoffrey Keynes, the editor and bibliographer of Donne, Browne, and William Blake, is a distinguished Harley Street surgeon, and the late Aleyn Lyell Reade, who did more than anyone else to retrieve the circumstances of Dr. Johnson's early life, was a Liverpool architect. Sir Edmund Chambers and John Dover Wilson, two of the greatest twentieth-century students of the Elizabethan drama, were officials in the Board of Education; a third, R. B. McKerrow, was a member of a publishing firm, as was Michael Sadleir, the leading specialist in the bibliography of Victorian fiction and the author of the standard bio-bibliographical study of Trollope.

to manual skill ceased the day instruction sheets no longer came with screwdrivers, there is satisfaction in gaining steadily greater command of the techniques of finding out what he wants to know; in proceeding with the least number of missteps to the most productive sources of information; in providing, off the cuff, a bibliographical clue to a riddle that has baffled a colleague or a professional librarian. From daily trial-and-error eventually develops a sense of mastery: one no longer feels lost and helpless among the reference shelves and miles of library stacks but is complacent monarch of all the books he surveys. It is a delight comparable to that which a visitor to London achieves when he is finally able to start from Oxford Circus, stride through the crooked streets and byways of Soho and Covent Garden, and emerge exactly where he had planned, at the Temple.

Among the readers of this book there probably are under-graduates contemplating careers as students and teachers of literature, and graduate students, some of whom may be wondering, as we all do now and then, whether they have chosen the right profession. A bit of self-examination therefore is in order. What are the chief qualities of mind and temperament that go to make up a successful and happy scholar?

I have often thought that the ideally equipped literary scholar should have come to his profession after serving a practical apprenticeship in one or the other of two occupations: law and journalism. The practice of law requires a thorough command of the principles of evidence, a knowledge of how to make one's efficient way through the accumulated "literature" on a subject (in legal terms, the statutes and decisions applying to a given case), and a devotion both to accuracy and to detail. It was perhaps no accident that James Boswell himself, who often would "run half over London, in order to fix a date correctly," was a lawyer by profession. Journalism, more specifically the work of the investigative reporter, also calls for resourcefulness—knowing where to go for one's information and how to obtain it, the ability to recognize and follow up leads, and tenacity in pursuit of the facts. Both professions, moreover, require organizational skill, the ability to put facts together in a pattern that is clear and, if controversy is involved, persuasive.

The ideal researcher must love literature for its own sake, that is to say, as an art. He must be an insatiable reader, and the earlier he has acquired that passion, the better. It was with good reason that André Morize, Harvard professor of romance literature, repeatedly insisted in his *Problems and Methods of Literary History* that the genuine scholar must love, and sensitively respond to, a work of art. The kind of work involved in meaningful literary study requires the peculiar impetus and intellectual sympathies that only devotion to an art can provide.

In the second place, the researcher must have a vivid sense of history: the ability to cast himself back into another age. He must be able to readjust his intellectual sights and imaginative responses to the systems of thought and the social and cultural atmosphere that prevailed in fourteenth-century England or early twentieth-century America. He must be able to think as people thought when Newton was educating them in the laws of physics, and to dream as people dreamed when Byron was spinning out his Oriental romances. Otherwise, he cannot comprehend the current attitudes or the artistic assumptions that guided an author as he set pen to paper. At the same time, he must retain his footing in the twentieth century for the sake of the indispensable perspective the historian needs. His sense of the past, then, must be a double vision—intimate and penetrating (in no way confined to the externals of an age, as that of historical novelists and popular biographers too often is) and yet detached.

Once there was an illusion, nourished by the plodding methodicalness of German philology, that literary research was an exact science. Unlike the natural sciences, however, literary scholarship tolerates to a degree the subjective impression, as is inevitable in a discipline that deals with the human consciousness and the art it produces. But as an assembler and assayer of historical facts, a literary scholar needs to be as rigorous in his method as a scientist. And indeed, a background in science is almost as good preparation for literary research as is one in law or newspaper work, because essentially the same qualities are required: intellectual curiosity, shrewdness, precision, imagination—the lively inventiveness that constantly suggests new hypotheses, new strategies, new sources of information, and, when all the data are in, makes possible their accurate interpretation and evaluation. A source overlooked, a wrong date, a carelessly transcribed document, a confusion of persons with similar names, an unsupported assumption silently converted into a certainty— these lapses on the part of a literary researcher are as much a violation of the scientific spirit as any analogous error committed in the laboratory.

Once in a while the substance, as well as the spirit, of such extra-literary training gives the scholar an advantage. The British scientist Desmond King-Hele, with his special knowledge of meteorology, was particularly well equipped to interpret such poems as the "Ode to the West Wind" and "The Cloud" (*Shelley: His Thought and Work*, 1960). And a few years ago a lawyer, reviewing a book on *The Keats Inheritance*, drew upon his professional knowledge to correct the author's misunderstanding. The latter had found what he took to be evidence of a family quarrel in the hostile tone pervading the principal document of a lawsuit involving the inheritance which the poet's grandfather left to the four Keats children. The reviewer pointed out that the phraseology was deliberately made hostile, as a conventional means of ensuring that the court would adjudicate on all issues. In the lack of any evidence to the contrary, he asserted, the suit seems to have been wholly amicable and designed simply to clarify the ambiguities of the will to the satisfaction of all concerned.[7]

Scholarship involves a great amount of detail work, in which no margin of error is allowed and over which the analytic intellect must constantly preside. It is no occupation for the impatient or the careless; nor is it one for the easily fatigued. A scholar must not only be capable of hard, often totally resultless work—he must actually relish it. "The test of a vocation," the aphorist-essayist Logan Pearsall Smith once wrote, "is the love of the drudgery it involves." The researcher pays for every exultant discovery with a hundred hours of monotonous, eye-searing labor. There are endless bibliographies to be searched, item by item if the indexing is undependable; calendars

7. John Rutherford in *Keats-Shelley Journal*, 15 (1966), 117-21.

of manuscripts, book auction records, lists of dissertations, long files of periodicals to be plowed through; boxfuls of fragile and half-illegible holograph letters to be examined in quest of a single clue; volumes upon volumes of dull reminiscences to be scanned for the appearance of a single name. Weariness of the flesh and congestion of the brain are inescapable occupational diseases. Yet, I hasten to add, they are not a high price to pay for the satisfactions people of a certain temperamental and intellectual constitution derive from research. If scholarship were not a delightful, as well as a demanding, mistress, I should not be writing this book.

Uniting all these qualities, and imparting coherence and meaning to the facts collected, must be a creative imagination. Without it the scholar is "lost," as Wordsworth put it, "in a gloom of uninspired research." Human limitations being what they are, the profession has always had its quota of members resembling Scott's Dr. Dryasdust and George Eliot's Mr. Casaubon. Their earnest labors have often furnished the foundation on which more imaginative workers have built, but they have been fact-grubbers, not scholars—pack-rats, not beavers. The true scholar, while conceding the apparent triviality of many of the individual fragments of data he gathers, always looks forward toward an eventual synthesis. He is constantly seeking that final substance which will precipitate from the cloudy solution of facts a crystal of significant truth. And from those crystals he or his grateful colleagues or successors will in time assemble the new masterpieces of literary history—the monumental overviews which radically revise our knowledge of the literary past.

Here, for example, is the famous manuscript of Malory's *Le Morte d'Arthur*, discovered at Winchester College, England, in 1934. Its great immediate importance lay in the fact that its text plainly was much closer to what Malory had written than was that of the edition Caxton printed in 1485. The theory at which scholars arrived was that the Winchester and Caxton versions each came from separate older versions, and that these older versions were both descended in turn from a single ancestor, which derived, ultimately, from Malory's own manuscript. But when a rare-book expert on the staff of the British

Library, which acquired the Winchester manuscript in 1976, noticed unexplained blots and smudges on many leaves, she subjected the manuscript to minute physical examination, including the use of mirrors, a binocular microscope, infra-red light, and photography, and finally a day-long visit to the forensic science laboratory at Scotland Yard. The smudges turned out to be "offsets" of printers' ink from types known to have been used by Caxton during the period when he printed *Le Morte d'Arthur*, the result, presumably, of the manuscript having been brought into repeated contact with freshly printed (and therefore still damp) pages from the press. The inescapable conclusion was that the manuscript had been in Caxton's printing house as early as 1483 and as late as 1489. Was it, then, the actual copy from which the printed text was set? Since it does not bear the usual marks of printer's copy, the supposition is that for printing purposes it was itself copied into another manuscript, which was edited to bring Malory's Midland language and spelling into conformity with the London English of the day. But no solid evidence identifies it as having come directly from Malory, and its precise place in the textual history of *Le Morte d'Arthur*—the line of descent from author to printer—has still not been determined.[8]

Here are Elizabethan documents: the prosaic records of the London theater business, which happen to include the names of the plays performed by the London acting companies during the years when Shakespeare was writing the tragedies and "dark comedies" which, according to some critics, testify to a deep personal crisis. On the state of Shakespeare's psyche at this or any other time, there is not a scintilla of biographical evidence, but on the other hand there is no reason to doubt that *Hamlet*, *Troilus and Cressida*, *Measure for Measure*, and *King Lear* reflect an anguished spirit. The theatrical records suggest that the mood which pervades those plays was not one playwright's alone; otherwise why would so many other plays laden with cynicism or the tragic sense have been as popular as the lists of their performances show

8. For details of these findings, see Lotte Hellinga and Hilton Kelliher, "The Malory Manuscript," *British Library Journal*, 3/2 (Autumn 1977), 91–113.

they were? This oblique testimony of a widespread spiritual malaise provides a salutary check to our inclination to over-simplify or sentimentalize. The fact seems to be that the somber spirit of those Shakespearean dramas was the product of the convergence of a private mood, however induced, with a public one. And with that knowledge, we look upon such plays from a new and stimulating perspective.

Here is the (incomplete) manuscript of Christopher Smart's *Jubilate Agno,* now in the Houghton Library at Harvard. It consists of three double and ten single folio leaves, and as first printed in 1939 by its discoverer, William Force Stead, it made only partial sense. Essentially it seemed to be a welter of fragmentary thoughts cast in lines beginning either "Let" or "For," as if Smart were trying in his mad way to emulate the antiphonal form of Hebrew poetry. A decade later, William H. Bond, theorizing that the order of the leaves had at some time been disturbed, rearranged them on the basis of watermarks, tears, and creasings. Thus reconstituted, in its original sequence, the manuscript revealed that Smart had been both systematic and brilliantly inventive. What he had set out to do was to compose a responsive reading: "a pair of poems, separate and yet intimately related, agreeing page for page and line for line." A comparison of Stead's edition of the poem as received with Bond's of the poem as restored (1954) dra-matically reveals how chaos can be reduced to order by a virtually microscopic physical analysis of a manuscript. [9]

Here is a list of misspelled words compiled from the manu-scripts of Keats's letters: *affod, depeciate, expession, gieved, peach, poof, procue, shot, surpised, sping, thead, thee, witten, wost.*[10] A mere case of careless orthography, of interest to the psychologist perhaps, but to no one else? Again, hardly. For Keats's obvious difficulty in writing *r* seems to point to an equal difficulty in pronouncing the sound, which in turn constitutes a valuable clue to his craftsmanship. As he composed, how did he hear—and pronounce—his lines? Seemingly with a minimum of *r*'s (he wrote *folorn* in the "Ode to a Nightingale"). In such

---

9. See also William H. Bond, "Christopher Smart's *Jubilate Agno,*" *Harvard Library Bulletin,* 4 (1950), 39–52.

10. *The Letters of John Keats,* ed. Hyder E. Rollins (Cambridge, Mass., 1958), I, 17.

a manner the evidence of a poet's manuscripts supplies a sort of vicarious recording of his voice, and we are enabled to reconstruct his melodic and rhythmic intention as he worked over the sound-texture of his verse.

In each of these four cases, material inadequately understood or considered irrelevant or trivial was precipitated into a critical product: clearer understanding of the genesis, intention, or nature of a work of literary art.

These are more or less random examples of the data and procedures that characterize literary research and of the results that make it something more. For although in this book I am using the words *research* and *scholarship* interchangeably, as is the common practice, much that I have said so far implies a distinction between the two which certainly exists, if not in the letter of present usage, at least in the spirit. It is pithily embodied in a proverb which H. L. Mencken attributes to the Japanese: "Learning without wisdom is a load of books on an ass's back." One can be a researcher, full of knowledge, without also being a scholar. Research is the means, scholarship the end; research is an occupation, scholarship is a habit of mind and a way of life. A scholar is more than a researcher, for while he may be gifted in the discovery and assessment of facts, he is, besides, a man of broad and luminous learning. He has both the wisdom and the knowledge that enable him to put facts in their place—in two senses. He is never either engulfed or overawed by mere data, because his mind is able to see them in the long perspective of man's artistic ambitions and achievements.

Especially memorable among the observations made on this distinction are those of John Livingston Lowes, spoken in 1933 but really dateless:

Humane scholarship . . . moves and must move within two worlds at once—the world of scientific method and the world, in whatever degree, of creative art. The postulates of the two are radically different. And our exquisitely difficult task is to conform at once to the stipulations of each without infringing on those of the other. The path of least resistance is to follow one and let the other go. Research, which is the primary instrument of science, is felt to be the easier and it is also the more alluring. I too have heard the Sirens sing, and I know whereof I speak. And so we tend to become enamored of the methods, and at times to forget the end; to allow, in a word, the fascination of the means to distract us from the very object for which they are employed. And that end is, in the broadest sense of the word, *interpretation*—the interpretation, in the light of all that our researches can reveal, of the literature which is our field.[11]

11. "The Modern Language Association and Humane Scholarship," *PMLA*, 48 (1933), 1403. The whole article, and most especially pages 1403–8, still is well worth reading.

CHAPTER TWO

The Spirit of Scholarship

~~~~~~

And as I would not take the least *Iota* upon Trust, if possible; I examin'd the *Original Authors* I could meet with: . . . I think a Writer of Facts cannot be too critical: It is *Exactness* I aim at, and would not have the least Mistake if possible pass to the World.

> —Thomas Prince, *A Chronological History of New-England* (Boston, 1736), pp. iv, ix.

However sensitive our esthetic perceptions, there is little use in talking about any topic associated with the circumstances or the result of literary creation if we do not have our facts straight. Criticism conducted in the shadow of error is criticism wasted. Douglas Bush quotes an "able critic" who, as he sketched the intellectual background of *Dr. Faustus*, asked: "Had not Harriot seen the satellites of Jupiter, and had not Raleigh come back from Guiana with reports [of a fabulous country]?" "Well," says Professor Bush, "if these questions are not merely rhetorical, the answer is 'No, they hadn't.' Raleigh did not set off for

Guiana until two years after Marlowe's death, and there seems to be no evidence that Harriot made any major observations until years later." [1]

A number of years ago F. R. Leavis, in *The Great Tradition*, praised the "sustained maturity of theme and treatment" in Henry James's first novel, *Roderick Hudson* (1876). To support the contention that even in this earliest stage of his career James was capable of a "formidable intellectual edge," Dr. Leavis quoted three long paragraphs from the novel. The only trouble was that he took the passage from the New York edition of 1907, in which *Roderick Hudson*, like the rest of James's work, had been subjected to detailed and extensive revision by the author. "This," says Gordon Ray, "leaves him [Dr. Leavis] in the position of having proved at length what nobody would think of denying, that James's writing at the age of sixty-four has all the characteristics of maturity." [2]

The scholar's business is in part constructive—to add to the sum of knowledge relating to literature and its makers—and in part constructively destructive—to expose and dispel the mistakes that, as the present chapter will show, fox the pages of the literary record. In the latter pursuit, the scholar wars upon the seemingly invincible legend (cultivated by the poet himself) that Burns was a barely literate plowboy, and seeks to cast in correct historical perspective Ben Jonson's remark, seized upon with glee by the "anti-Stratfordians," that Shakespeare had "small Latin and less Greek." Amassing his biographical facts and studying his texts with patient care, the scholar peels off the labels by which earlier critics simplified the reading of literature—"sensuous" Keats, "waspish" Pope, "ethereal" Shelley, and the rest—and reveals how resistant to facile categorizing are both the artist and his art.

1. "The New Criticism: Some Old-Fashioned Queries," *PMLA*, 64 (1949), Supplement, Part 2, p. 15.

2. "The Importance of Original Editions," *Nineteenth Century English Books* (Urbana, Ill., 1952), p. 22.

1. Error: Its Prevalence, Progress, and Persistence

To be a good researcher, one must be a thoroughgoing skeptic. Though in his personal relations he may be the most benevolent and trusting of men, professionally he must cultivate a low opinion of the human capacity for truth and accuracy—beginning with his own. The wellspring of wisdom in research, as elsewhere in life, is self-knowledge. Human beings, it seems, have an inherent tendency to shy away from the exact truth, and even though our profession enjoins upon us the most rigid canons of procedure, in research and writing (and, to carry it to the very end, proofreading as well) none of us, alas, is infallible.

Every practicing scholar, if he is candid, has a fund of instructive stories drawn from his own wry experience. In a travel book I wrote several years ago, I had occasion to recall the trip that Charlotte and Anne Brontë suddenly resolved to take in July, 1848, to reveal their true identities to their London publisher, who knew them only under their masculine pen names of "Currer Bell" and "Acton Bell." These were my words: "After tea, as Charlotte recounted it in a letter, they 'walked through a snow-storm to the station' (yes: in July) and took the night train for Leeds and London." The letter quoted is a long and famous one, dealing as it does with a dramatic episode, indeed a turning point, in the Brontës' lives. It was first printed—accurately, so far as the point at issue is concerned—by Mrs. Gaskell in her biography of Charlotte (1857). But beginning with Clement Shorter's edition of that book (1900), all writers on the Brontës as well as the editors of their letters, with a single honorable exception, have reprinted or quoted from the letter inaccurately. Like most writers who have used it, I was troubled by the July snow in Yorkshire, but, again like them, I failed to take the obvious and simple step of checking the newspapers or the meteorological records to verify that almost incredible freak of the weather. The fact is that "snow-storm" is a mistranscription, followed ever since 1900, of "thunderstorm." As Joan Stevens, the discoverer of the error, has observed, the fictitious snowfall provides "an Instant-Test for scholarly scrupulosity." [3]

Simply because we are made of mortal flesh, we have to reconcile ourselves to a small, irreducible margin of error in our work. But fatalism cannot under any circumstances rationalize carelessness. Granted that perfection is beyond our reach, we must devote every ounce of resolution and care to eliminating all the mistakes we can possibly detect. In the end, our consciences can be at rest. If a slip or two have survived our scrutiny, we can lay the omission to the postlapsarian state of the race to which we belong.

The long, broad stream of history has been contaminated from many sources. When we dip into it in the course of our research, whether we take but a thimbleful or enough to fill a gallon jug, our critical intelligence is the disinfectant that will make the water potable. It is impossible to count all the kinds of bacteria in the water we must perforce drink, nor can we fully catalogue their sources. An error in copying a document; moralistic, political, or personal bias on the part of an early witness; a biographer's striving for artistic effect at the expense of the facts; a slip in the memory of someone recalling an event that happened thirty years earlier; a misprint; a speculation that has been dignified into a "certainty"; an anecdote or an assumption of critics or literary historians which has gone unchallenged so long that it now seems as impregnable as an old-fashioned Gospel truth. . . .

The list is a lengthy one. In these pages, however, I have no intention of providing a systematic treatise on the critical examination of evidence; there are several good books on the subject, most of them written by and for professional historians. A few that are useful to literary students are mentioned on pages 242 – 245. Instead of a set of rules, I shall simply offer a selection of case histories and instances, small and medium-sized, which will suggest the variety of misinformation that lurks in the data we receive from our predecessors. In the end you will, I think, have a sense of the spirit of vigilance and skepticism that presides over every good scholar's desk.

3. "Woozles in Brontëland: A Cautionary Tale," *SB*, 24 (1971), 99–108.

The chronicles of literary scholarship are studded with stories that might be entitled "Five Little Half-Truths (or Non-Facts) and How They Grew." Once a mistake is set adrift, it not only harbors its original modicum of untruth but swells and proliferates. The oftener an error is repeated, furthermore, the more persuasive it becomes, and the more hospitably it extends its protective coloration over the additional mistakes that come to be associated with it. As a result, the story becomes increasingly difficult to discredit. The burgeoning of the myth of Christopher Marlowe's death, which I have narrated in another book, is but one instance out of many.[4]

Books and articles on Robert Louis Stevenson during the 1920's and 1930's contain much discussion of one "Claire," to whom Stevenson often alluded in his letters and poems. Who was she? Certain biographers thought she was an early sweetheart of R. L. S. or, even more excitingly, a prostitute whom the chivalrous young man-about-Edinburgh planned to rescue from a brothel. As it progressed, this legend of Stevenson's love acquired quite fancy trimmings. But in *Voyage to Windward* (1951), J. C. Furnas showed conclusively that "Claire" was simply Stevenson's name for Mrs. Sitwell, a woman some years older than he, who was his intimate confidante.[5]

One compelling reason why a myth persists despite exposure is that it is often so much more picturesque than the prosaic truth; a good anecdote, however doubtful its credentials, appeals to the romanticist in us. Thus a course of investigation sometimes results in a clash within us of two opposed inclinations—the scientist's devotion to austere fact and the artist's sense of the superior beauty that resides in what might have

key point

4. For others, in addition to the few included in the ensuing pages, see the list of further readings, pages 242–45.

5. Sentimentalism and slipshod scholarship have combined to populate literary biography with phantom lovers. The shortest lived, probably, was Louis Parensell. In a book called *The Life and Eager Death of Emily Brontë* (London, 1936), Virginia Moore announced her discovery of Louis, whose name she found noted at the head of one of Emily's manuscript poems. But in the *Times Literary Supplement* for August 29, 1936, a Brontë scholar, C. W. Hatfield, returned Louis Parensell to limbo by pointing out that what appeared to be his name actually was the phrase "Love's Farewell."

been. Our choice, as scholars, is clear, but our rejection of the palpably untrue or unlikely often is accompanied by a certain regret.

An interesting elementary example of the progress of error is embodied in a passage in Cecil Woodham-Smith's biography of Florence Nightingale (New York, 1951): [6]

Everything depended on War Office reorganization, and War Office reorganization could be pushed through by Sidney Herbert alone. "One fight more, the last and the best," wrote Miss Nightingale; let him nerve himself to this final task and he should be released.

The context is 1859–60. Yet Browning's "Prospice," from which Miss Nightingale's letter obviously quotes, was not published until May, 1864. Unless she was gifted with extraordinary foresight into the future writings of a poet, or unless (which is hardly conceivable) Browning somehow borrowed his phrase from a private letter she wrote to someone else, how can the quotation be reconciled with the date? Let us move a step backward, to Lytton Strachey's profile of Florence Nightingale in *Eminent Victorians* (New York, 1918). On page 185 occur these sentences:

At any rate, he [Sidney Herbert] could not resist Miss Nightingale. A compromise was arranged. Very reluctantly, he exchanged the turmoil of the House of Commons for the dignity of the House of Lords, and he remained at the War Office. She was delighted. "One fight more, the best and the last," she said.

At least no written document is in question here; Miss Nightingale "said," not "wrote." Still, the difficulty remains: how could she have anticipated Browning, and how did Strachey

6. Page 239. In the London edition of the preceding year, the passage occurs on page 353. Here is a good instance of why it is necessary to specify the edition from which one quotes. Although some books issued in England and America have identical pagination because they consist of the same sheets or are printed from the same plates, others are typeset independently and hence may be paged differently. Moreover, in the case of Woodham-Smith's *Florence Nightingale*, there was a big difference in text between the British and American hardbound editions, the latter being only two-thirds as long.

know she said what she "said"? A second step backward takes us to Strachey's major source, Sir Edward Cook's *Life of Florence Nightingale* (London, 1913). This is what Strachey had seen (I, 403):

> The cause of Army Reform would not be completed, the permanence of the improvements already made would not be secured, unless every department of the War Office was similarly reorganized under a general and coherent scheme. So Miss Nightingale urged her friend forward to "one fight more, the best and the last."

The solution is as simple as the moral to be derived from it. What Cook intended as merely an inlaid phrase, which every reader in 1913 would recognize as being quoted from a famous poem of Browning's, Strachey converted into words Miss Nightingale allegedly spoke, and Woodham-Smith into words she allegedly wrote. What began as a small artistic effect ended up as a putative quotation from a document which in all probability never existed.[7]

Although error has an inherent tendency to elaborate itself and to attract collateral untruths, like barnacles on a ship's bottom, sometimes it retains its original form through many repetitions. Such is usually the case with bibliographical "ghosts"— the inspired technical term for books, or particular editions thereof, which, though listed, were never seen by mortal eyes. (This is a spectral field of study—literally a never-never land— which Jacob Blanck once called "psychic bibliography.") The *Short-Title Catalogue of Books Printed in England . . . 1475–1640*, an indispensable guide to Renaissance studies, contains hundreds of ghosts, mainly of imperfectly identified editions but also including one created by an accident in setting type

7. Speaking of Florence Nightingale, two articles dealing with her biographers' numerous misdemeanors may be recommended as illustrating the sheer diversity of mistakes that can creep into biographies of a single person: Rosalind Nash, "Florence Nightingale According to Mr. Strachey," *Nineteenth Century*, 103 (1928), 258–65, and W. H. Greenleaf, "Biography and the 'Amateur' Historian: Mrs. Woodham-Smith's 'Florence Nightingale,'" *VS*, 3 (1959), 190–202. Further evidence of Strachey's free handling of facts in his profile of Miss Nightingale is found in Geoffrey Faber, *Jowett: A Portrait with Background* (London, 1957), pp. 308–11.

for the *Short-Title Catalogue* itself (see the preface). The editors, A. W. Pollard and G. R. Redgrave, were aware of the haunting when the book appeared, but perfection in an undertaking so vast as the *STC*, especially when done by only two men, was not to be sought for. These bibliographical apparitions are being laid as work on a revised edition progresses. Meanwhile, one ghost the *STC* happily does not contain is that of a certain edition of Chapman's *Bussy d'Ambois*. Here is what the principal authorities, 1812–1900, say about the dates of the various seventeenth-century editions of the play:

Baker: *Biographia Dramatica* (1812), II, 73:	1607	1608	1616	1641		1657
Watt: *Bibliotheca Britannica* (1824), I, 212:	1607	1608	1613*	1641	1646	
Hazlitt: *Hand-Book* (1867), p. 82:	1607	1608	1616	1641		1657
[In his *Bibliographical Collections and Notes* (2nd ser., 1882), p. 90, he added . . .					1646	]
Lowndes: *Bibliographer's Manual* (1869), I, 410:	1607	1608	1616	1641	1646	
Fleay: *A Biographical Chronicle of the English Drama* (1891), I, 50:	1607	1608	1616	1641		1657
Greg: *List of English Plays* (1900), pp. 19, 20:	1607	1608	1616	1641	1646	1657

* This is probably simply a misprint for "1616". At least, it was one ghost that did not prove viable.

Two years after his *List of English Plays* appeared, W. W. Greg pointed out (*List of Masques*, p. cxxiii) that the 1616 edition was probably a mistake of Baker (1812) for 1646, an edition which, significantly, Baker failed to include in his list. George Watson Cole, from whose article on bibliographical ghosts (*PBSA*, 13 [1919], 87–112) I have taken this example, says that neither Baker nor Watt "makes any pretense of locating copies nor even lays claim to having seen a single copy of any of these early editions. . . . Hazlitt . . . appears to have been one of the earliest English bibliographers who attempted to locate copies of the works he describes. Lowndes occasionally gives the location of a copy, as in the Bodleian or British Museum; Fleay makes no such attempt." Greg, on the other hand, systematically lists locations. His failure to find a single copy of the 1616 edition, or in fact any reference to it earlier than Baker's, made him suspect it to be a ghost. And though Greg's subsequent distinguished career as a bibliographer lasted for almost sixty more years, he never did run across a copy of the 1616 edition; it is not listed in his monumental *Bibliography of the English Printed Drama* (1939–59). In such a fashion a misread date, committed to type in 1812, "created" a book that nobody ever saw but that everybody, presumably, believed in until its non-existence was made reasonably clear ninety years later.

The lesson is really twofold. In the first place, notwithstanding the Bellman's familiar assertion, what is told three times is *not* true. A rumor, no matter in what various contexts it appears and at what intervals of time, can rise no higher than its source, and a mistake, no matter how often repeated or under whose auspices, remains a mistake. In the second place—but I can do no better than to quote a writer in the *Monthly Review* more than two centuries ago (16 [1757], 531):

. . . in proportion as History removes from the first witnesses, it may recede also from truth,—as, by passing thro' the prejudices, or the mistakes of subsequent Compilers, it will be apt to imbibe what tincture they may chance to give it. The *later* Historian's only way, therefore, to prevent the ill effects of that decrease of evidence which the lapse of years necessarily brings with it, must be, by punctually referring to the spring head from whence the stream of his narration flows; which at once will cut off all appearance of partiality, or misrepresentation. As in law, the rectitude of a person's character is not alone sufficient to establish the truth of a fact, so in history, not merely the Writer's testimony, be our opinion of his veracity ever so great, but collateral evidence also is required, to determine every thing of a questionable nature.

One necessary consequence of this advice is that researchers must be careful to use only the most dependable text of a literary work or a private or public document. Young scholars especially tend to forget that there are good texts and bad, incomplete editions and definitive ones. It is a scholarly axiom that no edition of an author's letters published before the 1920's, at the earliest, can be relied upon. William Mason's simultaneous mangling and "beautifying" of Gray's letters (1775) is one of the most notorious examples of editorial malpractice in literary history. Lockhart touched up the style of Scott's letters, silently omitted portions (thus changing their meaning), and cut them apart and recombined them, irrespective of date or recipient, into new letters.[8] In fact, every scholar who has had occasion to compare the pre-1920 printed texts of a literary man's private papers with the manuscripts themselves has blood-curdling tales to tell of the liberties their editors took. Sometimes, to be sure, the printed deviations from the original are accidental, the result of the editor's misreading. One of the most charming instances of this occurs in the *Life, Journals, and Correspondence of Samuel Pepys* (1841), where Sir Robert Southwell is represented as saying in a letter to Pepys that he has lost his health "by sitting many years at the sack-bottle." Reference to the manuscript reveals that what Southwell really sat at was not the sack-bottle but the "inck-bottle," which is a quite different kind of companion.[9]

In any event, one must make sure that the edition he uses, whether of an author's published works or of his letters, is the best available—which means, among other things, that the editor has scrupulously reproduced the text. Pope's poems should be quoted from the Twickenham edition, Jonson's plays from the Herford-Simpson edition, Spenser's works from the Johns Hopkins Variorum, Swift's prose from Herbert Davis' edition, Burns's poems from Kinsley's, Arnold's prose from Super's, the works of American authors from the CEAA and, since 1976, the CSE editions whenever these exist (see below, pages 71 and 72).

---

8. On Mason's misdeeds, see Paget Toynbee and Leonard Whibley, *Correspondence of Thomas Gray* (Oxford, 1935), I, xiv–xv; on Lockhart's, Davidson Cook, "Lockhart's Treatment of Scott's Letters," *Nineteenth Century*, 102 (1927), 382–98. Another instructive case in point is the history of the successive editions of Pepys's diary: see *The Diary of Samuel Pepys*, ed. Robert Latham and William Matthews, I (Berkeley and Los Angeles, 1970), [lxviii]–xcvi.

9. William Dunn Macray, *Annals of the Bodleian Library Oxford* (2nd ed., Oxford, 1890), p. 236n.

Similarly, part of a scholar's basic equipment is a knowledge of the authoritative editions of literary correspondences. Pope's letters should be quoted from Sherburn, Johnson's and Jane Austen's from R. W. Chapman, Walpole's from Wilmarth Lewis (the magnificent Yale edition, still in progress), Keats's from Rollins (no longer from Buxton Forman, whose texts and datings, as Rollins had plentiful occasion to show, are unreliable), Coleridge's from Griggs, Byron's from Marchand, George Eliot's from Haight, Thackeray's from Ray, Meredith's from Cline, Swinburne's from Lang, Emerson's from Rusk, Cooper's from Beard, Whitman's from Miller, Dreiser's from Elias. Where no authoritative editions are in existence, the scholar has no choice (short of finding the original manuscript) but to quote a letter in its received form; but he should do so in full awareness that all older editions of many important correspondences, such as Cowper's, Edward FitzGerald's, Ruskin's, Stevenson's, and the Brontës', abound in misreadings, silent omissions, stylistic revisions, transpositions, and every other variety of what we today consider editorial irresponsibility.[10] Remember the July snowstorm in Yorkshire.

The mere fact that an edition contains an elaborate apparatus of footnotes and textual variants is no absolute guarantee that the text is indeed accurate, though nowadays the presumption lies that way. In the most imposing piece of machinery there may be flaws that are revealed only with use. Nor may we trust, without putting them to the test, the assurances which editors—especially of former generations—give us of the accuracy and thoroughness of their work; their performance may have fallen considerably short of their ambition.

10. Even "definitive" editions, however, often prove to be incomplete. The DeSelincourt edition of Wordsworth's letters is being replaced by a fuller and more accurate one; Grierson's of Scott's is known to be seriously incomplete; and the edition by Frederick L. Jones of Shelley's letters lacks a large number owned, and to be published separately, by the Carl H. Pforzheimer Library in New York. Notable editions in course of preparation or actual publication include, on the English side, the correspondences of Burney, Crabbe, Cowper, Lamb, Dickens, Disraeli, Trollope, the Carlyles, Newman, Browning, Tennyson, Shaw, Yeats, Lawrence, O'Casey, and Synge; on the American side, those of Hawthorne, Bryant, Whittier, Longfellow, Howells, Henry James, and Mark Twain.

In the preface to his edition of Gray's works (1884), Edmund Gosse wrote: "As far, then, as regards the largest section of Gray's prose writings,—the letters which he addressed to Thomas Wharton [*sic*],—I am relieved from the responsibility of reference to any previous text, for I have scrupulously printed these, as though they never had been published before, direct from the originals, which exist, in a thick volume, among the Egerton MSS., in the Manuscript department of the British Museum." What Gosse did not know was that the person he had employed to transcribe the text "direct from the originals" had tired of reading Gray's writing and, finding that the letters had been printed by John Mitford in 1816, had taken the far easier course of copying them from the printed version—which happened to swarm with errors! [11]

While it is true, in general, that modern scholarly editions are more dependable than earlier ones, the hard words some editors have for their predecessors should not be taken as proof that their own work is unexceptionable. It is only natural to be impatient with a careless editorial job; it is equally natural to overlook one's own deficiencies. Sometimes an earlier text is not as bad as it is said to be, or its successor may turn out to be no better. In his *Bibliographical and Critical Account of the Rarest Books in the English Language* (1865), John Payne Collier attacked Thomas Park for the inaccuracy of his edition (*Heliconia*, 1815) of the Elizabethan poetical miscellany, *The Phoenix Nest*. Among other malfeasances, Park had omitted six stanzas from the text of a certain poem.

Thereupon [writes Hyder E. Rollins, in his definitive edition of *The Phoenix Nest* (Cambridge, Mass., 1931), pp. xiii–xiv] he proceeds to make up for the deficiency by giving an "accurate" reprint of the missing stanzas. He says that Park's first omission comes after the eighteenth stanza, when he should have said the seventeenth, and in printing the seven omitted lines he departs four times from the original. In reprinting the next two stanzas that Park leaves out he varies fifteen times (twice deliberately). In restoring the lines of the third omission (following stanza twenty-nine, which he calls twenty-six), he makes five errors. In filling the gap after stanza thirty-nine (which he calls thirty-five) he makes fourteen mistakes,

11. Evan Charteris, *The Life and Letters of Sir Edmund Gosse* (New York, 1931), p. 188.

and seven more in printing the fifty-ninth stanza. Thus in reprinting the six stanzas left out of *Heliconia* by Park,—a "brave scholar," he admits, "but a somewhat careless superintendent of reprints,"— Collier is himself guilty of forty-five blunders in the text plus three more that he slips into in counting the stanzas.

The lesson to be learned from this story is substantial: skeptical awareness provides an indispensable safeguard when dealing with "classroom" and "standard" texts and with scholarly editions which appear "definitive." The *Variorum Walden* (1962), for example, contained sixty-four erroneous readings of the first edition.[12] Although rigorous editing practices have significantly lessened the likelihood of such errors in the most recent scholarly editions, questions may arise in entirely different quarters, centering upon, for instance, the editorial principles used to determine copy text. The CEAA editions of *Walden* (1971) and of Stephen Crane's *Maggie* (1969) created controversy not because of inaccuracies but because of the methods adopted to establish the texts. Yet another, but far from the only other, category of potential difficulty involving texts is that associated with facsimiles, including microfilm reproductions—principally, the fact that they cannot always be trusted where minute details are in question.[13]

In using the work of an intervening historian, biographer, or editor, then, it is best practice for the scholar always to allow for the possibility of error or questionable editorial procedure. Usually the former is the more critical. By accepting on faith something we would have discovered was an error, had we but checked it, we become an inadvertent *particeps criminis* in passing the mistake one step further down the line. And often the pleasure of exposing an inaccurate statement or a slippery assumption is reward enough for the labor it has cost. In an article on the circulation of newspapers in eighteenth-century England (*RES*, 22 [1946], 29), a respected modern historian,

12. Joseph R. McElrath, Jr., "Practical Editions: Henry D. Thoreau's *Walden*," *Proof*, 4 (1975), 178.

13. See Fredson Bowers's assault on the Yale facsimile edition of the Shakespeare first folio (*MP*, 53 [1955], 50–57); Laurence A. Cummings, "Pitfalls of Photocopy Research," *BNYPL*, 65 (1961), 97–101; Franklin B. Williams, Jr., "Photo-Facsimiles of *STC* Books: A Cautionary Check List," *SB*, 21 (1968), 109–30.

Arthur Aspinall, says that "at no time were newspapers beyond the reach of town workers," and he supports his point, or seems to, by saying that "the very slaters had the newspapers brought on to the roofs of the houses on which they were working, that they might read them." The unqualified plural suggests a common practice, so common, indeed, that one can conjure up the vision of all the slaters in London dropping their tools to bury their noses in the paper. But when one turns to the author's source, Montesquieu's fragmentary notes on a visit to London about 1730, he finds that Montesquieu had written: "*Un couvreur se fait apporter la gazette sur les toits pour la lire.*" [14]

All that the cautious can infer from this statement is that Montesquieu saw one, but not necessarily more than one, slater reading a newspaper. While perhaps other slaters did in fact read, up there on the roof, Montesquieu's statement, couched in the singular, is no positive evidence of it. To be sure, a generalization is implied—the single slater, Montesquieu seems to suggest, is typical of many. But is it true, as Aspinall's acceptance and enlargement of it tempts us to believe? A reasonable interpretation of the statement must take into account all the independent evidence that bears on it, for an assertion is good only so long as no evidence substantially contradicts it. In this case, evidence does substantially contradict it, for enough is known about the availability of newspapers in the London of the 1730's and the extent of literacy among the artisan class to cast serious doubt on the historical accuracy of Montesquieu's observation. Furthermore, Aspinall failed to take into account the foreign visitor's characteristic readiness to convert the exceptional into the rule. In evaluating any piece of historical information, especially when it occurs in a primary source, a good working knowledge of human nature is one of the most effective pieces of equipment a scholar can possess. "Man," as George Eliot remarked in *Felix Holt*, "cannot be defined as an evidence-giving animal."

14. Montesquieu, *Oeuvres Complètes*, ed. Edouard Laboulaye, VII (Paris, 1879), 189.

2. Examining the Evidence

So back to the sources it is, then, if scholars wish to erase the mistakes that are all too likely to have occurred in the process of historical transmission. Back to the documents (or, in practice, to a thoroughly reliable printing thereof, if one exists); back to the people with whom our information began; back to the "collateral evidence" which, according to our sagacious *Monthly* reviewer in 1757, is needed to "determine every thing of a questionable nature." But primary and collateral evidence needs to be weighed every bit as carefully as the statements of intermediate sources. A document's age and unchallenged authenticity are no warrant of the truth of its contents. Again the scholar must bring into play his sense of the manifold ways by which people can, whether unconsciously or with full deliberation, distort the facts—or imagine them.

Valuable though authors' autobiographical narratives may be, we can never accept them at their face value. Apart from their frequent unreliability as to specific dates, places, and other historical facts, they usually are idealized, embroidered through sheer exuberance of the artistic imagination, colored by compelling motives such as the desire for self-justification (or in Carlyle's case, public expiation—for his ill-treatment of his wife during her lifetime), or simply undependable because of the lapse of time between the events narrated and the moment they are set on paper. Just about every conceivable kind of memorial lapse or embellishment can be illustrated somewhere in the autobiographical writings and oral reminiscences of English and American writers. Whitman, Mark Twain, Shaw, Yeats, Sherwood Anderson, J. M. Barrie, Faulkner, Thomas Wolfe—to mention only a few—are a source of constant exasperation to their biographers because they recurrently, for whatever reason, deviated from what is demonstrably the truth about their lives.

And the scholar's task is no easier when a great writer leaves behind him several discrepant versions of a single episode. Shelley told the story of his expulsion from Oxford at least five different times, never twice in exactly the same way. Add four more versions from other sources, also disagreeing in certain details, and you have a real puzzle on your hands. Confronted with several variant accounts, one can seldom reconcile the conflicts by counting the number of times each detail occurs and accepting the most frequently recounted one as the truth. Majority rule is an admirable foundation-stone of democratic politics, but a slippery procedure in scholarship. Instead, one must carefully examine the probability of each detail as well as the circumstances under which each version was uttered (was there any reason why Shelley, on a given occasion, should have altered this detail or that?). And the man's own versions must then be compared with the testimony of others—testimony which must in itself be delicately evaluated for a possible tincture of fanciful elaboration, slips of memory, personal bias, and so on. In the end, it is not usually possible for a scholar to say with absolute confidence that this, and this alone, is what happened in a given episode; the best he can do is assert that, everything considered, the probabilities favor one set of details more than another.

Consider the famous anecdote told by Boswell, which, he says, he gives "authentically from Johnson's own exact narration":

I received one morning [said Johnson] a message from poor Goldsmith that he was in great distress, and, as it was not in his power to come to me, begging that I would come to him as soon as possible. I sent him a guinea, and promised to come to him directly. I accordingly went as soon as I was drest, and found that his landlady had arrested him for his rent, at which he was in a violent passion. I perceived that he had already changed my guinea, and had got a bottle of Madeira and a glass before him. I put the cork into the bottle, desired he would be calm, and began to talk to him of the means by which he might be extricated. He then told me that he had a novel ready for the press, which he produced to me. I looked into it, and saw its merit; told the landlady I should soon return, and having gone to a bookseller, sold it for sixty pounds. I brought Goldsmith the money, and he discharged his rent, not without rating his landlady in a high tone for having used him so ill. [15]

Thus James Boswell, offering a direct quotation from Johnson. But Mrs. Thrale also printed an account of this charitable

15. *Life of Johnson*, ed. G. Birkbeck Hill, re-ed. L. F. Powell, I (Oxford, 1934), 416.

transaction. Boswell called it "a specimen of the extreme inaccuracy with which all her anecdotes of Dr. Johnson are related, or rather discoloured and distorted," but the antipathy
of one biographer toward another must not be allowed to affect
our own judgment:

I have forgotten the year, but it could scarcely I think be later than
1765–6, that he was called abruptly from our house after dinner, and
returning in about three hours, said, he had been with an enraged
author, whose landlady pressed him for payment within doors,
while the bailiffs beset him without; that he was drinking himself
drunk with Madeira to drown care, and fretting over a novel which
when finished was to be his whole fortune; but he could not get it
done for distraction, nor could he step out of doors to offer it for
sale. Mr. Johnson therefore set away the bottle, and went to the
bookseller, recommending the performance, and desiring some immediate relief; which when he brought back to the writer, he called
the woman of the house directly to partake of punch, and pass
their time in merriment.[16]

So much for Mrs. Thrale, offering not a verbatim quotation
from Johnson, but the next thing to it. A third version, also
attributed to Dr. Johnson himself, was printed by the dramatist
Richard Cumberland in 1807:

I have heard Dr. Johnson relate with infinite humour the circumstance of his rescuing him [Goldsmith] from a ridiculous dilemma
by the purchase money of his Vicar of Wakefield, which he sold
on his behalf to Dodsley, and, as I think, for the sum of ten pounds
only. He had run up a debt with his landlady for board and lodg-
ing of some few pounds, and was at his wit's-end how to wipe off
the score and keep a roof over his head, except by closing with a
very staggering proposal on her part, and taking his creditor to
wife, whose charms were very far from alluring, whilst her demands
were extremely urgent. In this crisis of his fate he was found by
Johnson in the act of meditating on the melancholy alternative
before him. He shewed Johnson his manuscript of The Vicar of
Wakefield, but seemed to be without any plan, or even hope, of
raising money upon the disposal of it; when Johnson cast his eye
upon it, he discovered something that gave him hope, and immediately took it to Dodsley, who paid down the price above-mentioned
in ready money, and added an eventual condition upon its future
sale. Johnson described the precautions he took in concealing the

16. *Anecdotes of the Late Samuel Johnson* (London, 1786). Quoted here
from the "new edition" (London, 1822), pp. 94–95.

amount of the sum he had in hand, which he prudently administered to him by a guinea at a time. In the event he paid off the landlady's score, and redeemed the person of his friend from her embraces.[17]

In addition to these extended narratives, there are several anecdotes which contain some, but not all, of their components. Johnson's pre-Boswellian biographer, Sir John Hawkins, says simply:

Of the booksellers whom he [Goldsmith] styled his friends, Mr. Newbery was one. This person had apartments in Canonbury-house, where Goldsmith often lay concealed from his creditors. Under a pressing necessity he there wrote his Vicar of Wakefield, and for it received of Newbery forty pounds.[18]

Nothing is said of Johnson's intervention. Nor does Johnson figure in William Cooke's account of the composition of *The Vicar of Wakefield:*

The doctor [i.e., Goldsmith], soon after his acquaintance with Newbery, for whom he held "the pen of a ready writer," removed to lodgings in Wine Office Court, Fleet-street, where he finished his "Vicar of Wakefield," and on which his friend Newbery advanced him *twenty guineas:* "A sum," says the Doctor, "I was so little used to receive in a *lump,* that I felt myself under the embarrassment of Captain Brazen in the play, "whether I should build a privateer or a play-house with the money." [19]

On the other hand, Goldsmith does not appear in an anecdote, also involving a necessitous author's captivity for non-payment of just debts, rescue by a comparatively affluent friend, and application to a bottle of wine, which George Steevens, a member of the Johnson circle, alleged Johnson told of himself, referring to his early London years:

Richardson, the author of Clarissa, was his constant friend on such occasions. "I remember writing to him (said Johnson) from a spunging-house; and was so sure of my deliverance through his kindness and liberality that, before his reply was brought, I knew I could afford to joke with the rascal who had me in custody, and

17. *Memoirs of Richard Cumberland, Written by Himself* (London, 1807), I, 372–73.
18. *Life of Samuel Johnson* (2nd ed., London, 1787), p. 420.
19. *European Magazine,* 24 (1793), 92.

did so, over a pint of adulterated wine, for which, at that instant, I had no money to pay." [20]

In this welter of discrepancies and outright contradictions, where is the truth to be found?

1. *Did the episode happen at all?* Almost certainly, yes; for we have Boswell's word that Johnson described the incident, and Boswell is a remarkably dependable biographer whose testimony has withstood close scrutiny time after time. Mrs. Thrale to some extent corroborates him, though her knowledge can only be second-hand. Independent evidence proves the transaction took place in 1762, and Johnson did not begin to frequent her household until January, 1765. She could not, therefore, have been an eyewitness to his departure "after dinner" (note that Johnson, quoted by Boswell, says "one morning") or his return.

2. *How much did Goldsmith—with or without Johnson's aid—collect for "The Vicar of Wakefield," and from whom?* (Boswell: £60, "bookseller" unidentified; Cumberland: £10, from the bookseller Dodsley; Hawkins: £40, from the bookseller John Newbery; Cooke: twenty guineas, from Newbery.) Goldsmith's regular publisher was Newbery. The total amount paid for the novel seems to have been sixty pounds or guineas (the terms were used more or less interchangeably in the period), because an entry in the accounts of the Salisbury printer who brought out the first edition of the *Vicar* says that he bought a one-third share in the work for £21, or twenty guineas. Either Hawkins' figure of £40 or Cooke's of twenty guineas may be reconciled with the total of £60, given by Johnson, if we assume that Johnson garbled the story slightly, and that his true mission was to collect from Newbery the *remainder* of the £60, part of which Goldsmith had already received.

3. *Where was Goldsmith at the time the manuscript was sold?* (Hawkins: Canonbury House [in the then suburb of Islington]; Cooke: Wine Office Court, Fleet Street.) Wine Office Court, where, as attested by Newbery's papers, Goldsmith was living in October, 1762. A few months later he

20. *London Magazine*, n.s. 4 (1785), 253.

moved to Canonbury House, where, as Hawkins says, Newbery also had rooms.

4. *What about Cumberland's version, which is conspicuously
different from the others?* Probably sheer embroidery and
careless variation on the better attested facts. No other evidence suggests that Dodsley was a party to the transaction, and
the landlady whose charms were less than compelling seems
so patently a stock character from comic fiction and drama
(remember that Cumberland was a playwright) that very
likely we are justified in dismissing her with the same alacrity
that Goldsmith, according to Cumberland, did.

5. *Might not the story of Richardson's rescuing Johnson have
colored the Johnson-Goldsmith anecdote?* Possibly, though the
story seems to have come from George Steevens, a very unreliable witness who may well have based it, instead, on the
Goldsmith episode. However, if Steevens can be relied upon
and Johnson did celebrate over a bottle of wine, it is conceivable that in telling the Goldsmith anecdote to Boswell, Johnson contributed the Madeira bottle from his own analogous experience. Such accretions, as all of us know who tend to
elaborate a story in the telling, almost inevitably accompany
the making of anecdotes.[21]

These plentiful discrepancies remind us of the story, famous
in the annals of psychology (and told, appropriately, of more
than one pioneer psychologist) of a fracas staged in a classroom,
and of the wildly different versions of the event that all the
student-spectators gave when asked to tell what really happened. Every man views every other man, and every event,
through his own unique set of mental lenses. Hence, whenever we are dealing with the evidence left by people who
participated in or witnessed an event—or by people who knew,
or recorded contemporary information about, an author in
whom we are interested—we must ask a few simple questions,
very much in the manner of an attorney interrogating a witness.
What, for one thing, is the man's general reputation and capac-

21. For a closer analysis of this tangle, which has many parallels in
literary history, see Temple Scott, *Oliver Goldsmith Bibliographically
and Biographically Considered* (New York, 1928), pp. 166-72. Scott's
discussion well exemplifies the method of sorting out the various strands
of asserted "fact" and, so far as possible, reconciling them.

ity for accuracy? If he has been proved wrong on other points, he is not automatically disqualified as a witness, for as Browning was fond of pointing out, a large muddy blob of error may well conceal a precious grain of truth. But evidence from such a source must be scrutinized with extra care. For another thing, was the witness in a position to *know* the facts of which he speaks? Can it be demonstrated that he was present (and attentive, and sober, and with good eyesight and hearing), or is there irrefutable evidence that he was a hundred miles away that evening? Is it possible that the events he describes "first-hand" were, in fact, described to him by people who were there, and that the story suffered heaven knows what changes in the telling?

If a witness was clearly in a position to know the facts, there is still the possibility that his testimony is biased. This is one of the chief booby traps that biographers have to keep alert for as they delve into the lives of English writers who were embroiled in the religious and political controversies of their times. The polemical nature of the documentary sources—pamphlets, newspaper attacks, personal letters, and the rest, vehement in their denunciation of the personal character and deeds of their victims—beclouds the study of Dryden, Defoe, and Fielding as men. A modern French biographer, for example, asserts that Defoe owned a mistress as well as a tile works at Tilbury, but the only evidence for such a statement, John Robert Moore says, "is that such a charge appeared in *The True-Born Hugonot*, a doggerel poem expressing the attitude of extremists who hated the reformation of manners as much as they hated political freedom and religious toleration" and who therefore sought to smear a fellow-pamphleteer who espoused those causes.[22] The student of Pope, likewise, finds himself floundering in what George Sherburn has called a "morass of attack and counter-attack," with the air above him, one might add, filled with flying libels—"a perpetual reciprocation," said Dr. Johnson, who nearly always can be allowed the last word, "of malevolence." Where, in all this furious sniping, can the truth of men and events be discovered? It takes years of patient analysis of personalities and motives, and of the

22. *Daniel Defoe: Citizen of the World* (Chicago, 1958), p. 286.

public issues that brought out the worst side of all the people involved, to get anywhere near it.

American literary biography has been relatively free of political or religious prejudice, but these are not the only kinds of bias that detract from a witness' credibility. One of the many species of legends that flourished in Poe lore until Arthur Hobson Quinn's ruthlessly skeptical biography appeared in 1941 was the series of descriptions of Poe's deathbed given to the press by the Baltimore physician who attended him. The authenticated circumstances of the poet's end are sufficiently harrowing, but Dr. J. E. Snodgrass embellished them as he went along. That Poe was "rather the worse for wear" is made certain by the note that summoned Snodgrass to Poe's aid. In a New York temperance paper, in 1856, Snodgrass was more specific: "The muscles of articulation seemed paralyzed to speechlessness, and mere incoherent mutterings," and Poe was afflicted with "deep intoxication." In *Beadle's Monthly* eleven years later, Snodgrass turned the "deep" into "beastly" and maintained (as the Puritan narrators of Christopher Marlowe's demise had done, many years earlier) that as Poe died, he uttered "scarcely intelligible oaths and other forms of imprecation"—which does not quite jibe with the earlier "mere incoherent mutterings." The reason for this intensification of effect, Quinn shows, was that the estimable Snodgrass was a temperance lecturer, who made his account more vivid—and to him, at least, probably no less credible—the oftener he repeated it.[23]

Nor is animus on principle the only reason for doubting the veracity of a contemporary account. There are also distinctly personal considerations. Literary men probably have disappointed as many women, per capita, as any other class of beings; they have certainly owed as much money; they have uttered their quota of slanderous remarks; they have betrayed, or, Joycelike, simply abandoned friendships. On the other hand, they have also left behind them adoring wives and children, friends whom they aided beyond their deserts, acquaintances who fell under their spell as conversationalists and bon vivants. All of which adds further complications when one is faced

---

23. *Edgar Allan Poe: A Critical Biography* (New York, 1941), p. 639n.

with a cloud of memoir-scribbling witnesses to the personal
life of a great author. After Byron, Shelley, Poe, and D. H.
Lawrence came hundreds of men and women who sooner or
later recorded their memories of them—and not one of whom
can be said to have been thoroughly disinterested. The more
colorful and complicated the author's personality was, and the
more troubled his relationships with other people, the harder it
is to distinguish the motivations behind each account of him
that survives. The governing prejudices range over the whole
spectrum of human partiality, from the vindictive to the adula-
tory; to filter them out requires an expert knowledge not only
of the facts but of psychology. And, in the midst of complex
jealousies and desires for self-justification, the eternal juxtaposi-
tion of the whitewash brush and the tar bucket, we never can
be sure either of all the relevant facts or of the true motives of
people long dead. All we can do is try to see things as clearly as
we can, removed as we are from the agitating spell of the
writer's presence.

One of the most vexing problems in English literary history
is the character and career of Byron, over whose grave an
extraordinary warfare has raged without intermission for the
last 150 years. Byron's life story is, of course, inseparable in
its later phase from Shelley's; and inseparable from both is the
swashbuckling figure of Edward John Trelawny, whose chief
distinction is that he wrote the most detailed description of the
burning of Shelley's body on the beach near Pisa. During his
long life he wrote ten separate versions of the pyre scene, each
differing to some extent from all the rest. The discrepancies
of detail are enough to bewilder any seeker after the truth, but
troubles multiply with our knowledge that Trelawny's contemporaries regarded him as an indefatigable liar. When he was
a member of the Shelley-Byron circle he had already, according
to himself, served an exciting life before the mast, deserted his
ship in Bengal, turned pirate, and embarked on a series of
romantic and sometimes melodramatic attachments to women,
the first of which was a Haidée-like idyll in the South Seas.
Persisting in his adventurous habits, Trelawny subsequently
became involved in the Greek War of Independence, and
took, as his third wife, the half-sister of the revolutionary
leader Odysseus. In 1831, at the age of thirty-nine, he pub-

lished his autobiography, *Adventures of a Younger Son,* which, if literally true, commemorates one of the most remarkable careers a red-blooded Englishman has ever survived.

As biographers delved ever deeper into the lives of Byron and Shelley, the question persisted and grew more urgent: How far could Trelawny be trusted? Some time ago, two investigators, Leslie Marchand and Lady Anne Hill, examined his narratives afresh. Lady Hill was inspired to check the assertions in *Adventures of a Younger Son* against unimpeachable British Admiralty documents in the Public Record Office. Episode by episode, she sailed in Trelawny's wake, and concluded that "the proportion of truth to fiction in *The Adventures* turns out to be small, no more than one tenth"—the latter fraction representing his astonishingly accurate memories of his pre-nautical childhood. If he was capable of telling the exact truth, why did he spin such outrageous yarns? Lady Hill suggested, in essence, that it was to compensate for his sense of inferiority in the company of well-educated and sophisticated men like Byron and Shelley. His one asset was his career as a sailor, and he not only exploited such excitements as he had had far beyond their worth but actually invented the saga of himself as buccaneer.[24]

The question then arises, did the same incurable bent for romancing about his personal adventures affect his veracity when he told of the last days of Byron and Shelley? Marchand, after minutely comparing the multiple versions of the seaside cremation, concluded that those written nearest to the event are the most credible (as such accounts ordinarily are) and the most consistent in detail, one with the others. It is mainly those written from thirty to fifty years later that are suspect—the result of a failing memory, a "lazy disinclination to check anything," and concern for the susceptibilities of the Victorian audience, which resulted in his omitting some of the grisly details he had included in earlier descriptions. The famous volume of Sophocles (or was it Aeschylus?) that Shelley was

24. "Trelawny's Family Background and Naval Career," *Keats-Shelley Journal,* 5 (1956), 11-32. For an expanded discussion of the *Adventures* and of the life generally of this notorious figure in literary history, see William St. Clair, *Trelawny: The Incurable Romancer* (London, 1977).

alleged to have had in his pocket was a late addition (1858) to the story.[25]

Fortunately, biographers do not often have to contend with witnesses as extravagantly romance-prone as Edward John Trelawny, though he has his rivals; one thinks, for instance, of Ford Madox Ford, to whom H. G. Wells attributed "a copious carelessness of reminiscence," and of Frank Harris, a celebrated liar who, energetically assisted by the tendentious and discrepant memoirs of other participants in the events, managed (among other accomplishments) to becloud the history of Oscar Wilde's last years so thoroughly that it probably never will be entirely straightened out. But most scholars must, from time to time, cope with dubious testimony of some sort. Poe's more romantic biographers, notably Hervey Allen, made much of the story of his courtship of "Mary Devereaux," the purported details of which Mary, then aged seventy-one, related to a writer who printed them in *Harper's Magazine* in 1889. Poe, according to Mary, was desperately in love with her, and "cowhided" her uncle, who took exception to the proposed match. But, as Arthur Hobson Quinn wrote (*Poe*, p. 196), "If there is any form of evidence that is fundamentally unreliable, it is that of an elderly woman concerning her youthful love affair with a man who has since become famous."

Day by day, if we keep our eyes and ears open, we can behold myth in the making. Colleges and universities from coast to coast have their stories of Dylan Thomas and other spectacular literary characters who have enlivened poetry readings and receptions by their unconventional, and more often than not alcohol-induced, behavior. The anecdotes seldom lose anything, except accuracy, in the telling or in the process of transmission down through the years. When they are finally dignified by print, they are often grotesque distortions of what really happened.

Responsible scholars therefore seize every chance they get to correct misstatements before they can take root and grow. In the *Times Literary Supplement* (October 31, 1958), Sir Shane Leslie wrote that Monsignor Fay and the Newman

25. "Trelawny on the Death of Shelley," *Keats-Shelley Memorial Bulletin*, 4 (1952), 9–34.

School "trained and civilized" the Scott Fitzgerald who came "from the wilds of Minnesota"; that he, Leslie, corrected and sent to Scribner's the manuscript of *This Side of Paradise*, 40,000 copies of which were sold in Chicago alone; and that during the Fitzgeralds' visit to London, "Zelda very nearly had a baby" on the Leslies' best sofa. Immediately Fitzgerald's biographer, Arthur Mizener, wrote to correct Sir Shane's manifold errors (*TLS*, November 14, 1958). The fifteen-year-old boy who came from Minnesota—hardly "the wilds" thereof—to the Newman School may have been naive, he said, but the St. Paul Academy, which he had formerly attended, was the better school, and "if Fitzgerald was ever 'trained and civilized' . . . it was mostly by Princeton." The book that Leslie corrected was not *This Side of Paradise* but *The Romantic Egotist*, and *This Side of Paradise*, far from selling 40,000 copies in Chicago alone, had a total sale for the year of less than that figure. As for the alleged peril to the Leslies' sofa, the truth was that "the Fitzgeralds were in London for ten days in June of 1921; their child was born four months later, on October 26th, in St. Paul, Minnesota." In reply (November 21) Sir Shane took solace in the thought that "it is only by hashing up memories that the finality of biography is prepared for the biographers." Since, even in this scientific age, accuracy on the part of the witnesses is too much to hope for, scholars must examine evidence relating to recent authors as carefully as they have long been accustomed to do with stories told of Shakespeare and Milton.

The problem of evaluating primary evidence is complicated, of course, when several firsthand witnesses, all presumably of the same dependability, differ among themselves. Those who knew the mature Wordsworth left a remarkable variety of impressions. The favorable reactions added up to the image of a modest poet, receptive to honest criticism, generous to younger men, possessed of wide sympathies and an open mind on political and religious questions. But an equally large body of evidence supports the idea that Wordsworth was egotistic, intolerant of criticism, a religious bigot, and a political renegade. Obviously one version is nearer the truth than the other—but which is it? The source of every statement has to be analyzed in view of the character, reliability, temperamental sympathy, and possible bias of the contributor. Edith Batho, who performed the task in her provocative book *The Later Words-worth* (1933), concluded that the favorable report of Wordsworth is derived from the testimony of "a heterogeneous assemblage of people . . . all of marked independence of judgment" and therefore trustworthy, while the unattractive image was the product of a closely knit group that included Leigh Hunt, Keats, and Hazlitt. Thus, Batho argued, Wordsworth's reputation as a man has suffered because of the animus of a small but influential coterie operating in the limited period 1818–25. I do not happen to subscribe to her conclusion, but her method, which boils down to an exhaustive inquiry into Exactly Who Said What, is the right one.

"Exactly Who Said What?"—and, as we have seen, it is equally important to ask When: soon after the event, or at a long remove from it? Moreover, as we analyze primary evidence, we must also consider How and Under What Circumstances. The very language of a statement sometimes is a clue to its veracity. The more emotional a person is, the less likely is he to provide an objective version of an event or a judicious opinion; and the overwrought terms in which a piece of evidence is phrased may well cast doubt upon its dependability except as an index to the witness' state of mind. More subtly, there is always the problem posed by the elusive quality of words. In letters between intimates, only the recipient has the full key to the special implications and connotations of the writer's language; the subsequent reader can only infer the subsurface meaning from whatever else he knows. Swift's letters to Stella are an extreme case of what I am talking about, but much more common is the irony, the private joke, the concealed affectionate or knife-twisting phrase—a knowledge of which may alter the whole residual meaning of a statement. This sensitivity to tone extends, also, to what has been called period style. Gordon Ray has pointed out that the high-flying sentimentality of Victorian correspondence between a man and a woman may easily be misinterpreted; in that era, as in the Elizabethan, the plumes of rhetorical smoke did not inevitably denote the presence of amorous fire, though they may well have done so in the case of Thackeray and Mrs. Brookfield.[26] The conventionalities of contemporary discourse, then, must be allowed for in interpreting evidence. And it sometimes happens that the unwary scholar is betrayed by a single word. I once read a paper in which a graduate student argued that a certain Victorian journalist and sensational novelist was despised by the working classes because in their newspapers he was referred to as a "trump." Evidently assuming that "trump" is a portmanteau word amalgamating "tramp" and "chump," the student took it to be a term of opprobrium; whereas the fact is that to call a chap a "trump" was just about the highest praise the Victorian man in the street could bestow on another. A whole argument undermined by one misunderstood word!

Finally, the immediate circumstances under which a statement was made may provide a clue to its veracity. Innumerable nineteenth-century biographies are laden with character sketches and other memoirs contributed, at the request of the widow and children, by friends of the subject who could be relied on to tell only as much of the truth as would be appropriate—and perhaps to enhance the floral atmosphere with a few blooms of non-truth as well. Hallam Tennyson's two-volume monument to his father (1897) is smothered under such tributes, the evidential assay of which is depressingly low. The grim truth about Tennyson's upbringing in a country rectory dominated by an alcoholic and psychotic father was first revealed in 1949, in an excellent biography by his grandson, Sir Charles Tennyson, to whose cooperation and generosity many modern scholars are deeply indebted. (Sir Charles, incidentally, was not an academic himself but a distinguished lawyer and holder of high offices in British government and industry.)

A letter, likewise, must be read in the light of its immediate purpose and the relations that existed between writer and recipient. Is the writer attempting to justify himself, to win sympathy for his cause, to persuade the other person to a certain course of action? May he be, for whatever reason, distorting the facts? And is the friend one to whom the writer is accus-

26. Gordon N. Ray, *Thackeray: The Age of Wisdom* (New York, 1958), p. 80.

tomed to unbosom himself—or is their relationship such that we may suspect a certain reticence, or even a deliberate reshaping of the facts?

3. Two Applications of the Critical Spirit: Fixing Dates and Testing Genuineness

Throughout this chapter, underlying all the diverse illustrations, we have heard one persistent theme: *Be sure of your facts —and if in the slightest doubt, take another look.* (Even if you have no doubt, take another look anyway.) Now, before we turn to the way the critical spirit operates in several broad fields of research, we should look briefly at two problems which are often met in all of those fields, from determination of text to source study. These topics are, to use the formal designations, chronology and critical examination of a document's authenticity.

Nowadays, when most people's historical perspective is so limited that all events which happened before 1900 seem to have been roughly contemporary with one another, scholars must take particular care to cultivate an acute awareness of time. By very definition, the concern of literary history is with events that occurred in a certain order and are often causally related. Chronology often provides a decisive answer to questions of relationship where other evidence is vague, ambiguous, or simply non-existent. By applying our sharp time-sense to the documents and received narratives before us, we can often place an event more precisely in the sequence to which it belongs, and even more important, we may thereby prove or disprove a doubtful statement.

For a long time, the accepted story behind "The Triumph of Time," Swinburne's lyric lament over a broken love affair, was that the poet had been in love with Jane Faulkner ("Boo"), the adopted daughter of an eminent London pathologist. According to Edmund Gosse, Swinburne proposed to her "in a manner which seemed to her preposterous and violent. More from nervousness, probably, than from ill-will, she broke out laughing in his face. He was deeply chagrined, and . . . he showed his displeasure, and they parted on the worst of terms." Swinburne went into Northumberland and there poured out his embittered heart in "The Triumph of Time." This is a moving and plausible story, which has but one flaw in it, as John S. Mayfield learned when he found the official record of Jane's birth. She was born on February 4, 1852, and since the year in which she allegedly laughed in Swinburne's face was 1862, the conclusion is fairly obvious. It is not unlikely, to be sure, that a girl of ten *would* have responded thus to a proposal from a man of twenty-five, but it is highly doubtful that Swinburne, whatever his other sexual proclivities, would have proposed to a girl of ten in the first place. Thus "Boo" has been discredited as the inspiration of "The Triumph of Time," and although it is generally agreed that the poem, along with others from the same period, is the product of a deeply traumatic experience, the girl who inflicted the damage has not yet been positively identified. [27]

Chronological considerations sometimes may lead us into deeper waters than we anticipate. When writing his *Crusader in Crinoline*, Forrest Wilson closely inspected the series of events preceding and following Harriet Beecher Stowe's publication of the story of Byron's incest as she had heard it from his widow. The article that contained the dark narrative appeared in the *Atlantic Monthly* for September, 1869, and at once the press on both sides of the ocean denounced Mrs. Stowe as a vicious scandalmonger. When, the following year, she published a book on the subject, *Lady Byron Vindicated*, Mrs. Stowe declared that she would never have written her *Atlantic* article had she not been moved to do so by some aspersions on Lady Byron's character printed in *Blackwood's Magazine* for July, 1869. But by examining the records of Fields, Osgood, and Company, the *Atlantic*'s publishers, Wilson

27. Mayfield's article, "Swinburne's Boo," *English Miscellany* [Rome], 4 (1953), 161–77, is a good example of the way a researcher assembles documentary evidence to piece together the record of an obscure life. Cecil Y. Lang, "Swinburne's Lost Love," *PMLA*, 74 (1959), 123–30, proposes Swinburne's cousin, Mary Gordon, for the place left vacant by Mayfield's dethronement of the prenubile Boo.

was able to show that Mrs. Stowe did not tell the truth, for she had in fact delivered her manuscript to the editor in late June, before any copy of the July *Blackwood's*, or any word of its contents, could possibly have arrived in the United States. Actually, Wilson maintained, her whole purpose in writing the article was to proclaim "the glamorous, stupendous fact that she . . . had been the bosom friend of Byron's wife and widow, the sharer of her most intimate secrets." [28]

The exact order in which events occurred may thus lead a scholar to reconsider an author's motives, and this, in turn, may affect his final estimate of the author's character. Dates have a way of opening whole new realms of fruitful exploration. Even when the chronological test has apparently only destructive results, the erasure of a palpably untrue story may leave a gap that must be filled by renewed inquiry. If the event did not happen as alleged, did it happen at all? And if it did happen, what were the *true* circumstances?

In addition to chronological problems involving events whose dates are on record or can be inferred from existing information, there are those presented by undated or questionably dated books and manuscripts. Take as an example, for simplicity's sake, an undated letter by a famous romantic poet. How can one supply the day, month, and year when it was written? There are several kinds of physical evidence. A postmark, naturally, is a great help, but even assuming (which we have no right to do) that the letter was mailed the day it was written, the practices and accidents of the post office in its earlier days were such that a postmark may have been applied two or three days after the letter was handed in. If the paper's watermark bears the year of manufacture, one can say with confidence that the letter was not written *before* that year, and probably no more than five to eight years later; it is simply a question of how long a supply of such paper would normally have lasted in the warehouse, the stationer's shop, and the purchaser's writing desk. Handwriting is a possible clue: if enough dated specimens are available for comparison, it may be legitimate to

28. *Crusader in Crinoline: The Life of Harriet Beecher Stowe* (Philadelphia, 1941), pp. 535–51.

say that a given document is in the handwriting the poet is known to have used at the age of twenty rather than that which is characteristic of him at the age of fifty. But handwriting varies so much—a man in a hurry, for instance, may write a quite different hand from that which he used an hour earlier, when he was at leisure—that no conclusions can be reached without expert knowledge and an abundance of documents to examine, and even so, they must remain tentative.[29]

One is on firmer ground in attempting to date a letter from its contents. Allusions to contemporary events can be pinned down by reference to newspapers, diaries, and other firsthand sources for the period. (Large-scale chronological dictionaries or "annals" are often useful also, but their accuracy should be checked against sources close to the event.) Similarly, references to situations and incidents in the writer's personal life, when clarified by other biographical material such as letters and diaries, either those of the writer himself or of his friends, may provide the key to the letter's exact or approximate date. And sometimes it is possible to date a letter by fitting it into the sequence to which it belongs; if it alludes to a statement made in a letter received from a friend of the writer and dated September 18, and if a question it contains is answered by that friend in a letter of October 3, it must have been written some time between September 19 and October 2. Additional evidence, such as knowledge of the respective whereabouts and activities of the correspondents during the period (how long would a letter have taken to pass between them? was one away from home and his mail not forwarded? was he ill and unable to write?) and acquaintance with their habits as letter writers (was the one usually dilatory, the other a prompt

29. The editors of the Pilgrim edition of Dickens' letters rely heavily, for dating purposes, upon the steady changes in his characteristic embellished signature: see Volume I, p. xxiv and the facing plate. The dating of Emily Dickinson's poems is both assisted and complicated by her altering handwriting and the fact that her manuscripts were divided into little packets consisting of various kinds of paper; the problem is to find some kind of rational sequence amidst the variables. See R. W. Franklin, *The Editing of Emily Dickinson: A Reconsideration* (Madison, Wis., 1967). In her *Arthur Hugh Clough: The Uncommitted Mind* (Oxford, [1962], pp. 264–66) Lady Katharine Chorley dates certain of the poet's manuscripts by reconstructing the folding of the paper.

answerer?), might narrow down the probable date still further.[30]

The same genera of techniques, though of course different species thereof, are used to unknot problems of date presented by books. Incunabula (books printed before 1501) and six-teenth- and seventeenth-century books often bear no dates or places of printing, or if they do, this information may be con-veyed in a mysterious fashion. The title page motto GUSTAVUS ADOLPHUS GLORIOSE PUGNANS MORITUR may conceal the fact that the book was printed in 1632 (add up the letters that are also Roman numerals, counting the U's as V's), and an English book purporting to have been issued at "Malborow" actually was printed at Cologne—although "Malborow" means "Mar-burg"! Chronograms, as exemplified by the Gustavus Adolphus motto, and fictitious imprints, usually intended to conceal the origin of obscene, seditious, blasphemous, or otherwise sub-versive literature, such as the Martin Marprelate tracts, are two of the many riddles the bibliographical sleuth must be prepared to solve in order to ascertain a book's probable date. Others relate to the book's physical characteristics: its paper (watermarks are an important form of evidence), typography, and ornaments and illustrations. Borderlines, title page devices, elaborate initial letters, and even, in the earliest period of print-ing, illustrations were kept in stock and used over and over by the same printer. Hence, by minutely examining the degree of wear exhibited by such components in an undated volume and comparing it with that shown in dated specimens, it is possible to establish the approximate year when a book was printed. The progressive wear exhibited by individual pieces of type is now being used to distinguish between early and late states of sheets in copies of the Shakespeare first folio.

Many of the critical techniques used in determining date are applied to the detection of forgeries. As I have described in

30. Individual literary works are sometimes dated, or re-dated, accord-ing to the same principles. Constance Drake, "A Topical Dating for 'Locksley Hall Sixty Years After,'" *Victorian Poetry*, 10 (1972), 307–20, analyzes a number of topical allusions in Tennyson's late poem to demon-strate that it was written sometime between 1882 and 1884, and not in 1886, as a statement in Hallam Tennyson's *Memoir* of his father has led scholars to assume. For a description of the various kinds of evidence used to date Coleridge's notebooks, see Kathleen Coburn, *The Notebooks of Samuel Taylor Coleridge*, I (New York, 1957), xxii–xxvii.

detail in my book, *The Scholar Adventurers,* John Carter and Graham Pollard exposed Thomas J. Wise's long career as a manufacturer and seller of spurious rarities by showing that neither the type nor the paper used in his fake "first" and "private" editions had been introduced at the dates given on the various title pages. And in the case of the most famous forgery, Mrs. Browning's *Sonnets from the Portuguese* (allegedly printed at Reading in 1847), one of the most damning bits of evidence was the fact that Mrs. Browning first showed her poems to her husband *in manuscript* in 1849.

Out-and-out forgeries turn up most frequently in connection with authors who are, or have been, fashionable among collectors and whose holographs have therefore brought unusually high prices. Burns students are often bothered by unauthentic letters, and even today a relic of the spate of bogus Shelleyana that polluted the market in the 1920's occasionally turns up. In the early 1950's there was a flurry of excitement over a group of letters by and to Smollett that an American student had published in *Notes and Queries* and later in a monograph which, though it bore "Madrid" on its title page, seemed actually to have been printed in Brooklyn, New York. Still later the student used one of the letters to argue that Smollett's translation of *Don Quixote* was largely the work of someone else. After the genuineness of the letters was challenged on stylistic grounds by two other Smollett specialists, their owner was prevailed upon to have them examined in a laboratory, where they were proved to be forgeries.[31]

But these are isolated instances. Scholars encounter forgeries by no means as often as writers about the adventurous side of literary research, eager for a touch of melodrama, may imply. Nevertheless, every investigator must, as a matter of prudent routine, keep alert to the possibility that a manuscript or book he is examining was produced with deceptive, if not

---

31. But what's done cannot be undone, and the letters remain in print in at least four places (a monograph and three articles) without anything to warn the unwary that they are not what they purport to be. For a summary of this unhappy episode, see *PQ,* 31 (1952), 299–300, where references are given to the previous attacks on the letters and their sponsor's replies.

clearly criminal, intent. The date may be erroneous; the document's handwriting may not be that of the putative author; a "new edition" of a book may contain a text that has been reprinted without change or, on the other hand, has been silently abridged. All that glisters is not gold, and as James Sutherland observed when he was writing about the progress of error in biographies of the actress Mrs. Centlivre, "the price of . . . truth appears, indeed, to be eternal vigilance, and eternal skepticism."

CHAPTER THREE

Some Scholarly Occupations

~~~~~~

"You may observe [said Sir Arthur Wardour, speaking of
Jonathan Oldbuck] that he never has any advantage of me
in dispute, unless when he avails himself of a sort of
pettifogging intimacy with dates, names, and trifling matters of fact, a tiresome and frivolous accuracy of memory . . ."
"He must find it convenient in historical investigation,
I should think, sir," said the young lady.
—Sir Walter Scott, *The Antiquary*, Ch. 5.

In the preceding chapter, the spirit of scholarship was illustrated chiefly from one kind of research, the biographical.
Now we shall look at several other important branches of
literary investigation: the establishment of a dependable text,
the determination of authorship, source study, the tracing of
reputation and influence, and, finally, at the contiguous fields
of history in which the literary student often travels. That

these branches are treated *seriatim* does not imply, however, that literary scholarship is in any way compartmentalized. They are all interdependent and mutually contributory, as fundamentally related as, say, organic, inorganic, and physical chemistry. Like a chemist, a literary scholar must command all the basic techniques of his profession, so that he is competent to deal with whatever unforeseen problems may arise as his investigation proceeds. Settling a question of authorship may call for detailed biographical research as well as the expertise of the textual student. Each of a number of different kinds of problems—textual accuracy, disputed authorship, a novelist's indebtedness to one of his predecessors, or a dramatist's influence on his successors—calls for the skillful evaluation and interpretation of internal evidence. The key to an obscure passage in an author's poetry or to a crucial aspect of his thought may lie in an odd corner of intellectual or social history. Seldom is an investigation so neatly delimited that it does not require borrowing data and techniques from adjoining areas.

A good scholar therefore has to be versatile. But at the same time, work in the different branches of literary research to be touched upon in the following pages has a single necessity: observance of the cardinal rules of evidence and reasoning. The fact that one body of law governs all makes it possible for any intelligent scholar to range freely and with reasonable confidence over the whole territory. A clear head and an undeviating adherence to the canons of historical criticism will not make him a master in any field, but they do entitle him to his journeyman's papers.

In view of the tendency of its several sections, this chapter might just as well be called "Further Applications of the Critical Spirit." For while, like Chapter Two, it makes no pretense of offering either a systematic or an exhaustive decalogue of scholarly procedure, it contains, however informally presented, the essence of such a code. Implicit in the examples and the discussion of problems that are characteristic of one or another of the major scholarly occupations are a few governing principles which will be summarized at the end of this chapter and in the opening pages of the next.

1. Textual Study

Nobody yet knows how it happened, but happen it did: in the first American edition of Henry James's *The Ambassadors*, Chapters 28 and 29 were reversed. Whether or not James was somehow responsible, we do not know; he supervised the first London edition, published two months earlier in 1903, and there the chapters were in the right order. Whatever its cause, the transposition persisted in all American editions, and not until 1950 was attention called to it. In 1955 the publishers, Harper and Brothers, announced that the forthcoming reprinting of *The Ambassadors* in their Modern Classics Series would finally present the chapters in the right order. *Hubris* is as sure an invitation to disaster in the publishing trade as elsewhere,[1] and Harpers promptly had a great fall; in the new edition, Chapter 29 once again preceded Chapter 28. After corporate prayer and fasting, Harpers sent the book back to press in 1957, and, to their relief, the chapters finally came out in the right order. But the next year the firm leased the rights to Doubleday for an Anchor paperback edition. "That edition," they wrote in their house organ in November, 1958, "has just been published and with a flourish (how well we recall *our* April, 1955 announcement) the Anchor people have proclaimed to the world that *here* is an edition of the novel with *all chapters in their proper sequence*. And you know what? They aren't."

Subsequently, to bring the story down to date, several paperback *Ambassadors* have had the chapters in correct sequence. But it would be a rash prophet who could assure the world that henceforth, without fail, Chapter 28 will precede Chapter 29.[2]

1. Further disaster was narrowly averted when this very sentence appeared in the first edition of the present book. A nodding professional indexer wrote a slip reading "*Hubris* (Henry James)," and so it appeared in the galley proofs of the index. Only the vigilance of the proofreading author forestalled a fictitious addition to the James canon. This is one way, though admittedly not a common one, by which bibliographical ghosts are made.

2. For a review of this curious story, see Leon Edel, "The Text of *The Ambassadors*," *Harvard Library Bulletin*, 14 (1960), 453–60.

This example suggests that (as has already been intimated in Chapter 2) some errors are, in the strictest sense, incorrigible. They simply refuse to give way to truth. This bibliographical comedy supplied a powerful impetus to the movement for authoritative texts. Although scholars had long been insisting on textual accuracy, the stress upon close reading that resulted from the so-called "new criticism" in the 1940's and 1950's focused interest as never before on the very words the author wrote. More than once in the course of those years, critics were unlucky in their choice of texts from which to quote; the word they celebrated for its aptness or ambiguity or irony or simple depth of meaning happened not to be the one that the author wrote. The classic case—it has been cited so often as to be a chestnut by now, but no other example makes the point quite so well—was that of F. O. Matthiessen, who lavished much admiration upon what he took to be the *discordia concors* of the "soiled fish" image in Melville's *White-Jacket* (Chapter XCII). His admiration unfortunately was misplaced. "Soiled" was a printer's error; the word Melville actually had written was "coiled." [3]

But if critics, in pursuit of hidden subtleties, often failed to distinguish between the author's true intention and a fortuitous misprint, with every passing year scholars have become more conscious of the number of error-spotted versions of masterpieces that have passed down to us through the hands of careless printers and easygoing editors and, in lack of better ones, remain the texts upon which critical discussion rests.

If misapprehension about a text is sometimes responsible for errors in interpretation and criticism, it also may result in a mistaken understanding of the history of a book's early reputation. In 1832 Edward Bulwer's novel *Eugene Aram*, a popular success, came under severe critical attack because of the author's sympathy with the murderer-hero and, therefore, his presumptive encouragement of any number of readers to go and do likewise. But modern readers find it hard to understand the basis of this attack, because in the copies of the novel they read, Aram—a historical figure—is not guilty of murder. The

3. John W. Nichol, "Melville's '"Soiled" Fish of the Sea,'" *AL*, 21 (1949), 338–39.

answer is that when the novel was to be reissued in 1849, Bulwer-Lytton (as he had then become) considerably revised it. "In the new preface . . . he announced that he had changed his mind about Eugene's guilt: having restudied all the evidence, he had concluded that Eugene Aram was an accomplice in the robbery but no more. In the text . . . Bulwer changed the substance of the criminal's confession, made his attitudes more palatable both before and after the crime, and altered some passages which had been interpreted as showing the author's admiration for the criminal. Aram looked, after all this, a different man indeed." [4] It was this revised text of 1849, with its crucial alteration of viewpoint, that was followed in all subsequent editions, thus giving the reader a totally false impression of the original.

Today we realize that accurate texts, and knowledge of which text of a particular work has a bearing upon a given problem, are indispensable to the progress of literary study. It is pointless to try to interpret and evaluate any work of art, whether a poem, a painting, or a sonata, on the basis of an imperfect reproduction, or of a reproduction which does not represent it as a certain critic or audience knew it. Before we presume to judge a work's meaning, its artistic strategy, or the response of its readers from its first appearance down to the present, we must have its *exact* words before us. [5]

Shakespeare offers the most bountiful case in point. The textual history of his plays is incredibly complicated. Half of them appeared in one or more quartos (small-format printings of individual plays) which preceded the first collected ("folio")

4. Keith Hollingsworth, *The Newgate Novel* (Detroit, 1963), p. 94. For other examples from the same period of the trouble caused by failure to use the right edition see Ellen Moers, *The Dandy: Brummell to Beerbohm* (London, 1960), pp. 69, 78, 174 (on Bulwer's *Pelham*) and Robert Blake, *Disraeli* (London, 1966), pp. 37–44 (on Disraeli's *Vivian Grey*).

5. As M. J. C. Hodgart has observed, however ("Misquotation as Recreation," *Essays in Criticism*, 3 [1953], 28–38), inaccurate quotation on the part of both poets and critics sometimes has its own critical significance, representing an attempt at "creative rewriting." But the inadvertent emendations are seldom as good as the authentic originals.

edition of 1623, and the readings of which differ among themselves as well as from the folio. Moreover, we now know that even among individual copies of the same printing, which one would expect to be identical, there may be hundreds of textual variations. This discovery was made possible by the invention of the Hinman Collating Machine, an ingenious optical device which, by superimposing on a mirror the images of two different copies of a printing, opened at the same page, shows up minute differences of typesetting. And besides the quartos and the four seventeenth-century folios, there have been scores of eighteenth-century and later editions whose editors have constantly introduced their own readings or emendations. During the past sixty years, enormous effort has gone into straightening out this confusion and establishing as nearly as possible what Shakespeare presumably wrote. Scholars and the ordinary reader alike have profited from this effort; the Shakespeare texts commonly found in the classroom have been scrupulously re-edited and now reflect and incorporate this new knowledge.

Although for sheer prolific quantity of error and more or less capricious emendation the Shakespeare canon is probably unmatched in the history of English literature, many other classic texts have suffered the same way, beginning with the original printer's misreading of copy and continuing through subsequent misadventures in the printing house and at the nodding or overingenious editor's desk. Between 1711–12, when the *Spectator* papers were first printed, and 1868, when Henry Morley prepared what remained until recently the best critical edition, some 3,000 corruptions worked their way into the text.[6] Except for Jane Austen, no nineteenth-century English novelist can be read in a textually reliable collected edition. Modern trade editions of Dickens, for instance, usually trace their text back to one or another of the editions published in his lifetime, not necessarily representing either the version that the first readers saw or the last version Dickens approved, and

6. Donald F. Bond, "The Text of the *Spectator*," *SB*, 5 (1952/3), 109–28. Bond's definitive edition (5 vols., 1965) is an exemplary work of scholarship.

are disfigured by a generous accretion of subsequent printer's errors. Only now are the Clarendon Press editions of Dickens and the Brontës and the highly praised Wesleyan edition of Fielding beginning to provide scholars with texts comparable in reliability to those of *Hard Times* and *Bleak House*, both edited by George H. Ford and Sylvère Monod, in the Norton Critical Editions series. Other inexpensive editions whose texts range from acceptable to very good include certain titles in Houghton Mifflin's Riverside series (*Vanity Fair*, *The Mill on the Floss*), the Oxford English Novels (*Jane Eyre*, *Cranford*), and the Penguin English Library (*Shirley*, *Daniel Deronda*).

American editions of nineteenth- and early twentieth-century British writers are notoriously undependable, since they were often set from uncorrected proofs or advance sheets of the British edition and suffered further indignities at the hands of American editors and printers. Hardy's American admirers, as Carl J. Weber demonstrated with many examples, seldom read exactly what their English contemporaries did; in the Harper edition of *The Return of the Native* that was long current, a whole page was missing, and until recently all of the American editions of *The Woodlanders* reproduced the novel's magazine text, without taking account of the numerous changes Hardy had made in successive London editions.[7]

The list of great literary works which until lately have been, and in many cases still are, read in undependable texts could be extended almost indefinitely. One instance is that of *The Scarlet Letter*. Beginning with the second edition, the type for which was set hastily to meet an unexpected demand and was not proofread by Hawthorne, the text became more and more corrupt, until the "standard" text of 1883 contained many hundreds of variants from the first edition. Only in 1961 did the first-edition text, the only one Hawthorne corrected, become available in a modern printing. David Daiches has pointed out that "in the first one-volume American edition of the collected poems of W. B. Yeats there are at least half a dozen misprints

7. "American Editions of English Authors," *Nineteenth-Century English Books* (Urbana, Ill., 1952), pp. 27–50 *passim*. For more on Hardy, see Robert C. Schweik, "Current Problems in Textual Scholarship on the Works of Hardy," *English Literature in Transition*, 14 (1971), 239–46.

which completely change the meaning of the passages in which they occur, and in some cases critics have actually analyzed the misprinted poems unaware of the errors, and have justified and even praised the mistaken words. The printing of 'he' as 'she' at the end of the second stanza of 'Crazy Jane on the Day of Judgment' changes the meaning of the whole poem, for the poem is a dialogue and the misprint transfers a key statement to the wrong speaker." Similarly, the substitution of the sixth line for the second in another dialogue poem, "Cuchulain's Fight with the Sea," had the effect of attributing every subsequent speech to the wrong speaker.[8] But this is only one aspect—the most accidental—of the perplexity that attends a study of Yeats's texts, for he was a ceaseless reviser and his poems, even after publication, were in a constant state of flux.

The best text of *The Great Gatsby* is found in Fitzgerald's posthumous *Three Novels*. Of the seventy-five significant changes between the first edition and the latter text, thirty-eight were suggested by Fitzgerald, the rest being inserted by the publisher without his authorization—and, conversely, a number of other corrections which the novelist proposed were *not* made. Thus even the "best" text does not represent the way Fitzgerald wanted his book to read.[9]

In this highly unsatisfactory state of affairs, the textual scholar has acquired greatly enlarged importance. It is he who produces a certified copy of a literary text, so that the interpretive critic has an absolutely authentic basis for his exegesis. But to identify or reconstruct a "sound" or "pure" text is a complicated job, because the histories of individual books vary greatly and it is often hard to decide which of several available versions should be used as "copy text." The three earliest printings of the *Spectator*—the original folio sheets (contemporary newspaper format), the first collected edition (in octavo volumes), and the second (in duodecimo)—"differ widely," as Donald Bond has reported, "not only in punctua-

8. *Critical Approaches to Literature* (New York, 1956), pp. 332-33. See also Russell K. Alspach, "Some Textual Problems in Yeats," *SB*, 9 (1957), 51-67.
9. Bruce Harkness, "Bibliography and the Novelistic Fallacy," *SB*, 12 (1959), 59-73.

tion, spelling, and capitalization, but in phrasing, in grammatical construction, and in literary style. For how many of these changes—in spelling, for example—were Steele and Addison responsible? How many were due to the style of the printing-house, or to the care—or negligence—of the compositor?"[10] Sometimes complexity is heaped on complexity by the existence of manuscript and other versions which deviate at many points from the received printed text. The editor of John Stuart Mill's *Autobiography*, for example, must cope with at least four versions: an early manuscript draft (printed for the first time in 1961), a second draft (from which the "Columbia" text of 1924 was printed), a copy prepared for the press after Mill's death (and containing over 2,650 variants from the manuscript on which it was based), and the printed first edition of 1873.[11]

Sir Walter Greg, whose article on "The Rationale of Copy-Text" (*SB*, 3 [1950/51], 19–36) is widely regarded as a *locus classicus* for modern methodology, generally preferred the earliest printed text as the most authoritative, because it was closest to the writer's manuscript. A reprint whose text has been thoroughly revised by the author, however, seemed to Greg to have at least the authority of a first edition. He concluded, therefore, that "it seems impossible to lay down any hard and fast rule as to when an editor should take the original edition as his copy-text and when the revised reprint. All that can be said is that if the original be selected, then the author's corrections must be incorporated; and that if the reprint be selected, then the original reading must be restored when that of the reprint is due to unauthorized variation [such as a compositor's error or a publishing-house editor's "improvement"]. Thus the editor cannot escape the responsibility of distinguishing to the best of his ability between the two categories."

Greg's preference was adopted, with modifications, as the policy of the Center for Editions of American Authors, to be discussed shortly. But the contrary preference also has many adherents: that is, the view that the text of the last edition the author supervised in his lifetime is the most authoritative.

10. Bond (cited in note 6), p. 112.
11. Jack Stillinger, "The Text of John Stuart Mill's *Autobiography*," *Bulletin of the John Rylands Library*, 43 (1960), 220–42.

It is impossible to fix upon a hard-and-fast rule, because individual cases offer special problems. Thus, although the definitive edition of Browning's poetry now in progress adopts the last edition published in the poet's lifetime as the copy-text, it can be maintained that despite Browning's many subsequent revisions, the first edition of *The Ring and the Book* is historically the most significant because it represents the poem as it was read by the wary audience—"British Public, who may like me yet"—to whom Browning committed his reputation as a poet. It was upon the basis of this text, rather than any later one, that the British public of 1868–69 decided that he was, after all, a great poet. Similarly, Henry Binder has argued that the manuscript version of *The Red Badge of Courage* is the text which most faithfully reflects Crane's intentions, not that published by Appleton in 1895. Crane severely altered and excised material in the manuscript, Binder claims, in order to meet the demands of the contemporary audience as they were perceived by his editor, Ripley Hitchcock.[12]

Greg was one of the pioneers (R. B. McKerrow and A. W. Pollard being two noteworthy coadjutors) of the so-called "new bibliography," a British-made discipline as sophisticated, and in its own sphere as epoch-making, as the American-bred "new criticism" was to be somewhat later. Reconstructing the steps by which an early author's manuscript found its way into print, they sought to discover what vicissitudes the text may have suffered in the process. Their laboriously acquired knowledge of the conditions and practices that prevailed in the

12. "The *Red Badge of Courage* Nobody Knows," *Studies in the Novel*, 10 (1978), 9–47. Binder's views have not gone unchallenged, however; for a defense of the published text as that representing Crane's intentions, see Donald Pizer in *Studies in the Novel*, 11 (1979), 77–81, and Binder's reply later in the same volume, pages 216–23. Examples of solutions to problems involving the selection of copy text and the determination of authorial intention abound in the volumes of *Studies in Bibliography*, *Proof*, and *Papers of the Bibliographical Society of America* published in the 1960's and 1970's. An excellent guide to and through material on this subject is G. Thomas Tanselle's article, "The Editorial Problem of Final Authorial Intention," *SB*, 29 (1976), 167–211. Scholarship on other aspects of textual editing, for example the extent and nature of apparatus desirable in a critical edition, the treatment of accidentals (spelling and punctuation), and the function of mechanical aids (collators, scanners, computers) is well surveyed in "The Center for Scholarly Editions: An Introductory Statement," *PMLA*, 92 (1977), 583–97.

English book trade during the sixteenth and seventeenth centuries made possible the production (by themselves and others) of editions of Renaissance literary works, most notably the printed drama, that are closer to the authors' manuscripts than are any previous editions. In the last four decades or so, editors have turned their attention to establishing the texts of writers since Dryden, for they recognize that the corruptions in the received versions of post-1700 literary works are as numerous, and often have as much effect on meaning, as those which marred the now-superseded editions of earlier writers.

Hard physical evidence, higher mathematics (the title of a basic book in the field—another of Greg's works—is *The Calculus of Variants*), and rigorous logical procedures dominate the bibliographical techniques that are preliminary to textual study. Although most bibliographers today resist claims that their discipline is a "science," on the ground that the results they obtain lack absolute certitude, their procedures are thoroughly scientific.[13] Success in textual study requires talents similar to those the scientist possesses: among them endless patience in dealing with the minutiae of physical and textual differences in books, a gift for detecting significant relationships in a seeming chaos of fragmentary data, and the ability to re-create the often complicated printing history of a literary work on the basis of these technical data.

The specialized knowledge necessary to study the textual history of printed books lies in the province of "analytical," "descriptive," and "critical" bibliography. These are Fredson Bowers' terms. *Analytical* bibliography is the "technical investigation of the printing of specific books, or of general printing practice, based exclusively on the physical evidence of the books themselves"; *descriptive* bibliography involves using all the data and methods of analytic bibliography to describe the physical format (and thus the printing history) of

13. For an excellent historical survey, beginning early in the nineteenth century, of the ways *science* has been linked with *bibliography* and how the two words have shifted their meanings in discussions where similarities have been asserted, see G. Thomas Tanselle, "Bibliography and Science," *SB*, 27 (1974), 55–89.

a given book; *critical* bibliography is "the application of the evidence of analytical bibliography . . . to textual problems where meaning of some sort is involved." [14]

For many years, the standard guide to this field was R. B. McKerrow's *An Introduction to Bibliography for Literary Students* (1927). Concentrating on the early (hand press) period of book production, McKerrow showed how a reconstruction of the way a book was set in type from the author's manuscript and then passed through the press could provide the essential information on which a study of the history of its text could rest. The most serious limitation of the volume was its neglect of most eighteenth-century developments and its total omission of the subsequent history of printing, from the beginning of the machine-press era down to the present age of composition by film and computer. This gap has been filled, and McKerrow's work amplified and corrected in the light of recent research, by Philip Gaskell's *A New Introduction to Bibliography* (1972), which is distinguished by copious illustrations and an excellent reference bibliography. Every prospective literary scholar, even one with no immediate plans to do textual work, should master its contents.[15]

In all literary study there are few more absorbing topics than the hazards an author's manuscript underwent between the time he delivered it to the printer and the moment the printed and folded sheets of the book were ready for the binder. There was the form of the manuscript itself, fit to baffle any typesetter— illegible handwriting, cryptic interlineations, balloons in the margins, additional matter (inadequately indicated) on the other side of the leaf, abbreviations to be interpreted. There were the manifold accidents of typesetting—reaching into the wrong

---

14. "Bibliography, Pure Bibliography, and Literary Studies," *PBSA*, 46 (1952), 191–96. This and many other important discussions of textual matters are reprinted in Bowers's *Essays in Bibliography, Text, and Editing* (Charlottesville, 1975).

15. For important reviews of Gaskell, see Fredson Bowers, "McKerrow Revisited," *PBSA*, 67 (1973), 109–24 and G. Thomas Tanselle, "Philip Gaskell's *A New Introduction to Bibliography*," *Costerus*, N. S. 1 (1974), 129–50.

compartment (or into the right compartment, into which a printer's devil had negligently put the wrong type) and consequently setting a wrong letter; the "memorial" errors attendant on trying to keep too large a phrase of the copy in mind before taking another look at the manuscript; distractions of every sort, including the many occasions that called for a drink or two (a newly qualified journeyman, completion of a big job, a religious or civic festival). The history of literary texts was deeply affected by what we may call the factor of the trembling hand and the blurred eyesight, as well as by all the other human conditions that conspired to produce an imperfect book: "a harassed author, a testy master printer, a stupid proofreader, a love-sick compositor, a drunken pressman, a newly-articled apprentice." [16] The wonder is not so much that early books contain so many errors, as that, given the conditions under which their type was set, they contain so few. Although many authors supposedly were indifferent to the state in which their well-chosen words finally were set before the public, from the very beginning there were occasional tense scenes in the printing house, such as the one suggested by Thomas Heywood's bitter words:

The infinite faults escaped in my booke of *Britaines Troy*, by the negligence of the Printer, as the misquotations, mistaking of sillables, misplacing halfe lines, coining of strange and neuer heard of words. These being without number, when I would haue taken a particular account of the *Errata*, the Printer answered me, hee would not publish his own disworkemanship, but rather let his owne fault lye vpon the necke of the Author. . . . [17]

Our knowledge of the way printers worked in the earlier centuries is still far from exhaustive, but it is steadily growing, and as it does, the assumptions on which we base our recon-

---

16. R. C. Bald, "Evidence and Inference in Bibliography," *English Institute Annual 1941* (New York, 1942), p. 162.

17. *An Apology for Actors* (London, 1612), sig. [G4]^r.

struction of a book's textual history have to be revised. One recent discovery, the implications of which are unusually far-reaching, is that type was not necessarily set in consecutive page order, as one would copy a manuscript on the typewriter. Instead, Elizabethan printers sometimes were governed by the fact that the composed type for all the pages that would make up one side of a printed sheet had to be arranged in a certain systematic, but non-progressive, order in the frame upon which the sheet was laid to receive the inked impression of the type. Thus, if "setting by formes," a compositor might first set page 6, then pages 7, 5, 8, 4, 9, 3, 10, 2, 11, 1, and 12; or if two men were working, the first would set 6, 5, 4, 3, 2, and 1, in that order, while the other set 7, 8, 9, 10, 11, and 12.

This system meant, of course, that the foreman had to "cast off" copy beforehand—that is, go through the manuscript or printed book and mark off as much copy as he expected to occupy each page of the new setting. The state of the copy naturally affected the precision with which this could be done. If the type were to be set from a printed book or a reasonably clean manuscript, an experienced printer could predict fairly accurately how much matter would go into a single page. Such would be the case, also, if the copy to be set were in verse, with its easily countable lines, rather than in prose. But, as Charlton Hinman, who made this discovery, said, "real difficulty would probably be encountered . . . in copy very untidily made up from various sources, interlined, supplied with marginal annotations partly in verse and partly in prose, and so on"; hence, "miscalculations would be inevitable and gross inaccuracy would be more likely to occur with edited than with unedited copy." To take up slack or, on the other hand, to pack more matter into a page than had been allowed for, the typesetter resorted to various typographical or outright verbal alterations—dividing a line into two, running two lines into one, omitting a word (or line) or two, and so forth. The more evidence that is found of forced expansion and compression in response to the arbitrary space requirements imposed by casting-off, the greater the likelihood that a book was set from copy that was hard to estimate and to follow. [18]

By similar analysis of evidence, Hinman and other modern specialists have also shown how many compositors set a given book, and for which pages or formes each was responsible. It was previously known that the tragedies in the Shakespeare First Folio were set by three compositors, one of whom probably was an apprentice (each typesetter's work has its own peculiarities). But Hinman went a step further by identifying parts of *Hamlet*, *Othello*, and *Lear* which the apprentice seems to have composed. His work was most inexpert, requiring constant correction before printing (the signs of which are readily evident to an expert), and Hinman concluded that because of his incompetence he was not allowed to set copy from manuscript but was, instead, limited to relatively easy-to-follow printed text. [19]

The intricate reasoning by which specialists arrive at such conclusions is fascinating to watch, but the results are what count. Inferences derived from the practice of casting-off and from the habits and competence of individual typesetters, fitted in with various other kinds of textual evidence, are the closest we can get to establishing the nature of the copy from which a Shakespearean play was set—whether an earlier quarto (which may have been comparatively unmarked or, on the other hand, lavishly corrected), or a clean manuscript, or a much battered and amended one, or a bewildering patchwork made from two or more of these. And the nearer we come to deciding what that copy was like, the more confident can be the subsequent process of deducing, from the printed text that eventually emerged, the exact words the typesetter had before him.

The changes that have occurred in the publishing trade and

18. "Cast-off Copy for the First Folio of Shakespeare," *Shakespeare Quarterly*, 6 (1955), 259–73. This and the article cited in the next note were among the numerous by-products of Hinman's work toward the famous Norton Facsimile Edition of the First Folio (1968), each page of which represents the most nearly perfect of the several states of that page that are found in various copies of the Folio. The Norton Fascimile, in effect, reproduces a book that never was; it might be called a Platonic-construct, or Ideal, First Folio.

19. "The Prentice Hand in the Tragedies of the Shakespeare First Folio," *SB*, 9 (1957), 3–20.

printing techniques since 1800 have complicated the textual editor's task. Although the invention of stereotyping early in the nineteenth century tended to stabilize a text, since there was no longer any standing type to be reset every time someone wanted to make an alteration, the fact that successive editions of popular books were printed from the same plates does not eliminate the possibility that changes were made in those plates between printings, or the further possibility that, as one error was corrected, another was invented. The use of duplicate plates for large press runs, one set of which is corrected and the other not, as in the case of Sinclair Lewis' *Babbitt*, adds one more complexity to the textual study of modern authors.[20] Again, in the nineteenth century as well as the early twentieth, many books first appeared as serials in periodicals, and often, as was true of Hardy's novels, important changes were made in the text when it was reprinted as a volume. Hence, the editor must meticulously compare the magazine text with that of the first and subsequent editions in book form.

In the United States, there is the further complication that many important men of letters wrote for newspapers—ephemeral journalism for the most part, but also, sometimes, stories and essays which were later revised and collected in volumes as part of the author's canon. Publication of three volumes of the University of Virginia's edition of Stephen Crane was delayed for several years while its editors searched the files of thirty newspapers to which he had contributed, and established the original texts of his short stories and sketches.

From early in the 1960's until 1976, the Center for Editions of American Authors, an institution sponsored by the Modern Language Association of America and supported by grants from the government and private foundations, initiated or assisted with a series of ambitious editorial projects. The very latest methods of textual analysis and reconstruction were applied to the works of Melville, Hawthorne, Mark Twain, Emerson, Crane, Howells, Whitman, Thoreau, and Irving. (In Mark Twain's case, there is also a separate edition of his

20. Matthew J. Bruccoli, "Textual Variants in Sinclair Lewis's *Babbitt*," *SB*, 11 (1958), 263–68.

papers, and in Emerson's, the journals, notebooks, and later lectures are being edited as well as his printed works.) By an exhaustive comparison of all versions of a text with which the author had something to do, as well as those into which variants were later introduced by the printer, the editors attempted to "achieve a text which matches no existing text but which comes closer to the author's hand and his intent than any previous printed version." [21] When the CEAA ceased to exist in August 1976 at the expiration of its operating grant from the National Endowment for the Humanities, it was succeeded by the Center for Scholarly Editions, also under the aegis of the MLA. The CSE differs from the CEAA in two principal respects: it places no restrictions on the type of document to be edited (the CEAA, of course, was limited to American authors); and its role is wholly advisory.[22]

Thus far I have been talking about textual study as if it were primarily concerned with printed books and the evidence they can be made to yield about the nature of the (no longer extant) manuscript which lay before the original compositor. This kind of textual work is at present more in the scholarly limelight because of both the novelty and sophistication of its methods and the dramatic results it has produced. But textual criticism of another sort is much older: the branch that deals with the history and relationships of existing, and sometimes also of hypothetical, manuscripts. It began as long ago as the early Renaissance, with the humanists' attempts to determine, from a critical examination of codices (manuscripts), the oldest of which were still several centuries removed from the originals, the text of the books of the New Testament and of the Greek and Latin classics.

At the end of the nineteenth century, the techniques that had been developed in Biblical and classical studies began to be applied to English literature, especially to works written before the printing press was invented and of which, therefore, a

---

21. William M. Gibson, "The Center for Editions of American Authors," *Scholarly Books in America* (January, 1969), p. 8.

22. "The Center for Scholarly Editions: An Introductory Statement," *PMLA*, 92 (1977), 583. This full "statement" and description of the CSE and of the "state of the art" of textual editing is available as a separate pamphlet under the same title from the MLA Publications Center.

number of manuscript copies were made. The essential problem was—and is—to establish the date and place of origin of each manuscript and thus, eventually, to construct a pedigree (technically known as a *stammbaum* or *stemma codicum*), at the top of which will stand the manuscript which presumably is closest to the lost original. Sometimes this genealogical diagram will involve hundreds of manuscripts, each with its peculiar variants of phraseology and dialect, its omissions and insertions and different placements of specific lines or passages, its obvious mistakes, and all the other idiosyncrasies that help the scholar to determine its place in the history of the author's text. Of Chaucer's *Canterbury Tales*, there are some ninety manuscripts and early printed versions, either of groups of tales or the whole sequence. An examination of the Manly-Rickert edition based on all these texts will give as impressive an idea as one could wish of the problems an editor faces as he seeks to work back through the maze of later versions to Chaucer's own words.

Needless to say, this kind of research, which ordinarily concentrates on medieval and early Renaissance texts, is not for the novice. One must be able to interpret the significance of scribal errors, dialectal variations, and other varieties of characteristic corruptions for the sake of placing each manuscript in its appropriate chronological-genealogical slot and, more important, of suggesting emendations that will clarify the meaning. In addition, an expert knowledge of paleography, a science which includes the study of medieval and Renaissance handwriting, is essential. A certain amount of the requisite knowledge and technical skill can be acquired by reading, but only experience with actual manuscripts, under firm guidance, can produce a finished textual critic.

The complete textual scholar must of course be at home among both manuscripts and printed books. In some types of investigation he has to deal with only one category: a student of *Piers Plowman*, for example, has little to do with printed texts, but his hands are full enough with the sixty-odd manuscript copies that represent three different versions of the poem. In Donne's case, on the other hand, only a single holograph of one of his English poems is known to survive; for the rest, the texts we have "depend on seventeenth-century transcripts made at several removes from the original copies."[23] But from about Donne's time onward, authors' manuscripts begin increasingly to survive side by side with the printed texts, and these supply the indispensable basis of any authoritative edition.

In recent times, just as in earlier centuries, there have been plenty of slips and second thoughts in the interval between completion of copy for the printer and the emergence of the book from the press. Wherever possible, the textual student must examine the correspondence exchanged by the author and his publisher or editor, for the sake of whatever discussion of alterations it may contain, and the printer's proofs may provide vital evidence of the way an author's creative powers kept working even after his book was set in type. Some years ago the proof-sheets of the first eight books of Pope's translation of the *Iliad* were discovered in the Bibliothèque de l'Arsenal in Paris. Although the proofs of Books I–IV contain Pope's corrections of typographical errors only, the remainder show him painstakingly reconsidering his artistry, "from emendations of a single word to cancellations and revisions of quite long passages."[24] The corrected proofs of John Gibson Lockhart's life of Scott throw light on both his biographical craftsmanship and his desire, strengthened by advice from friends, not to give offense. As late as proof-stage Lockhart was busily touching up dialogue and description and altering the text of Scott's journals and letters so as to add consistency and vividness to the idealized conception of his father-in-law which he strove to present throughout his long biography; and at the same time he tactfully adjusted many details relating to Scott's financial transactions, and cut out numerous painful references to the novelist's mental deterioration during his final months.[25] Comparison of a set of unrevised galley proofs of Faulkner's *Sanctuary* with

23. This holograph was discovered as recently as 1970, lying miscatalogued among the family papers of the Duke of Manchester which had been in the Public Record Office for over eighty years. See A. J. Smith in *TLS*, January 7, 1972, p. 19.

24. Norman Callan, "Pope's *Iliad:* A New Document," *RES*, n.s. 4 (1953), 109–21.

25. Francis Russell Hart, "Proofreading Lockhart's *Scott:* The Dynamics of Biographical Reticence," *SB*, 14 (1961), 3–22.

the printed book has revealed a striking instance of a novelist's completely changing the focus and manner of a book after type was set. In Faulkner's own words, he "tore the galleys down and rewrote the book." [26]

The contributions which textual study makes to our understanding of literature, then, are twofold. In the first place, an authoritative text may reveal the author's intentions, purged of the blemishes and misrepresentations that crept into a book after he ceased to control it. It is, in any event, a *sine qua non* for the informed criticism of a work considered solely as a finished product. Secondly, an examination of manuscripts, proofs, or successive printed versions or, in unusual cases, all three is a matchless means of watching the whole process of literary creation. Such studies, to borrow Jack Stillinger's words in his *The Texts of Keats's Poems* (1974), aim "to determine the relationships among the extant MSS (who copied what from whom), the sources of the earliest published versions (how the poems first got into print), and the relative authoritativeness of the various texts that might have claims to be the standard (which versions are 'the best')." In this case, the end product was Stillinger's edition (1978) of the 150 poems reasonably presumed to be Keats's. By presenting the three separate forms (1798–99, 1805, 1850) of Wordsworth's great autobiographical poem *The Prelude*, the Norton Critical Edition, edited by Jonathan Wordsworth, M. H. Abrams, and Stephen Gill, vividly reveals the way the poet's intellect and sensibility both mellowed and hardened over a long span of years. The Victoria and Albert Museum's rich collection of Dickens' memoranda, manuscripts, and proof sheets (including his rough working plans and passages that were discarded for lack of space) permits us to watch a great novelist at work under the new pressures of serial publication: "how he responded to and conveyed 'the feelings of the day', what methods of work he evolved as best suited to his own genius and to the demands of monthly or weekly publication, and above all, how he [learned] to combine the 'circumspection' of preparation with the immediate

26. Linton Massey, "Notes on the Unrevised Galleys of Faulkner's *Sanctuary*," SB, 8 (1956), 195–208.

and intimate relation to his readers which he valued so highly." [27]

Equally valuable, for other reasons, is the comparison of successive printed texts in each of which the author has exercised his privilege of retouching. T. S. Eliot's *The Waste Land*, for instance, appeared in two periodicals (the *Criterion* and the *Dial*), then had a number of separate editions in book form (both British and American), and, in due course, was included in the poet's collected poems. The variant readings in all of Eliot's texts, as one scholar has noted, afford "added insight into recurrent phrasing and themes in the poems and plays and a stricter sense of their chronology and possible interrelationships," as well as "the alterations in phrasing which borrowings from other authors have undergone." [28]

27. John Butt and Kathleen Tillotson, *Dickens at Work* (London, 1957), p. 9. Additional discussion of Dickens' composing techniques can be found in three articles which focus directly on the memoranda and working plans: Harvey Peter Sucksmith, "Dickens at Work on *Bleak House*: A Critical Examination of His Memoranda and Number Plans," *Renaissance & Modern Studies*, 9 (1965), 47–85; Paul D. Herring, "Dickens' Monthly Number Plans for *Little Dorrit*," *MP*, 64 (1966), 22–63; and Ernest Boll, "The Plotting of *Our Mutual Friend*," *MP*, 42 (1944), 96–122.

28. Robert L. Beare, "Notes on the Text of T. S. Eliot: Variants from Russell Square," *SB*, 9 (1957), 21–49. A representative sampling of studies of authors' habits of composition and their revisions in manuscript and proof would include: B. C. Southam, *Jane Austen's Literary Manuscripts: A Study of the Novelist's Development Through the Surviving Papers* (Oxford, 1964); Jon Stallworthy, *Between the Lines: Yeats's Poetry in the Making* (Oxford, 1963) and its sequel, *Vision and Revision in Yeats's "Last Poems"* (Oxford, 1969); Matthew J. Bruccoli, *The Composition of "Tender Is the Night"* (Pittsburgh, 1963); John Paterson, *The Making of "The Return of the Native"* (Berkeley and Los Angeles, 1960); Jerome Beaty, *"Middlemarch" from Notebook to Novel* (Urbana, Ill., 1960); James A. Winn, "Faulkner's Revisions: A Stylist at Work," *AL*, 41 (1969), 231–50; T. C. Duncan Eaves and Ben D. Kimpel, "The Composition of *Clarissa* and Its Revision Before Publication," *PMLA*, 83 (1968), 416–28; the same authors' "Richardson's Revisions of *Pamela*," *SB*, 20 (1967), 61–88; Robert Peters, "A. C. Swinburne's 'Hymn to Proserpine': The Work Sheets," *PMLA*, 83 (1968), 1400–1406; and Martin C. Battestin, "Fielding's Revisions of *Joseph Andrews*," *SB*, 16 (1963), 81–117. Valuable discussions of current problems and methods in the editing of texts from various periods of English and American literature are found in a series of volumes originating in conferences held at the University of Toronto. See below, pages 246–48 under Baird, Bentley, Domville, Halpenny, Lancashire, Millgate, Rigg, Robson, Schoeck, and Smith.

Textual criticism is not a labor to be undertaken lightly. It is among the most demanding of all branches of literary scholarship. The technical knowledge, the infinite patience, and the reasoning powers which the ideal editor brings to his task are found combined in few men or women. And sometimes, it must be admitted, these gifts are squandered on unworthy causes; a fourth-rate example of literature does not repay the labor of a first-class editorial job, and candid critics, in such instances, can scarcely be blamed for remarking that it takes more than a meticulous determination of text to make a bad novel better. (This has been one of the points made by critics of the CEAA projects.) But at its best, when it enables us either to behold a work of art exactly as it left its author's pen or to watch it in the very state of "becoming," textual study has, in Fredson Bowers' words, the dignity of "an independent act of critical inquiry into the author's mind and art." [29]

Of all the literary scholars practicing today, comparatively few have either the training or the occasion to do such extensive work in textual criticism and editing as to qualify as specialists. (The present-day application of computer technology to complicated textual problems requires that specialists have even more expertise than before. For the "computerization" of *Ulysses*, see below, pages 149–50.) But the exacting standards of modern textual study embody a responsibility to which everyone who deals with literary works and their history, for whatever purpose, is subject. The expert's *summum bonum* is the non-expert's working rule. Few of us may dedicate our energies to the patient unraveling of the knotty textual history of a work; all of us, however, have an inescapable obligation to base our scholarly and critical activity upon the most authentic text that is available and to reproduce it with the utmost fidelity in whatever we publish for the use of others.

2. Problems of Authorship

After I. A. Richards dramatically demonstrated, through the university students' papers quoted in his *Practical Criticism*

29. *Textual and Literary Criticism* (Cambridge, 1959), p. 17.

(1929), how deeply readers' judgments of a poem are affected by their knowledge of its author, some critics urged that authorship be disregarded altogether and the poem treated as if it were an artifact as anonymous as a primitive statuette from Polynesia. But this extreme view, though it had considerable influence, has lost favor, and rightly so. We have an ineradicable and perfectly valid desire to know what fellow human being created the work of art we admire. Even more important is the fact, once more, that seldom is an artistic work an isolated entity which can be explained and judged solely in terms of itself. It is, on the contrary, one among several or many productions of the same creative intelligence; sound criticism requires our placing it among the other works which preceded or followed it and our using to the full the insights they afford both into it and into the mind that produced them all.

Knowledge of authorship, then, far from diverting the critic from his proper business, lights him on his way. The research that substantiates, or corrects, this knowledge has three chief objects: to identify the author of anonymous or pseudonymous works (or of works attributed to the wrong writer); to decide which parts of a work written by two or more authors belong to whom; and to remove from the received list of a writer's works whatever pieces are not his, thereby purifying his canon (the roster of his *authentic* writings).

Positive as we are that Chaucer wrote *The Canterbury Tales*, Thackeray *Vanity Fair*, and Hemingway *A Farewell to Arms*, we tend to forget how many cases of undecided paternity crowd the docket of literary history. In some ages the conditions under which literature was written often encouraged, if they did not actually require, concealment of authorship. Before the Renaissance, the poet behind the poem was of little consequence; it was the poem's content and its intended effect that counted, not the negligible human personality which happened to create it. Only during the Tudor period did readers begin to think it important to know who wrote the books they read. But this growing curiosity was frustrated in the case of gentleman authors, who, shrinking from what they considered the vulgarity of public print, circulated their work in manuscript. When the anthologies derived from these manuscripts were printed, the authorship of many individual poems, if it had not already been deliberately concealed or lost in the course of circulation, was now suppressed, hidden under initials, or simply misreported, and in later editions the original mystery often was deepened by the unexplained shifting of ascriptions.

Until at least the mid-eighteenth century, the polemicism of some of the books and pamphlets composed by leading literary figures, Dryden, Defoe, Swift, and Fielding among them, made anonymity or pseudonymity the best policy. And then, just as the repressive climate of political and religious opinion was beginning to clear, a strong new force leading to concealment of authorship appeared in the form of journalism. Since the Queen Anne period, many men of letters have been prolific contributors to newspapers and magazines, and only gradually, during the later Victorian age when the profession of journalism had gained respectability, did their work come to be signed as a matter of custom. Finally (though this does not exhaust the motives authors have had for dissociating themselves from their writings), there is the element of hack work. Authors of high critical stature may write potboilers or books in genres outside that in which they own their reputation, and to keep their literary personalities separate, among other reasons, they use a pseudonym. The mild deceptions occurring on the title pages of detective novels (a future Poet Laureate, an Oxford don, and a Columbia University professor of English, writing, respectively, as Nicholas Blake, Michael Innes, and Amanda Cross) are merely the best-known modern instances of an old practice.[30]

But many writers have become detached from their work or, just as often, have had their names attached to someone else's work, through no desire of their own. There was a particularly fertile breeding ground for incorrect attributions in the hundreds of poetical miscellanies published from the Elizabethan era down to the middle of the eighteenth century. Their compilers matched poems and authors on grounds varying from the comparatively responsible (the existence of a signed manuscript—

30. An interesting earlier example is the author of *Little Women*. For details of the blood and thunder novels Louisa May Alcott wrote anonymously or pseudonymously and for the text of four of these, see Madeleine B. Stern, *Behind a Mask: The Unknown Thrillers of Louisa May Alcott* (New York, 1975).

even though the wrong name may have been signed!) to the whimsical (a fancied resemblance to the known work of the author, or a sentimental legend that attributed the poem to him).

Another frequent source of misattribution has been commonplace books, in which poems written by the man who kept the book are indiscriminately mingled with poems from other pens. The sonnet called "The Poet," hitherto assumed to be Keats's, on the ground that it appears in the so-called "Woodhouse Commonplace Book" into which many of Keats's authentic poems were transcribed, has been shown to be by his friend and publisher, John Taylor.[31]

False ascriptions occasionally result from the fortuitous binding together of several works, some the authentic work of the announced writer, the others unsigned; the latter thus acquiring a putative father by association. Thus, a volume entitled *Tales of Terror* (1801) has repeatedly been attributed to Matthew G. ("Monk") Lewis. The fact is that this is a collection of parodies by various unknown hands which was issued as a companion volume to the second edition of Lewis' authentic *Tales of Wonder*. Lewis' 1839 biographer mistakenly assumed that both were by Lewis, and the error was solidified when, in 1887, they were reissued under a single title.[32] And especially in the eighteenth century, when editors of newspapers and magazines inserted poems as fillers, they did not hesitate to append the name of a celebrated author who may well have never seen the verses credited to him. So too with anthologies: several spurious poems of Dr. Johnson entered circulation by way of the aptly named *New Foundling Hospital for Wit* (1771).

The "big name," in fact, has loomed large in publishers' calculations ever since the Tudor era. The sales of seventeenth-

31. The evidence was provided by Mabel A. E. Steele, "The Authorship of 'The Poet' and Other Sonnets," *Keats-Shelley Journal*, 5 (1956), 69–80, after E. L. Brooks had questioned Keats's authorship for another reason ("'The Poet': An Error in the Keats Canon?," *MLN*, 67 [1952], 450–54). These articles, along with the items to be cited in the next dozen notes, provide a good survey of the ways in which the authorship of texts can be critically examined.

32. See Louis F. Peck, *A Life of Matthew G. Lewis* (Cambridge, Mass., 1961), p. 311, and Morchard Bishop, "A Terrible Tangle," *TLS*, October 19, 1967, p. 989.

century anthologies presumably benefited by the inclusion of poems blandly and mendaciously attributed to Spenser and Sidney, the printer's commercial instincts (as Francis Davison, the first editor of the *Poetical Rhapsody* [1602], complained) overruling the compiler's express wishes. Astute publishers sometimes cashed in on the current popularity of an essayist by issuing a volume, or indeed a whole "collected edition," which was padded with work lifted from other writers, but vended (and thence introduced into the canon) as his genuine production. Sterne's vogue in the latter half of the eighteenth century was responsible not only for the publication of some ninety imitations of his works, but for the outright forgery of scores of letters which were put forth as his in various published volumes.[33] The same mercantile motive led time after time to the placing of the wrong author's name on the title pages of printed Elizabethan and Jacobean plays, the result being some of the most recalcitrant of all authorship mysteries. Of the fifty-two plays in the second folio (1679) of Beaumont and Fletcher, fewer than twelve actually are by the two dramatists in collaboration. The rest are by Fletcher alone or in collaboration with Massinger or with one or more of a dozen other Jacobean playwrights. The attempt to match plays and authors, and to determine what share each collaborator had in a given play, continues to be a major occupation among specialists in the drama.[34]

Old book-lists, again, have been a constant source of misattribution; the bibliographies included in the various dictionaries of English authors, from Bale's *Scriptorum Illustrium Maioris Brytanniae* in the middle of the sixteenth century to ponderous compilations like the six-volume *Biographia Britannica* of 1747–66, are replete with false ascriptions, as are the catalogues of seventeenth-century booksellers and collectors, who, when in doubt, had a regrettable tendency to assign a play to the most celebrated name that could plausibly be suggested.

33. Lewis P. Curtis, "Forged Letters of Laurence Sterne," *PMLA*, 50 (1935), 1076–1106.
34. A noteworthy attempt to disentangle the authors of this "whole library of Stuart drama," as it has been called, is Cyrus Hoy's series of articles, "The Shares of Fletcher and his Collaborators in the Beaumont and Fletcher Canon," *SB*, 8 (1956) –15 (1962). Hoy's evidence is wholly linguistic.

Compounding these opportunities for mischief has been the credulity or enthusiasm—or both—of some editors, who, by failing to scrutinize the evidence closely enough, have given unwarranted authority and undeserved life to patently false attributions. A notably copious example is Sir Walter Scott's edition of Swift.

Despite all this mischief, remarkable progress has been made toward clarifying the record. On matters of authorship we are much better informed than our great-grandfathers were. A hundred years ago, it was still believed that Chaucer had written *The Testament of Love*, *The Cuckoo and the Nightingale*, *The Court of Love*, and other poems that had become attached to his name through the centuries. These have now been rejected, and the status of *The Romaunt of the Rose* is doubtful. On the other hand, a scientific treatise brought to light in the library of Peterhouse College, Cambridge, in 1951 is now generally accepted to be Chaucer's, though the evidence is by no means conclusive. Over a dozen plays once attributed to Shakespeare, among them *Arden of Feversham*, *Mucedorus*, *The Puritaine*, *Locrine*, and *The London Prodigall*, have been removed from his canon, but the riddle of how much, if anything, he had to do with *Pericles*, *Henry VIII*, *Edward III*, *Sir Thomas More*, and *The Two Noble Kinsmen* remains *sub judice*.

Daniel Defoe's output, which never was deemed negligible, has turned out to be more prodigious with every generation's study. In 1790 George Chalmers credited him with ninety-nine works, of which twenty-two were not certainly his; in 1830 Walter Wilson raised the total to 210; by 1913 W. P. Trent could name 370 titles; and in the 1960's John Robert Moore, who had devoted thirty years' work to the subject, announced a grand total of some 560 pieces known, or credibly supposed, to have been written by Defoe. Other specialists have considered Moore's total to be on the exuberant side, but even the most conservative estimates still credit Defoe with an almost superhuman productivity.

In recent years, a number of Coleridge's hitherto unknown essays and even a few poems have been located and identified in the periodicals to which he contributed them. Concurrently, however, more than a few pieces previously ascribed to him, sometimes on the strength of his own signature, have been shown to be by other hands.

Some mysteries of attribution are not likely ever to be solved. Examples of Samuel Johnson's hack work await discovery in eighteenth-century newspapers and magazines, though in some cases this discovery in turn awaits the finding of the papers themselves, such as the missing *Birmingham Journal* for 1732–33, in which Johnson's earliest writing was printed.[35] Much of William Cullen Bryant's work is still unretrieved from the files of the *New York Post*, and William Dean Howells' journalism is distributed among the files of sixty American newspapers.

It is quite possible that, in instances like Bryant's, the labor involved in excavating his routine journalism would not be justified by the results. But sometimes the game proves eminently worth the candle. Harry Stone has added a quarter of a million words to the fringes, so to speak, of the Dickens canon in the form of essays and sketches printed in the novelist's weekly, *Household Words*, between 1850 and 1859. These are all works of composite authorship. By his extensive alterations Dickens, as editor, often made himself an informal collaborator with the author who submitted the original piece. Combining internal and external evidence, such as the *Household Words* contributors' book and Dickens' editorial correspondence, Stone was able to ascertain with a fair degree of confidence just what parts of a given essay were from Dickens' pen.[36]

Who wrote *A Tale of a Tub?* When it appeared, the publisher Edmund Curll claimed that it was written jointly by Jonathan Swift and his cousin Thomas. But Jonathan brusquely

35. Johnson signed only a small portion of his work. For a good idea of the sources and variable reliability of Johnsonian attributions, including those by Boswell, see Donald J. Greene, "The Development of the Johnson Canon," in *Restoration and Eighteenth-Century Literature: Essays in Honor of Alan Dugald McKillop*, ed. Carroll Camden (Chicago, 1963), pp. 407–27.

36. *Charles Dickens' Uncollected Writings from "Household Words"* (2 vols., Bloomington, Ind., 1968). Instant fame awaits the discoverer of the long-lost contributors' book for *All the Year Round*, which Dickens edited after he killed off *Household Words*.

dismissed the assertion: "If any Person will prove his claim to three lines in the whole Book, let him step forward . . ." Since Curll—"the Unspeakable," as he was called in his time—was a notoriously unreliable witness, subsequent scholarship accepted the more famous cousin as the sole author. Thomas' annotated copy, however, is now at Cornell, and it substantiates Curll's claim. But was Thomas any more dependable a witness than Curll? That was the problem Robert M. Adams set out to solve. By correlating various kinds of internal and external evidence, he made a persuasive case for Thomas' having actually written no fewer than fifty-five of the 161 pages comprising the first edition of *A Tale*.[37]

Of the two kinds of evidence employed in determining authorship, internal is the more slippery.[38] The premise underlying its use is that every author's work has idiosyncrasies of style, such as preference for Latinate instead of vernacular words, or for certain turns of expression which he repeats time after time. If these characteristics are found in the writings that are unquestionably his, then, the argument goes, their occurrence in an unsigned or questioned work is good ground for attributing that work to him also. The process is analogous to fitting a piece into a jigsaw puzzle on the basis of matching colors. A noteworthy example of such a proceeding is Stuart M. Tave's work on De Quincey. We probably will never know how many of De Quincey's essays and other journalistic pieces are buried forever in the potter's field of ephemeral periodicals. The author himself forgot them once they had earned him a few pounds, and almost no external clues to their whereabouts exist. Tave, however, was able at least to identify his contributions to the *Edinburgh Saturday Post* and the *Edinburgh Evening Post* in 1827–28 by making literally thousands of cross-references from the undisputed De Quincey canon to the suspected essays in the newspapers' files. Such a feat was possible only because he had made his mind a sensitive detecting device by saturating it with De Quincey's char-

37. See "Jonathan Swift, Thomas Swift, and the Authorship of *A Tale of a Tub*," *MP*, 64 (1967), 198–232. Dipak Nandy, though, has expressed some reservations: see his identically titled article, *ibid.*, 66 (1969), 333–37.

38. The two standard treatments of this topic are Erdman-Fogel and Schoenbaum: see below, page 249.

acteristic ideas and peculiarities of style.[39]

Many authorship studies, particularly in the later nineteenth century and the early twentieth, laid claim to scientific rigor, and were published with an imposing panoply of statistical charts and tables. F. G. Fleay's *Shakespeare Manual* (1878) is an easily accessible example of such work.[40] Elaborate versification and vocabulary tests, however, are only quantitative, not qualitative; they constitute a crude, unimaginative approach to material that by its very nature defies complete statistical reduction.

Versification and vocabulary used to be the two staple categories of stylistic evidence employed in authorship study. In the 1930's a third was brought into prominence: imagery. In an age as conscious as ours of the way that an individual man's or woman's personality and interests are mirrored in metaphorical habits, the techniques available for ascertaining authorship were bound to be enlarged and enriched by Caroline Spurgeon's systematic demonstration, in her *Shakespeare's Imagery* (1935), that Shakespeare had a marked fondness for specific images, or clusters of related images, which, being used repeatedly in the plays, constitute a hallmark of his style. Subsequent analyses of the imagery of Bacon, Marlowe, and Dekker, among others,

---

39. *New Essays by De Quincey* (Princeton, 1966).

40. In Shakespeare's case, the metrical tests were directed primarily toward establishing the order of the plays, although they were also used in the effort to differentiate Shakespeare's work from that of supposed collaborators or revisers. For one trenchant criticism of some of these tests, see H. T. Price, "Towards a Scientific Method of Textual Criticism for the Elizabethan Drama," *JEGP*, 36 (1937), 151–67. With other authors, however, the tests of meter and vocabulary have been employed chiefly to determine authorship. The most elaborate of all such pre-computer exercises is G. Udny Yule's *The Statistical Study of Literary Vocabulary* (Cambridge, 1944), an attempt to decide whether Thomas à Kempis or Jean Gerson wrote *De Imitatione Christi*. "The book," as the *TLS* remarked in a monumental understatement, "is not for the non-statistical reader." The observation could be applied with equal force to the computer-assisted "stylometry" described and demonstrated in A. Q. Morton's *Literary Detection: How to Prove Authorship and Fraud in Literature and Documents* (New York, 1978). One noteworthy result of the application of Morton's technique has been what Morton regards as the confirmation, on stylistic grounds, of a theory first advanced a century ago on the grounds of handwriting: namely, that the play *Sir Thomas More*, the manuscript of which is in the British Library, was written by Shakespeare. For more on the contribution of computer science to this kind of study, see below, pages 148–52.

revealed pronounced differences in the subjects of their respective metaphors. Given enough material to permit statistically acceptable conclusions, the test of unique imagery is a valid aid in discriminating the work of the author from that of another. But the method has obvious dangers. Image strains are less amenable than either metrical patterns or vocabulary to mechanical classification. Images, like other stylistic qualities, are easy and tempting to imitate, as is shown by the plays of the lesser playwrights who flocked to exploit Marlowe's great success. But probably the greatest peril in image-study as an instrument of deciding authorship is that of confusing the uniquely personal image with one which is in the wide literary domain. The occurrence in a disputed play of the figure of a dog slavering over sweetmeats dropped from a banquet table may be scored in favor of the play's being by Shakespeare, who was demonstrably fond of the image, but the likening of the hair of one's beloved to golden wires and her lips to ripe cherries merely suggests that the author was an Elizabethan. Midway between these two extremes lies a broad expanse of imagery which cannot positively be identified as either idiosyncratic or conventional, and for that reason, among others, whatever evidence imagery provides must be treated as at best collateral, never conclusive.[41]

In bringing stylistic evidence to bear on problems of authorship, therefore, the scholar must meet and answer such insistent questions as these: Are his touchstones—the criteria derived from a close examination of the author's authentic works—valid? Are the peculiarities of versification and language and imagery demonstrably characteristic of that writer *alone*—or are they found, to a significant extent, in the works of others? If

41. Two critiques of the assumptions and methods of image-study are Lillian Herlands Hornstein, "Analysis of Imagery: A Critique of Literary Method," *PMLA*, 57 (1942), 638–53, and Moody E. Prior, "Imagery as a Test of Authorship," *Shakespeare Quarterly*, 6 (1955), 381–86. The student about to undertake the study of imagery, for whatever purpose, should also read R. A. Foakes, "Suggestions for a New Approach to Shakespeare's Imagery," *Shakespeare Survey*, 5 (1952), 81–92; Edward B. Partridge, *The Broken Compass: A Study of the Major Comedies of Ben Jonson* (New York, 1958), Chapters 1–2; and the relevant parts (see index) of D. V. Erdman and E. G. Fogel, *Evidence for Authorship* (Ithaca, N.Y., 1966).

these "peculiarities" are, in fact, common property—the characteristics of period style (such as that of Augustan verse) or of a school (such as the Della Cruscans or the Spasmodics)—then their occurrence in the work under consideration is, of course, not very helpful in establishing the identity of the author, whatever they may incidentally reveal of his literary affiliations and predilections. Sometimes, too, the styles of several authors, all of whom may have contributed to a work, are so similar that differentiation of their respective portions is impossible. Though we know that half a dozen men (Swift, Arbuthnot, Pope, Gay, Parnell, and the Earl of Oxford) composed the *Memoirs of Martinus Scriblerus,* we cannot positively isolate the contributions of any one of them.

Methodical comparison of style (the disputed work laid alongside the settled canon) can take us some distance toward establishing authorship, but it can never be wholly free of impressionism. Impressionistic judgments have their place in literary study if they rest on a solid foundation of knowledge and esthetic perception. Long and intensive study of an author's works attunes the scholar's ear, as no amount of mechanical analysis can do, to his true and subtle accents. The scholar seeking to decide the genuineness of a literary work is in the position of an art expert called in to authenticate a museum's new acquisition. Other tests proving inconclusive, he must finally rely upon his knowledge of the way the artist customarily worked. When a specialist who has spent years reading and re-reading an author declares that a disputed piece is genuine, his intuitive expertness must be given respectful attention. Yet no such verdict can ever be regarded as final. One of the leading modern Keats scholars defended the authenticity of "The Poet" on the ground that it was "so much in accord with other passages in Keats's poetry that it is difficult to doubt his authorship." But the external evidence subsequently produced seems to require that doubt.

We turn the coin over, and the same caveats persist. In stating our conviction that a work is *not* by the writer to whom it has been credited, we may have to fall back on the assertion that it is simply "not like him"—that it does not ring true. But, though it may very well not be "like him" as we ordinarily conceive him, can we not assume circumstances in which his manner would markedly change? It is hardly credible that the same poet who wrote

> O darling room, my heart's delight,
> Dear room, the apple of my sight,
> With thy two couches soft and white,
> There is no room so exquisite,
> No little room so warm and bright,
> Wherein to read, wherein to write

also was responsible for the melancholy magic of

> Dark house, by which once more I stand
>   Here in the long unlovely street,
>   Doors, where my heart was used to beat
> So quickly, waiting for a hand,
>
> A hand that can be clasp'd no more—
>   Behold me, for I cannot sleep,
>   And like a guilty thing I creep
> At earliest morning to the door.
>
> He is not here; but far away
>   The noise of life begins again,
>   And ghastly thro' the drizzling rain
> On the bald street breaks the blank day.

But Tennyson wrote both poems, and at a remove of no more than fifteen years. Nor is an author's style consistent even within a short span of time; one day he may write prose that his critics readily identify as characteristic of his ripest genius, and the next he may turn out slovenly stuff reminiscent of the time he was a penny-a-line hack. There are therefore numerous reasons why, despite our feeling that a questioned work is "uncharacteristic" of its putative author, it may nevertheless be genuine. Although the presence of features not usually found in a writer's works (or, conversely, the absence of features that are normally present) may be a point against its inclusion in the canon, we must remember that no artist is wholly consistent or predictable, and a poem or novel which has little in common with the rest of his work may yet be his.

Luckily, another kind of internal evidence—contentual—is often available to substantiate or control a judgment reached by the analysis of style. For one thing, the ideas put forth in a disputed piece may closely resemble those expressed in a writer's authentic work. How much weight this similarity will carry in the total argument depends on the number of resemblances and, even more, on the degree of idiosyncrasy, the special angle and emphasis, that set this man's opinions apart from those of others who think in generally the same way. For another, there may be intimate allusions to persons, such as patrons or close friends, which only he would be likely to make, or to fairly obscure authors for whom he is known to have cherished an eccentric preference; or the text may contain mention of events that have special meaning to him and that no other writer would refer to precisely as he does. Sometimes, too, there may be references to other works which are surely his, but which were then unpublished and which he alone would have known about. These are examples of what we might call the test of unique knowledge, a sort of corollary to the test of unique style. To the stylistic question, "Could any other author have written this way?" it adds: "Could any other author have known what this writer knew?" If the answer to either query is "yes," then we must look elsewhere for our proof, namely, outside the text.

Again like the art expert, the literary scholar trying to solve a problem of authenticity ransacks external sources for possible support of his attribution. Perhaps the piece in question is referred to by the author in a private document or in another literary work—Chaucer left valuable lists of his poems in the Introduction to *The Man of Law's Tale* and the Prologue to *The Legend of Good Women*. Ordinarily, if an author says he wrote such-and-such a work, we can believe him, although writers have been known to claim books that were not theirs, and others have refused to acknowledge books that were.[42] Or,

42. It is advisable, though, to be sure he said what he is represented as saying. The printed text of a letter of February, 1792, has Robert Burns asserting that, of the bawdy songs in *The Merry Muses of Caledonia*, "A very few of them are my own." This may be, and has been, read in two ways: either as a confession or as a denial of more than minimum guilt, depending on how one feels about Burns. But no such statement appears in the holograph; it was inserted when Burns's first biographer, Dr. Currie, printed the letter. "It is now plain," wrote De-Lancey Ferguson, who discovered the original (*MLN*, 66 [1951], 471–73), "that Burns neither affirmed nor denied having enriched his collection with additions of his own . . . The student must therefore

at least as often, someone who was in a position to know recorded that a given poem or essay was written by so-and-so. (Milton's nephew and pupil, Edward Phillips, for example, left a valuable list of his uncle's writings.) Such statements are useful, if true, but each must be evaluated according to the rules of evidence described in Chapter Two. Was the witness in a position to know the truth? Is his statement founded on accurate knowledge or simply a report of hearsay? Had he any reason not to tell the truth?—and so forth. Many of the false or dubious ascriptions in the poetry of the sixteenth through the eighteenth centuries can be traced to erroneous statements made, in however good faith, in commonplace books and other personal memoranda and letters.

Publishers' records, where they survive, sometimes provide information on the authorship of anonymous and pseudonymous books. They are even more useful in identifying unsigned contributions to periodicals. The marked files and account books left by publishers or editors have enabled us to identify the contributors to the eighteenth-century *Monthly Review*, and the nineteenth-century *Edinburgh, Quarterly*, and *Dublin Reviews, Blackwood's Magazine, Punch,* and the *Athenaeum,* among others.[43] And where such records are unavail-

---

scrutinize with new alertness every bawdy lyric which survives in the poet's handwriting, or which contemporary opinion attributed to him. The pious defenders of the Burns legend can no longer brush these compositions aside as mere transcripts of folk songs. The burden of proof is shifted: unless the defenders can show that a given song was already known in Burns's day, we must assume that he wrote it." For later information, on the revised view of Burns's contributions that was made possible by the discovery of the Cunningham manuscript in the British Museum, see G. Legman's edition of *The Merry Muses* (New Hyde Park, N.Y., 1965). Legman's long introduction also describes the vicissitudes the collection underwent in the course of its many reprintings as a popular under-the-counter literary item.

43. A good instance is the recently discovered office set of the *Gentleman's Magazine* annotated and maintained through successive generations (1778-1863) by the Nichols family, owners and editors of that periodical for three quarters of a century. For the story of this important find and the history of the file as it passed from the family to an English provincial bookseller and eventually to the collection of Henry C. Folger (see below, pages 181-83), see James M. Kuist, "*The Gentleman's Magazine* in the Folger Library: The History and Significance of the Nichols Family Collection," *SB,* 29 (1976), 307-22.

able, the possibility still exists that a poem or essay originally published without signature was later included in a (signed) collection of its author's work. Although the reviews in the *Times Literary Supplement* were anonymous until June 1974, their authorship has sometimes been quietly revealed when they reappeared in the collected essays of such contributors as T. S. Eliot, John Middleton Murry, and Virginia Woolf.[44]

Failing these explicit clues to authorship, there remain various types of circumstantial evidence which permit plausible inference, if nothing better. If an author is known to have contributed to a certain periodical in a given span of years, we can at least assume that a questioned article, which appeared in that place at that time, *may* have been from his pen, and then follow the process of elimination. What other known contributors might have written it? We weigh the evidence in each case and in such a fashion reduce the field, perhaps narrowing it down to a single probable candidate. Again, if an unsigned or pseudonymous book came from the same publisher who issued the acknowledged works of the author we believe wrote it, we have a link of association which is interestingly suggestive, however inconclusive.

Even technical bibliographical evidence may help in author ascription. A number of years ago, Donald F. Bond, analyzing the typography and text matter (including advertisements) of the folio sheets that constituted the first printing of the *Spectator*, discovered that the essay-paper was produced by two different printers, who worked on alternate issues so as to have

44. All the varieties of external evidence just described, as well as several others, have been used in the compilation of the *Wellesley Index to Victorian Periodicals*, edited by Walter E. Houghton and Esther Rhoads Houghton (Toronto, 1966–   ), which identifies the authors of tens of thousands of articles and reviews printed in forty-eight English quarterlies and monthlies during the great era of "the higher journalism." The bibliographies of many Victorian authors have been enlarged by, in some cases, scores of hitherto unascribed items. The magnitude of the editors' achievement is suggested by the fact that approximately 90 percent of the periodicals' contents during this era (1824–1900) were unsigned. For a detailed consideration of the problem of anonymity in English periodicals, with numerous examples drawn from the Wellesley experience, see Mary Ruth Hiller's discussion in *Victorian Periodicals: A Guide to Research*, ed. J. Don Vann and Rosemary T. Van Arsdel (New York, 1978), pp. 123–48.

time to strike off enough copies to meet the demand. Evidently Printer A (Jacob Tonson) and Printer B (unknown) each received the work of a different set of contributors. Since the issues Tonson printed contained almost all that have been identified of the twenty-seven papers attributed in *Spectator* 555 to Eustace Budgell, it is logical to expect that Budgell's other papers, when they are identified, will be in Tonson's sequence. Discovery of this system of alternate printing, furthermore, is likely to alter the existing ascription of unsigned essays, because copy from Addison's friends seems to have gone to Tonson and that from Steele's to the other printer.[45]

On the very borderline between internal and external evidence—on the title page of a book or pamphlet, or at the foot of a periodical essay—lies the pseudonym: "Peter Parley" (Samuel G. Goodrich), "Olphar Hamst" (an anagram for Ralph Thomas), "Orpheus C. Kerr" ("office seeker": R. H. Newell), "Z" (Hannah More), "G. Forrest" (the Rev. J. G. Wood). Most pseudonyms of concern to a student of English or American literature, along with anonymous books whose authors have been identified, are listed in the standard reference work on the subject, Halkett and Laing's nine-volume *Dictionary of Anonymous and Pseudonymous English Literature.* While generally reliable, it is not infallible, because its identifications are uncritically derived from a wide variety of sources, some dependable, some not.[46]

By now it is apparent that the certainty of an ascription is proportional to the cumulative weight of evidence, both internal and external. Seldom can style or content, alone or in combination, be taken as virtual proof that a questioned work

45. Donald F. Bond, "The First Printing of the *Spectator*," *MP*, 47 (1950), 164–77.

46. Connoisseurs of adulterism, apoconyms, boustrophedons, demonyms, hieronyms, initialism, pharmaconyms, pseudandry, pseudojyns, pseudo-titlonyms, stigmonyms, syncopism, telonism, translationism, and kindred phenomena will find much to occupy them in Chapter III of W. P. Courtney's *Secrets of Our National Literature* (London, 1908) and in the Introduction to the current edition of Halkett and Laing, I, xi–xxiii. An amusing article on the same general subject is Franklin B. Williams, Jr., "Renaissance Names in Masquerade," *PMLA*, 69 (1954), 314–23.

was written by a particular author; and only the most unequivocal kind of external data can provide that near-proof where
internal evidence is ambiguous or lacking. Rather, it is the convergence of diverse types of evidence that comes nearest to
clinching an argument about authorship.[47]

The essence of what has been said in this section is illustrated
by a fairly romantic story. In 1628 the London printer Thomas
Walkley issued a volume of amatory poetry called *Brittain's
Ida*, "written," as the title page proudly averred, "by that
Renowned Poet Edmund Spenser," who had died twenty-one
years earlier. In a dedicatory letter to Lady Mary Villiers,
Walkley said that he was "certainly assured by the ablest and
most knowing men, that it must be a Worke of Spencers, of
whom it were a pitty that any thing should be lost." Nevertheless, not all students of Spenser in the following centuries
were willing to believe that the poem was a sibling of *The
Faerie Queene;* for one thing, Spenser's celebrity had been so
great that booksellers were sorely tempted to publish under his
name poems that were not his. Some editors of the poet's works
omitted *Brittain's Ida* altogether; others printed it, but with
reservations. A few critics, notably Thomas Warton, detected
occasional stylistic resemblances to *The Purple Island* (1633),
the most considerable poem by Phineas Fletcher, who was a
leading imitator of Spenser. In 1869 the Reverend A. B. Grosart
went a step further and tried to make a formal case for Fletcher's authorship. His fellow students of Elizabethan literature,
however, were not impressed. The author of the article on
Fletcher in the *Dictionary of National Biography* was non-
committal; George Saintsbury, who had read everything and
sometimes gave the impression that he knew everything, maintained that there was no real evidence for the attribution; and
Edmund Gosse somewhat perversely came out for Phineas'
brother Giles instead.

Forty years after Grosart's unavailing effort to add *Brit-*

---

47. This convergence is well illustrated in William H. Marshall, "An
Addition to the Hazlitt Canon: Arguments from External and Internal
Evidence," *PBSA*, 55 (1961), 347–70. For a later example involving the
same canon, see John O. Hayden, "Hazlitt Reviews Hazlitt?," *MLR*, 64
(1969), 20–26.

tain's Ida to the Phineas Fletcher canon, F. S. Boas tried again, founding his case wholly on the evidence in the text. In the poem, he argued, occurred passages that were remarkably similar to those in works which nobody doubted Phineas Fletcher had written. He cited scores of words which the author used in senses peculiar to Fletcher, and he showed too that many of the images were duplicated in exactly similar contexts in Fletcher's authentic pieces. But, like every argument based exclusively on stylistic resemblances, Boas' fell far short of certainty.

In the mid-1920's Ethel Seaton, rummaging through the library at Sion College, London, happened upon a manuscript volume composed of several sections bound together in fairly modern times and catalogued, vaguely, as "Latin and English MSS. on Paper, 17th Century." Its contents were variegated: mathematical calculations by some Elizabethan savants; two treatises on usury; a partial draft of a "Harmony of the Four Evangelists"—interesting pieces, perhaps, but hardly of literary importance. She turned to the last portion of the volume, badly stained by water during the Great Fire of 1666, which had destroyed part of the Sion College library. "English Pastorals," read the manuscript title. "Venus and Anchises, etc." There was no indication of authorship.

Seaton turned over the pages and quickly realized that, though she had never heard of "Venus and Anchises," she had read the poem; for here, under a title inscribed by some seventeenth-century pen, was *Brittain's Ida*, the poem Walkley had confidently attributed to Spenser. But Walkley had not printed all that the manuscript contained, and in the omitted portions lay the key to the real author. In two introductory stanzas, missing from the 1628 text, the author spoke of himself as "Thirsil" and referred to himself as writing on the banks of the Cam. As every student of early seventeenth-century literature knows, only one poet used the pseudonym of "Thirsil" time after time, and only one was so much in love with the Cam that it plays, as Seaton observes, "almost the part of a chorus" in his poetry. That one was Phineas Fletcher. Nor was this all. In the same manuscript volume, Seaton found several other poems whose authorship had never been doubted, because they had been printed in 1633, in the *Purple Island* volume. The internal and external evidence, in other words, converged upon one writer.[48]

3. *The Search for Origins*

"The poet's mind," wrote T. S. Eliot in "Tradition and the Individual Talent," "is . . . a receptacle for seizing and storing up numberless feelings, phrases, images, which remain there until all the particles which can unite to form a new compound are present together." The aim of the scholarly pursuit called source-study is to establish the nature of the ingredients that thus coalesced into a finished work of literary art. By identifying the antecedent of a striking phrase or metaphor, of a character or symbolic episode or pregnant thought, whether it is found in a single earlier work or simply hovering in the general literary tradition, we are often enabled to say more precisely what it meant to the author and what he, in turn, intended it to mean to his readers. When we determine where he heard or read it, and under what circumstances, we have moved a step further toward our scholarly-critical goal of comprehending the aura of emotional and ideological association that attended the creation of a poem or novel.

The possible sources of a literary work are as numerous and varied as the writer's whole experience of life. They may be people he has known, who have served him as prototypes for fictional characters; by learning all we can about his real-life models and his relations with them, as has been done with much success in the cases of Thackeray, Conrad, Joyce, and Thomas Wolfe, among others, we can reconstruct his own view of them and thus clarify the significance of their fictional counterparts. Sources may be, as well, visual impressions, whether direct observation of scenes (a distant prospect of Eton College, or Westminster Bridge in the early morning) or graphic representations (church windows, tapestries, statues, engravings in a favorite childhood book); or they may be a

48. The *Brittain's Ida* story is told in F. S. Boas' edition of the *Poetical Works of Giles and Phineas Fletcher* (Cambridge, 1909), II, xiii–xxi, and in Seaton's edition of the manuscript (London, 1926).

combination of sight and sound (Whitman's poetry sometimes reveals the effect of his attendance at the opera); or they may be contemporary events in which a writer has participated or about which he has read (the court-martial aboard the United States Navy brig *Somers*).

But while any kind of experience that has somehow affected the content and style of a literary work is, properly speaking, one of its sources, in practice source-study concentrates on literary origins: the fund of phrase, image, plot, character, device, and idea an author accumulated through reading. This is reasonable enough, for the chief debt any work of art owes is to its predecessors in the same medium—compare music, for example, or painting. In addition, the evidence of literary indebtedness as a rule is more concrete than that of other kinds of "inspiration," because we have, for whatever it may prove to be worth, the testimony of printed pages laid side by side. But, as we shall see, determining literary sources requires great tact and caution; intelligently conducted, it is anything but the mechanical exercise it is so often mistaken to be.

The whole topic of source-study enters the present pages, as it does any discussion of modern literary scholarship, trailing clouds of stigma. During the first third of this century, no branch of research brought the academic study of literature into greater disrepute among laymen. Like the mythical scholarly passion for counting the commas in *Piers Plowman*, the widely publicized, and admittedly all too prevalent, zeal for discovering the obscure places where a poet was alleged to have lifted his material became a symbol, to the world at large, of all that was niggling, pedantic, and futile in scholarship. While some such exercises were of indisputable value, far too many were pretentious wastes of time and misapplications of scholarly diligence. Although they were theoretically dedicated to revealing the ways of the imagination, their main effect was to disclose how little of that gift some professional students of literature themselves possessed and how inadequately they understood its operation in others. Too often, casual or unremarkable similarities were interpreted as evidence of one writer's dependence on another. Year after year, articles and monographs rested their proof that Author B had borrowed from Author A on such slender grounds as the fact that in their works both introduced precocious children or scenes in bawdy houses, or were anti-Gallic, or had a somewhat similar vein of humor, or displayed a marked familiarity with Chaucer or horsemanship, or were fond of exclamations like "By St. Paul!" and "I swear!", or had a habit of ending their sentences with prepositions.[49]

Today the criteria by which we judge the evidence of indebtedness are much stricter. Nor do we consider the satisfactory demonstration of a borrowing an end in itself, as did scholars working in the epoch when literary history, drawing much of its rationale from natural science, laid a disproportionate emphasis upon simple causality, without regard for critical significance. While the journals still occasionally print articles which are content to pinpoint a source and let it go at that, all good source-study is governed by the principles laid down by Rosemond Tuve in her study of the liturgical and iconographic background of George Herbert's "The Sacrifice." The first is that "Origins are relevant to criticism only if they illuminate meaning and thus deepen feeling"—if they help to explain the meanings a poem had for "one of its greatest readers—the author." The second is that "the biography of elements in a poem . . . must follow the same stern rules as biographical study of authors to be critically relevant."[50]

Above all, we must keep in mind, because the distinction is vital to the ultimate application of our results, the difference between a direct source or borrowing, on the one hand, and a parallel or analogue on the other. When we speak of a direct source, we usually mean that certain elements in poem y are

49. These are not exaggerations or fancies. They are among the seventy-odd "types of evidence employed by scholars concerned primarily with canons, literary influence, and source relationships" which George C. Taylor enumerated in "Montaigne-Shakespeare and the Deadly Parallel," *PQ*, 22 (1943), 330–37.

50. *A Reading of George Herbert* (London, 1952), pp. 92–93. Note also Mona Wilson's wise words (*Sir Philip Sidney* [London, 1931], p. 314): "The search for sources may become the dreariest form of pedantry when pursued by those who understand neither how a poet writes, nor even how an educated man reads. The literature of Italy and of antiquity was to the Elizabethans what Shakespeare and the Authorized Version became to later generations, the atmosphere they breathed, and not a topic to be got up for theses."

found elsewhere only in the antecedent poem x and therefore, barring independent invention,[51] must have been derived from x. But even if the elements that suggest the relationship are earlier found in other places besides x, it may still be likely that x was the immediate source; we may know, for instance, that the poet was reading x shortly before he wrote y, and hence the reasonable presumption is that he got his idea there rather than anywhere else. "Parallel" and "analogue," on the other hand, imply that neither internal nor external evidence is strong enough to make us confident that y derives from x. While certain features of poem y are indeed found in x, they occur fairly often in preceding or concurrent literature, and the fact that they are found in y may equally well—in the absence of more specific indications—be due to antecedents floating at large in the nebulous realm of literary tradition or intellectual milieu. Most people tend to value the more positive, specific identification over the second type, which necessarily seems vague and inconclusive. But once we realize that both kinds of answer— identification of a unique source and the conclusion that a given feature of a work can be found in many other places— have potential critical usefulness, we need not worry about the direction in which our evidence leads us. It is what we conclude at our journey's end that counts.

Here is a very elementary illustration of the problem posed by a resemblance between passages in two separate books. Douglas Bush (*The Renaissance and English Humanism* [Toronto, 1939], p. 18) speaks of "that old definition of a scholar—

---

51. Raymond D. Havens ("A Parallel That Is Not a Borrowing," *MLN*, 66 [1951], 271) cited a comment by John Henry Newman on Thomson's poetry which expresses "the same unusual idea—that poetry presents natural objects with a meaning, or glory, not their own —and end[s] with the same simple but striking phrase" as did Wordsworth in *The Prelude*, Book I. (Newman: ". . . a meaning, beauty, and harmonious order not their own." Wordsworth: ". . . with glory not their own.") The obvious conclusion is that Newman had read Wordsworth. But Newman's essay was printed in 1829, and *The Prelude*, though the lines in question were written in 1806, lay in manuscript until 1850. "The similarities," commented Havens, ". . . are closer than most of the parallels on which many, all too many, articles submitted to learned journals are based." Yet they cannot be used to prove anything except that coincidences do occur in literary history.

a siren which calls attention to a fog without doing anything to dispel it." Twenty-eight years earlier, Thomas Lounsbury (*The Early Literary Career of Robert Browning* [New York, 1911], p. 196) had written, "In fact, commentaries on Browning bear a close resemblance to foghorns. They proclaim the existence of fog; but they do not disperse it." The similarity can be explained in either of these ways:

1. Bush consciously or unconsciously remembered the words he had once read in Lounsbury and could have found the remark nowhere else.

2. The quip, at the time Bush wrote, was in oral circulation, a bit of change in the petty-cash drawer of academic wit. It may have originated with Lounsbury, or it may have existed earlier and merely happened to alight in print in his book; but in either case, Bush, in writing *The Renaissance and English Humanism*, was drawing upon the orally transmitted version—unassignable to any one person—rather than adapting Lounsbury's.

These, then, are the several possible routes of descent:

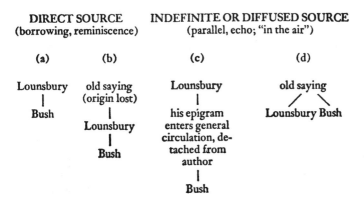

DIRECT SOURCE (borrowing, reminiscence)		INDEFINITE OR DIFFUSED SOURCE (parallel, echo; "in the air")	
(a)	**(b)**	**(c)**	**(d)**
Lounsbury	old saying (origin lost)	Lounsbury	old saying
Bush	Lounsbury	his epigram enters general circulation, detached from author	Lounsbury Bush
	Bush	Bush	

I shall not attempt to adjudicate among these possibilities—one unsolved question is whether the epigram originally was applied to scholars in general or commentators on Browning in particular—but they typify some of the alternatives presented by a question of derivation.

Of all the devices used by students of literary genetics, the most seductive and the most laden with potential fallacy is the parallel passage: two sequences of lines whose resemblances are such as to suggest that the author of one sequence knew, if he did not deliberately imitate, the other. No type of scholarly evidence has been more frequently (and sometimes ludicrously) abused than the parallel passage, chiefly because the desire to establish an open-and-shut case has obscured the true subtlety of the way the creative imagination works in the midst of a literary tradition and contemporary atmosphere. One common-sense question should accompany all attempts to establish the direct indebtedness of one author to another on the grounds of verbal similarities: Might not the resemblances be attributable to the fact that both Author A and Author B were nourished by the same culture?

In the Elizabethan age, for instance, there was a rich fund of expressions and images, originating everywhere from the classics to rural proverbial lore, which was available to and used by everybody from Ben Jonson to the earliest denizens of Grub Street. Shakespeare and his contemporaries constantly quoted or paraphrased the Bible or Ovid without much aware-ness of the eventual "sources" on which they were drawing. We do the same thing today when we employ phrases like "more in sorrow than in anger," "foul play," "the primrose path," "rich, not gaudy," "more honored in the breach than the observance," and "something is rotten in the state of Den-mark": none of which is evidence that we have read a single line of *Hamlet*. They are merely phrases that, like innumerable lines in the King James Bible, have long since become detached from their matrix and flowed into the broad stream of every-day English discourse. To interpret a set of similar expressions as evidence of a writer's knowledge of another's works may well be to assume derivation where there is only echo—the echo of scores of other writers who were using the same forms of language simply because it was the normal thing to do. "Like this, therefore derived from this" is the commonest of all the fallacies that tempt the inquirer after sources.

Although verbal parallels are the most familiar kind of source-evidence, all other components of literary works lend themselves to borrowing. Inevitably, writers in every genre are affected by what other writers in the same genre have already done. The plot of the cheater cheated, or the tables turned, goes back at least as far as Roman comedy and has been used by dramatists and novelists ever since. Such characters as the termagant wife, the pompous pedant, the comic manservant, and the country bumpkin are so commonly encountered in literature that to assert that they owe their appearance in one work specifically to their presence in another is foolhardy, unless there are strong grounds for asserting that particular association. The author may have found his suggestion in any, or all, of a dozen other works. Dickens, as a youth, read Smollett, Fielding, Goldsmith, Cervantes, LeSage, and other comic writers; though they deeply influenced his own comic imagination, it is well-nigh impossible to say which of his episodes and habits of characterization he derived from any of them.

We are coming more and more to realize, too, how large a debt some authors have owed to the popular, or sub-literary, reading matter that stimulated their imaginations, especially in their formative years. Shelley was an avid reader of the Gothic novels of his day; the imaginative bent of Scott, Coleridge, Wordsworth, and others was shaped by their childhood reading of ballads and chapbook romances; Mark Twain's genius was affected by the tall-tale humor of the frontier, expressed and transmitted by word of mouth, in newspapers, and in obscurely printed leaflets and books. Because the materials characteristic of these popular forms were so broadly disseminated, seldom being exclusively associated with one author or work, the result of source-investigations is often the statement that "*books of this sort*" suggested this manner of writing, or that kind of character, to a certain writer; to particularize is an impossibility.

And so with ideas. The literature of every age is permeated with opinions and assumptions that are nobody's, and everybody's: they are the freely circulated legal tender of a period's mind. In the past several decades the historians of ideas have amply demonstrated how widely diffused in a given period were dominant ideas that once were assumed to have been more or less the property of a few influential thinkers. The Renaissance man's mind was replete with standard (but not necessarily uniform) notions on religion, politics, science, cosmology, and every other topic of human interest, and the literature of the time is a bountiful expression of those opinions. Shakespeare may have read Montaigne's *Essais*, but even if he had not, his frequent echoes of the French philosopher's ethical observations might adequately be accounted for by the fact that these were favorite capsules of wisdom. We cannot hope ever to identify all the books that contributed, overtly or subtly, to the poems of Milton, one of the most erudite and assimilative of English authors. He was steeped in the literature of theology and travel and science, in the classic epic, in the numerous neo-Latin, French, and Italian works which contained, in one form or another, portions of the story of the Fall of Man. The existing scholarly discussion of his sources, in fact, is a small library in itself. Some sources can be identified by author and title, but much of the material Milton drew upon was so widely distributed—the same ideas about astronomy, for instance, are found in encyclopedia after encyclopedia that he could have seen— that the only sensible conclusion we can reach is that his genius had an extraordinary power of transmuting intellectual commonplaces into great art. [52]

The best safeguard against what André Morize called "the hypnotism of the unique source" is, therefore, a ceaseless awareness of the amount of verbal and conceptual material that in every age belongs to the common domain. Every writer's total debt as an artist is, on the whole, less to a handful of authors by whom he was especially influenced than to the mingled currents of art and ideas, traditional and new, in the midst of which he cannot help living.

All of which is not to say that direct borrowing does not play an important role in literary transmission. It does, and the quest for specific sources often is rewarded by discoveries of high critical value. The same principles of investigation and reasoning which we have already seen governing the determination of authorship operate here as well. A small, isolated similarity of

52. See Arnold Williams, "Methods and Achievements in the Study of Milton's Sources: A Defense," *Papers of the Michigan Academy of Science, Arts and Letters,* 32 (1948 for 1946), 471–80.

phrase proves little if anything. But the likelihood of direct relationship grows if two passages virtually match, or contain peculiarities (unusual words or idioms, out-of-the-way images or images with unaccustomed details or uses) which are associated only with the two specific authors under consideration. Similarly with the various non-verbal resemblances. Mere occasional likenesses of plot, character, artistic form, or ideas are individually of small significance, unless they all point unmistakably in the same direction. The likelihood of direct borrowing increases with the quantity of evidence. If, instead of a few casual, scattered parallels of phraseology or content, we discover many resemblances which are both idiosyncratic and fundamental, we have proportionally greater reason to believe that the later author drew from the source where all these elements are found.

The attempt to establish a particular source, again like the attempt to determine authorship, is aided by the convergence of evidence, both internal and external. The stronger the internal evidence, in nature and amount, the better the case; but the intuitive element cannot be wholly eliminated from such an argument. External evidence, therefore, has to be sought to substantiate the inferences made from a comparison of the text with its suspected source of inspiration and to serve as a check on whatever impressionism colors our thinking. The most important question to be asked is so obvious that it is sometimes overlooked: Did our author read the book from which he seems to have borrowed? If he owned a copy, as might be established by the catalogue printed when his books were sold after his death or by the survival of the copy itself, the presumption is that he did read it. But possession of a book is no positive proof of its owner's having even glanced inside it. More convincing evidence is the presence in the volume of underscorings and annotations, written by the owner himself. Some writers had such a habit (Coleridge, as Lamb attested, was given to scrawling lengthy marginalia in the books he borrowed from friends), and scholars who have followed such writers' reading, as thus marked out, have been in a peculiarly advantageous position to understand the movement of their minds and the way they transformed and incorporated the harvest of their reading into their art. [53]

Equally useful are the allusions authors make in their formal published work to books they have read. The letters and diaries of many writers also are replete with comments on the books they have been reading, and in addition, some authors, such as Milton, Coleridge, Shelley, and Matthew Arnold, kept commonplace books into which they copied extracts from their reading. Another avenue of investigation lies in the books an author would have had to read at school and university. The published curriculum and other contemporary school records are useful to discover these facts, though the extent and depth of an author's acquaintance with "required books" must be judged in the light of all we know of students' habits, then and now. [54]

Lacking more positive evidence, including the strong circumstantial variety, we must decide whether the books would at least have been available to the author who we think levied from them. One of the main arguments of those who cannot believe that the Stratford-born actor William Shakespeare wrote the plays attributed to him is that such a man could not

53. For some interesting examples of the scholarly work that has been done on identifying the contents of, and in some instances reassembling, great authors' libraries, see Geoffrey Keynes, *The Library of Edward Gibbon* (London, 1940), and the same editor's *Bibliography of Dr. John Donne* (3rd ed., Cambridge, 1958), pp. 204–22; John C. Hodges, *The Library of William Congreve* (New York, 1955); Allen T. Hazen, *A Catalogue of Horace Walpole's Library* (3 vols., New Haven, 1969); Walter Harding, *Emerson's Library* (Charlottesville, Va., 1967); Nancie Campbell, *Tennyson in Lincoln: A Catalogue of the Collections in the Research Centre*, I (Lincoln, 1971), 25–107; George Whalley, "Portrait of a Bibliophile VII: Samuel Taylor Coleridge, 1772–1834," *Book Collector*, 10 (1961), 275–90; and Volumes I and XI of the Herford-Simpson edition of the works of Ben Jonson. The twelve volumes of A. N. L. Munby's *Sale Catalogues of Libraries of Eminent Persons* (London, 1971–75) reproduce in facsimile the contemporary printed inventories of the books owned by a number of eighteenth- and nineteenth-century English writers.

54. Typical of the monographs and articles that gather evidence of the books authors read are Merton M. Sealts, Jr., *Melville's Reading: A Check-List of Books Owned and Borrowed* (Madison, Wis., 1966); Marion Kesselring, *Hawthorne's Reading, 1828–1850* (New York, 1949); Jack L. Capps, *Emily Dickinson's Reading* (Cambridge, Mass., 1966); Floyd Stovall, "Notes on Whitman's Reading," *AL*, 26 (1954), 337–62; and Hill Shine, *Carlyle's Early Reading, to 1834* (Lexington, Ky., 1953).

have known all the books the author of the plays obviously knew. But while it is true that we cannot tell precisely where or under what circumstances Shakespeare had access to them, those books were without exception available, at booksellers and in many private libraries, and there is no reason at all to suppose that a man in his position could not have read them. A more troublesome problem, where Renaissance authors are concerned, stems from the practice of circulating poems in manuscript long before they were printed. If a writer seems to have borrowed from another's works at a time when they were not yet printed but are known to have been circulating privately, painstaking biographical inquiries must be made to determine whether the suspected borrower belonged to a social circle in which one of the manuscript copies passed from hand to hand.

The most famous large-scale use ever made of this kind of evidence is John Livingston Lowes's. Beginning with the so-called "Gutch Memorandum Book," a ninety-leaf "catch-all for suggestions jotted down chaotically from Coleridge's absorbing adventures among books," and helped by such leads as the record of the poet's borrowings from the Bristol Library, Lowes followed Coleridge's trail through an incredible number of books on travel and science, emerging, finally, with a virtually line-by-line reconstruction of the way in which "The Rime of the Ancient Mariner" and "Kubla Khan" took form in the deep well of the poet's subconsciousness. The book in which Lowes described Coleridge's transmogrifying of hints found in his reading into the stuff of poetic art—and Lowes's own adventures in recreating Coleridge's—is *The Road to Xanadu* (1927), the greatest true-detective story ever written.[55]

The assumption of direct borrowing ordinarily can be well sustained if the internal evidence is sufficiently large and striking to rule out casual resemblance and if external evidence makes it sufficiently probable that the one author knew the other's works. But if unchallengeable dates or other circumstances make it impossible that the author should have known

55. In his remarkable—and controversial—*Coleridge, the Damaged Archangel*, Norman Fruman takes a darker view of Coleridge's liberal use of other men's writings. See below, page 243.

certain books at the time he wrote the work in which the presumed indebtedness occurs, the case collapses.

It is possible, too, that despite the seeming weight of other evidence, a specialist's intimate knowledge of an author's literary opinions and habits may persuade him that the writer would not have suffered himself to be influenced by another's practice. Both of these considerations proved fatal to one of Lowes's last ventures in source-attribution. In 1940 (*PMLA*, pp. 203–6) he called attention to "an extraordinary instance of Shelley's indebtedness to Keats"—thirty "borrowings" from *Endymion* and two from "Sleep and Poetry" in *The Witch of Atlas*. It was an impressive demonstration, except that in the following year David Lee Clark (*PMLA*, pp. 479–94) blew it sky-high. For one thing, he pointed out, Shelley, far from being a Keats enthusiast, "deplored . . . Keats's bad taste in poetry." For another, not one of the thirty-two "borrowings," according to Clark, "can confidently be said to have come from Keats; three could have been suggested by Keats; *the remaining twenty-nine had been used by Shelley in his own productions written before he had read Keats.* Of these twenty-nine, it appears quite certain that one was suggested by *Isaiah*, two each by Virgil, Euripides, Shakespeare, and Rabelais, and the others by Spenser, Diodorus, and Pliny" [56]—in all of whom Shelley was well versed, and of whom he held a far higher opinion than he did of Keats. The episode was a melancholy final chapter in Lowes's career, but it illustrates as well as any the pitfalls that await even the most experienced source-investigator.

When our research is done, and we have defined as closely as we can the nature and extent of a literary debt, our critical faculty takes over, to infer what the material thus acquired and filtered through the author's creative intelligence meant to him, and how it accords with the rest of the artistic composition. To interpret with psychological and historical accuracy the relation between what he read and what he wrote, we seek to understand as intimately as we can the way his mind grew, the habits of his mature intellect, and the stimulation and sustenance he drew both from the literary and intellectual tradition his age inherited and from the atmosphere that prevailed

56. Italics supplied.

while he wrote. It is not origin that matters in the long run—the literary imagination, as distinct from the historical mind, is indifferent to origins and pedigrees—but the comparison which discovery of the source makes possible. If an author derived a dominant idea from another, just how did he modify it and impress it with the stamp of his own intellect? If he took a character from the stock of a currently popular genre or, on the other hand, drew him from life, what in the process of adaptation is important to our understanding of his artistic technique and his attitude toward his fellow men? If his metaphors can be traced back through the generations, what meaningful differences can we discern in his use of them? "To see [a work] in relation to the tradition out of which it sprang"—I quote Tuve again—"is only to perceive with greater pleasure those leaps and those masterful ordering actions of the single human mind by which new relationships are made and new unities created."

The path of the source-student lies through the valley of echoes, the house of mirrors. But it is not the fact of imitation in which he ordinarily is interested, but its converse: the revelation of an artist's originality, and precisely wherein it resides.

4. Tracing Reputation and Influence

Another phase of the genetic study of literature, virtually inseparable from the search for origins, is the tracing of reputation and influence. The main difference is that while the investigator of echoes and borrowings moves backward in time, from the author to the sources that suggested vivid images or governing ideas to him, the student of reputation and influence ordinarily moves forward from the author, school, or movement to examine the effect they had on their contemporaries and on succeeding generations of critics, fellow writers, and ordinary readers. The history of a writer's reception during his lifetime, and of his subsequent fame (or neglect) from era to era; the study of the interaction, and sometimes the blunt opposition, of critical opinion and popular taste that determined the nature of that reputation at a given moment; the review of the fortunes of a single seminal work down through the years, with particular attention to the angle from which each generation viewed it; the reconstruction of an episode in literary adaptation, the way a certain epoch took up an old theme or convention and, by reshaping it to fit new conditions, gave it fresh vitality and significance—these are some of the concerns of reputation-and-influence study.

As Lionel Trilling said, the poem is, among other things, "the poem as it has existed in history, as it has lived its life from Then to Now, as it is a thing which submits itself to one kind of perception in one age and another kind of perception in another age, as it exerts in each age a different kind of power." [57] To find everything *Paradise Lost* contains today, we must read it not only in the way Milton intended his first readers to do and in the various ways that modern critics suggest, but also as men in the intervening three centuries, with their constantly changing standards of value, have done. Implicit within *Childe Harold* or *Moby-Dick* is the record of all it has meant to the intellects and sensibilities of the men who have read it from the day of its first publication to our own. To decipher that intricate narrative of the life and works of a great piece of literature, for the sake of the multiple levels of experience that reading it can afford, we must draw upon the data of history.

That same process of historical reconstruction has other, equally valuable, functions. Tracing the course of an author's reputation helps define the critical standards and popular literary tastes that prevailed in successive eras, beginning with his own. Both the novelty and the traditionalism of Wordsworth's early poetry become more apparent when we read what its first critics said of it, note which poets Wordsworth was compared with—and then find out what contemporary critics and readers thought of *them*, and why. In such a fashion a whole climate of literary opinion can be re-created, with the primary aim of establishing what, given the prevailing modes and tastes, the poet set out to do (Wordsworth's own statements in the Preface to *Lyrical Ballads* are not the whole story by any means) and how his audience interpreted both his intention and his

57. "The Sense of the Past," reprinted in *The Liberal Imagination* (New York, 1950), p. 186.

achievement. And the subsequent fluctuations of his fame permit us to read in microcosm the principal trends in nineteenth- and twentieth-century taste, as well as to explain more adequately the art of those poets who found Wordsworth a rich inspiration and useful model and of those others who participated in the inevitable reaction against him.

Although the usual movement of reputation-and-influence study is chronological, the same materials and methods, applied to simultaneous phenomena, can be used to reconstruct the literary atmosphere of an age and then to account for individual aspects of literary taste and practice at the time. Once we learn, for instance, which authors of the recent or more distant past were widely read and which were out of favor in the period, we are better equipped to account for the themes and devices, the spirit and purpose, of Victorian writers and genres. Remembering the decline in popularity Fielding, Smollett, and Sterne suffered after the first third of the nineteenth century, and realizing at the same time the popularity of the historical novel during and immediately after Scott's reign, as well as of "Newgate" (crime) and "silver fork" (high society) novels, we comprehend more clearly the expectations and requirements of the audience that welcomed Ainsworth, Disraeli, Dickens, Bulwer-Lytton, Thackeray, and Wilkie Collins. Recalling the excitement that the discovery of Keats, after decades of neglect, caused among the young poets of mid-century, we are better able to understand the poetic ideals and techniques of two of his most gifted admirers, Dante Gabriel Rossetti and William Morris. If we know what the contemporary critical attitude was toward Chaucer, Gray, Burns, and Byron, we can gauge the degree to which Matthew Arnold, writing of these poets, was merely echoing orthodox opinion and the degree to which he was independent of it.

The study of reputation begins, obviously, with contemporary reception, whether of a single work or of an author's book-by-book production from the beginning of his career to its end. If a poem was an immediate success, what did it contain that so delighted its first readers? If it failed, what ideas or literary qualities either alienated the audience or, at best, left it indifferent? What specific features of style and content were most commented upon? What kind of readers were most interested in it? How many other writers, in that first audience, were possibly affected by it? Study of the first reception of a work not only illuminates the nature of the work itself, by attempting to account for its success or failure on the basis of its adherence to, or deviation from, current fashion; in addition, it helps explain the impact of the same literary environment on other authors.

For the contemporary reception of most important books during the past two centuries, abundant documents are available. Heading the list are reviews, which give us a direct indication of what the arbiters of taste thought. Because there are no convenient printed indexes to such reviews in the eighteenth and nineteenth centuries, finding them usually requires us to examine every available periodical (monthly magazines, quarterly journals of opinion, intellectual or semi-popular weeklies, and some newspapers) for the appropriate period. For nineteenth-century works, *Poole's Index to Periodical Literature* lists some reviews but only if they are of considerable length, and in any event unsystematically. The *Wellesley Index to Victorian Periodicals* is partially supplying this deficiency so far as British reviews for the period covered are concerned. The twentieth-century *Book Review Digest* is helpful for reviews in popular and semi-popular periodicals, and the eight-volume *Comprehensive Index to English-Language Little Magazines 1890–1970* now provides easy access to reviews in some of the most symptomatic and (in the long run) influential organs in Britain and America, the so-called "little magazines." [58]

The judgments delivered in these reviews must be subjected to the same cool scrutiny that is applied to all other kinds of historical evidence. Is a certain reviewer acting as a faithful mouthpiece for the age, or does one detect a pronounced literary or political bias, or a personal dislike of the author?

58. Access to much contemporary criticism of a number of major English and American writers—e.g., Spenser, Milton, Swift, Fielding, Scott, Dickens, Thackeray, Trollope, George Eliot, Hawthorne, Melville, Joyce—has been made easier through the Critical Heritage series published by the London firm of Routledge and Kegan Paul. Varying with the writers covered, these volumes generally include a survey of the writer's critical reputation and selected important reviews of each major work, and they may also include comments from diaries, letters, and journals of important contemporaries.

Many kinds of prejudice, not all of them relevant to a book's merits, affect criticism. Moreover, editorial policy in various epochs has had a great deal to do with a critic's decision, as it still does in some quarters. Every schoolboy used to know that a Tory author could no more expect an enthusiastic welcome in the pages of the Whig *Edinburgh Review* than a Whig writer could look forward to liberal justice in the Tory *Quarterly*. Similarly, during some decades of the nineteenth century, in both Britain and America, a publisher frequently arranged for an appreciative notice of a new book. Caution is particularly desirable in the case of the periodicals owned by publishing houses; books published by the London firm of Bentley in the 1830's were extravagantly praised in Bentley's magazines, and in evaluating a notice in the *Atlantic Monthly* in the 1860's, it is useful to remember that the firm which owned the magazine also published many of the books it reviewed. Today, reviewing is much more independent, and the cruder forms of critic-influencing have almost wholly vanished. Still, it is not unknown for a friend of the author to suggest to a book review editor the name of a suitable (i.e., well-disposed) reviewer.

Just as important in rounding out our knowledge of how a book struck its first audience is the evidence found in the private papers left by its members—their letters and diaries and the records of their conversation. Thus we can ascertain how widely a book was discussed, by whom, and for what reasons. The farther back we go, of course, the scantier such records become. The history of sixteenth- and seventeenth-century authors' early reputations must be compiled from contemporary biographical-critical dictionaries, compilations of excerpts and criticisms (of which Francis Meres's *Palladis Tamia* [1598] is perhaps the best known), the commonplace books some readers kept (many of which are still unexamined), and scattered allusions in the imaginative, critical, and controversial writings of the time, such as Robert Greene's famous attack on young Shakespeare.[59]

59. Two good examples of collections of allusions to earlier writers are Caroline F. E. Spurgeon, *Five Hundred Years of Chaucer Criticism and Allusion* (3 vols., Cambridge, 1925), and Gerald E. Bentley, *Shakespeare and Jonson: Their Reputations in the Seventeenth Century Compared* (2 vols., Chicago, 1945).

Besides the quality of a book's early reception, there is its magnitude to consider. How many copies were sold? The answer, if found, will provide some indication of whether the broad public agreed with the critics and the intellectual élite. Here publishers' records are the primary source, if they are extant (many extensive and valuable archives have been lost through fire and bombing) and open to scholarly exploration. These figures can be depended on: there are no secrets between a businessman and his ledgers. Other sources purporting to give the sales figures of books and periodicals must be regarded with great skepticism, for book-trade gossip is notoriously unreliable. Hence sales figures reported in magazine articles or diary entries by people who had them from the customary "good authority" have little value unless they can be substantiated from a better source. Above all, one should not be misled by a recital of the number of editions a book went through, because an edition may consist of a few hundred or several hundred thousand copies. The number of *copies* sold is far better evidence of a book's popularity than the number of editions printed.

The same observation applies to the subsequent publishing record of a book. Scholars sometimes point to the number of reprints a classic like *The Vicar of Wakefield* went through in the nineteenth century as a sign of its enduring popularity. Actually, as I have written elsewhere, "practical considerations, such as the publishers' desire to get their full money's worth out of their investment in plates and stock, may well have caused certain old standbys, such as Dryden, Pope, Goldsmith, Johnson, and Cowper, to overstay their welcome." Thus economic expediency (as well as the empty dignity of received reputation), rather than genuine popular interest, often accounts for the year-in, year-out sale of many books. The *Sonnets from the Portuguese* still appeals to gift purchasers, but most copies sold nowadays remain unopened.

It is instructive, too, to go through anthologies of contemporary poetry and essays to study the selections which the editors, who presumably were good judges of what their readers wanted, made from authors who were in fashion. And, in the case of extremely popular writers like Byron and Dickens, the number and nature of adaptations that were made of their books, particularly dramatizations, plagiarisms, imitations, and spurious "continuations," are a valuable measure of the public's insatiable appetite for their work, even if what was offered under their names had never been touched by their pens.

The largest body of evidence bearing on an author's critical fortunes in later years is found in the books and articles that deal with or simply mention him. From these materials, which for major writers are often bewilderingly abundant, can be constructed a graph that will accurately reveal the ascents and declines his reputation has undergone. Prominent among them are books specifically about him—critical and interpretive studies and biographies (which often contain revealing, if sometimes oblique, glimpses of current critical opinion). In periodicals can be found not only formal articles but what in many instances are equivalent to critical essays: reviews of new biographical and critical volumes and editions of the author's works.

In addition to these books and articles devoted specifically to the topic, the majority of which can be found without too much trouble by consulting the standard bibliographical tools, a wealth of incidental comment is to be found simply by wide reading in the critical literature of whatever era one is concerned with. A general article on the English humorists may contain a suggestive paragraph on Ned Ward, and a book on Emerson, written in 1900, may prove to have a long digression that throws light on the way people at that time regarded Thoreau. Some bibliographies of writings about individual authors (Corson's *Scott*, Miller's *Dickens*, the Broughton-Northup-Pearsall *Browning*, for instance) are so broad in their coverage, listing everything from the most solemn critiques to caricatures, that they serve as shorthand histories of the author's critical and popular fame. The definitive bibliographies of Oliver Wendell Holmes and John Greenleaf Whittier contain sections cataloguing the sheet music that wafted the poets' lyrics from the library table to the pianoforte, and Lucille Adams' bibliography of *Huckleberry Finn*, published in 1950 by the Buffalo Public Library, reaches all the way down to comic-book versions of the novel. But even the most exhaustive guides cannot possibly record the existence of many casual, but frequently revealing, comments scattered through the printed diaries and private correspondences of readers. For these, the books themselves must be scanned, with the help, never to be too much relied upon, of whatever indexes they contain.

An author's work not only evokes response from critics and common readers as it passes down through time; as has been noted, it also affects new generations of writers. In measuring the effect a writer has on his younger contemporaries and his successors, we re-enter to some extent the territory briefly surveyed in the pages on the search for origins. But there is this difference: although the terms "source" and "influence" are sometimes used almost synonymously, the latter refers to the wider, more profound, more subtle and intangible effects that a knowledge of one writer's works has upon another, whereas "source" designates specific borrowings that may or may not be related to that larger debt.

Moreover, in tracing influences we find ourselves dealing not only with the relationship of one author to another (Sir Thomas Browne to Lamb, Ruskin to Proust) but, to a greater degree than is true in source study, with generalized forces—conventions (Petrarchism), genres (the pastoral elegy), schools and movements (the Scottish Chaucerians), clusters of ideas (New England Transcendentalism)—at both the transmitting and receiving ends. The author of an interesting theoretical discussion of the subject [60] notes that the emanators of influence may include, in addition to specific authors and works, "climate, mores or locale of a people"; historical events such as the Armada and the American Civil War; "some particular style or literary convention"; "a particular theory or idea"; a specific thinker; and a literary movement. Similarly, the influence may be exerted upon such broad entities as the age at large, the cultural tradition, or a literary movement.

It was with good reason, then, that André Morize wrote, "Influence by its very nature does not always declare itself by precise and well-defined signs; its study does not admit of the same exactness as, for instance, the investigation of sources. Frequently, it consists in following the capricious, unexpected meanderings of a stream whose waters are led hither and thither

60. Ihab H. Hassan, "The Problem of Influence in Literary History: Notes Towards a Definition," *Journal of Aesthetics and Art Criticism*, 14 (1955), 66–76.

by the accidental contour of the ground and take their color
from the various tributaries and the soil through which they
flow—at times even disappearing from view for a space, to re-
appear farther on." [61] Thus diffusion, cross-currents, the in-
extricable mingling of numerous impalpable elements in the
literary and intellectual atmosphere make the tracing of influence a delicate and uncertain business, most especially where
generalized forces are involved.

Since source- and influence-study use the same highway for
much of their distance, the same common-sense rules of the
road prevail, and the same caution signs are posted. Confining
ourselves to the kind of influence-study most commonly prac-
ticed—that involving the impact of a single author or work on
a later group or succession of writers—we need to ask three
main questions: Is there enough solid evidence to permit us to
convert our supposition of influence into a probability? If so,
by what means, such as general diffusion or transmission
through a series of identifiable intermediaries, was it carried
down, and how widely was it felt? Finally, and most pertinent
for the intentions of criticism, what was the precise nature of
that influence as revealed by the literary works where it can be
detected?

The first question can be answered by the techniques discussed above, on pages 102–6. As always, similarity does not
necessarily mean causal relationship, and once in a while a
tempting case involving source or influence is ruined by one or
more inconvenient facts. In two great Victorian novels of the
1840's, *Vanity Fair* and *Dombey and Son,* are memorable passages describing the sale by public auction of the luxurious
household goods of a wealthy man who has lost his fortune—a
modern version of the old "fall of princes" theme. Might not
Thackeray and Dickens have been inspired by what they read
in the newspapers of two widely publicized sales of the kind,
the dispersal of the contents of Stowe House, palatial home of
the bankrupt Duke of Buckingham, and of Gore House, site of
the London salon presided over by the now equally destitute
Countess of Blessington? The idea is almost irresistible. But
alas, the dates destroy the hypothesis. The pertinent chapter of

61. *Problems and Methods of Literary History* (Boston, 1922), p. 229.

Vanity Fair (17) was published in May, 1847; that of *Dombey and Son* (59) in April, 1848. The Stowe House and Gore House sales occurred in August–September, 1848, and May, 1849, respectively. Thackeray, therefore, could have had neither sale in mind; and while Dickens would have read of Stowe House's being taken over by bailiffs at the end of August, 1847, his description of the dispersal of Dombey's property could have owed nothing to the actual Stowe sale. Both novelists, we must conclude, simply drew upon their —and their readers'—knowledge of what, after all, were quite common events, given the risks of early Victorian business life.

The dates and other bibliographical and biographical facts must, therefore, certify that the supposed influence could have occurred. To flesh out this initial possibility into something closer to certainty, we follow the source-student's method. The most effective way to show that Shakespeare's dramatic techniques were often adopted by eighteenth-century novelists, or that Arnold's long shadow is detectable in the critical attitudes of Pater, T. E. Hulme, Eliot, Herbert Read, and the American "new humanists," is first to gather all relevant internal evidence from the writings in question. To this assemblage of internal evidence, which, however impressive, is seldom adequate in itself to justify a conclusion, must be added whatever external evidence can be found, in particular proof that the writers not only had read but were thoroughly acquainted with the contents of the earlier author's work, or with the writings through which his influence was mediated.

The second of our major questions, that of the breadth and intensity of an author's influence and the way it was transmitted, can be answered in large part by the methods of reputation-study. We can show, for example, how many writers or schools of writers were affected by his style, his formal techniques, his attitudes; and how many critics, sitting on the sidelines of literary creativity, urged their contemporaries to emulate him. But as we seek evidence of influence in a given period or down through the centuries, our eagerness to prove a thesis may dull our sense of caution and discrimination. Granting that many ideas and artistic devices, once introduced into the air of an age, gain wide circulation, we run the risk of thinking we detect influence where the resemblances are, in fact, unremarkable and probably fortuitous. Here is one of the many situations in research where tough-minded skepticism must hold a tight rein on the human tendency toward all-out enthusiasm.

If the evidence assures us that A's influence on B is no figment of the overeager imagination, we must try to decide whether it was exerted directly or in diffused or intermediary fashion. Eighteenth-century poetry often has a markedly Miltonic style. If we put aside the possibility that the resemblances are due to both Milton's and the eighteenth-century "Miltonists' " drawing upon a common fund of heroic style, two explanations are available: the eighteenth-century authors were intimately acquainted with Milton's works, and the influence was therefore exerted directly from him to them; or they were simply echoing the idiom and tone that are found in the poetry of their numerous predecessors who imitated him.

Seldom is a clear-cut answer possible. It is not a matter of "either/or," but far more likely of "both"; in which latter case, our job is to estimate, as best we can, the relative proportions of direct and of indirect influence in the relationship between one writer and another. It is a moot question how much of the unmistakable Browningesque element in T. S. Eliot's technique is traceable (despite his own disclaimer) to his reading of Browning's poetry itself and how much to his acknowledged indebtedness to Ezra Pound, whose early work, in turn, as Pound often said, was deeply influenced by Browning. A third possibility, which does not exclude the other two, is that Eliot's use of the dramatic monologue and of colloquial diction is simply one evidence of the influence Browning had upon poetic technique in general during the first decades of the twentieth century.

While the complex and elusive quality of literary influence makes any confident answer suspect, it is far from idle to raise such questions. The very attempt to decide whether an influence was direct or secondhand, or both—or indeterminate—forces us to examine more intently the character of that influence, which after all, is our final concern. By seeking to establish *how* and *why* it happened that one writer had an important role in the making of others, we come face to face with the problem of exactly *what* happened. And the quality of that influence is affected, obviously, by the channels through which it was transmitted. No two cases are the same. The results are as various as the number of intelligences that have assimilated certain of Writer A's artistic idiosyncrasies and ideas in their own work, modifying them as the conditions of their era and their temperamental bent required, and the number that they, in turn, have influenced.

Every manifestation of influence, whether simple or complicated, easily isolated or tantalizingly nebulous, is part of the record of literary tradition. In sorting out the tangle of relationships that tradition involves, we are ceaselessly clarifying the causes and the nature of change in literary art. Every poem or drama or novel belongs to a process that is both continuous and communal, and to trace its way down the stream of history —the new coloration it has acquired, the banks it has washed, the new growths it has nourished—is to define more precisely both its nature and that of all the subsequent literature it has touched.

5. Cultivating a Sense of the Past

Most questions of the kind discussed in the preceding sections —what is the best text of a work? who wrote it? what were its sources? how was it received, and what influence has it had?— can be answered from the materials associated with *literary* history. And it is with literary history, obviously, that as researchers we are most concerned. It enables us to place the author or work or tendency we are studying among all the other authors, works, and tendencies belonging to its time and, perhaps, to the preceding eras as well. The better our knowledge of literary genetics, the more surely can we distinguish between the individual, the original, the innovative on the one hand, and the commonplace and conventional on the other.

But the present chapter has, at the same time, implied another, closely related, point. Surrounding the specifically literary current of history have always been the manifold currents of ideas, the other arts, and everyday habit which constitute the milieu of a work of literature at the time of its creation. Sound scholarship, and in its turn sound criticism, demands that we comprehend as intimately as we can the atmosphere of contemporary and antecedent circumstance that enveloped the life and productions of an author. Textual study, for instance, requires us to know in microscopic detail the practices of printers and booksellers at the time a book was being transferred from author to audience; in dealing with matters of disputed authorship, we need to understand the prevailing social attitudes toward writers and the reasons—many of them far removed from literary history—why authors have concealed their identity or, on the other hand, have had works attributed to them that are not theirs; in examining sources and influences we deal constantly with the problem of taste, which is a resultant of many intellectual and social forces. And always, and most important, an awareness of historical environment is indispensable to a correct reading of the literary text itself. Only by reading Marvell's "Horatian Ode" also as a historical document can we read it accurately as a poem, for a knowledge of what Cromwell meant to Marvell, and why, is prerequisite to knowing what Marvell meant the poem to convey to his readers.

Every good literary researcher, then, trains himself to be his own historian. It is his grasp of history that tells him the full meaning of the facts he has unearthed and that at the same time prevents the misinterpretation which is often the result of historical naïveté.

The applications of historical knowledge to literary scholarship range in size from the minute to the panoramic, and their variety is endless. Acquaintance with the ideas and customs of an era may be drawn upon to explicate a tiny topical allusion. When a character in a Victorian novel is said to have taken a "Shillibeer," did he swallow it, board it, or sniff it? If we are to be genuine authorities on the whole body of an author's works, or on the literary productions of a certain epoch, we must not only take for our province all the knowledge that was then current, but synthesize it into an entity that represents our personal, well-informed reconstruction of "the medieval [or Restoration, or Augustan, or Victorian, or early twentieth-century American] mind." To know what the lines of Shakespeare's plays meant to their first audiences, we need a thorough acquaintance with Elizabethan medicine, religion, costume, superstitions, crafts, political theory, ornithology, music, law, sport, table manners, military and naval practices, and scores of other topics. And in studying sixteenth- and seventeenth-century poetry, our specifically literary orientation (knowledge, for instance, of the medieval conventions that survived into Tudor times, and of the classics that affected the whole face and spirit of Elizabethan poetry) has to be supplemented from many non-literary fields. No sphere of current intellectual interest was alien to those restless, questing poets, who wove ideas from everywhere into their pages: the Ptolemaic, and then the Copernican, cosmology that permeated the thought of Spenser, Donne, and Milton; Neo-Platonism, most particularly as it affected the poets' concept of human love; the philosophical symbolism of musical harmony, exemplified in Sir John Davies' "Orchestra," Milton's "At a Solemn Music," Dryden's "A Song for St. Cecilia's Day"; alchemy, somewhat discredited intellectually but a prolific source of metaphor, as in Donne; the whole system of medieval-Renaissance psychology and physiology (the theory of the humors, the "passions," and so forth).

But our historical lenses must, like those of television cameras, be capable of different ranges. Not only are literary works products of a long age: they are, far oftener than we customarily recognize, products of a decade, even of a year or a month. In studying many authors, both the long view and the short are indispensable to adequate comprehension. Milton O. Percival's *William Blake's Circle of Destiny*, which traces the age-old esoteric systems of thought upon which the poet-artist drew, is complemented by David V. Erdman's *Blake: Prophet Against Empire*, which focuses on the contemporaneity of Blake's message in the politically and socially critical years of the French Revolution.

Consider how much of the multiplex allegory of *The Faerie Queene* is overlooked if by concentrating on the wider set of ethical and philosophical themes we fail to see how immediately topical Spenser's religious and political shadow-references were to readers in the 1590's. Many an Elizabethan or Jacobean drama is as replete with the subjects of the day as a news broadcast—and for the beginning and end of each such story, of which the play provides only a tantalizing fragment, we must repair to the documents of history; otherwise its full meaning escapes us. Joyce's *Ulysses* is, among many other things, a colossal feat of retrospective journalism, preserving in the amber of its Homeric myth the streets and people of Dublin as they existed on June 16, 1904. One of the most noteworthy recent contributions historical scholarship has made to the explication of a major literary work has been the joint effort of many researchers who have combed newspaper files and interviewed virtually every surviving old-time Dubliner, for the sake of explaining Joyce's almost countless topical and local allusions.

Of peculiar importance to the correct reading of English literature in some epochs is a knowledge of contemporary politics. Research in the writings associated with Dryden, Defoe, Addison, Swift, Pope, and the pamphleteering Henry Fielding calls for a good working knowledge of who was who and what was what in court and Parliament during the Restoration and early eighteenth century. This is not easily obtained, because politics, religion, economics, and personalities were perhaps never more desperately entangled than in the years from the end of the Commonwealth to Sir Robert Walpole's administration.[62] Yet neither the controlling assumptions nor the point of individual passages in the writings of some of the age's greatest authors—not to speak of the mass of historical documents surrounding them—can be comprehended without such knowledge. This is true, above all, of the period's satire, whose subject generally is the moment and its fleetingly spotlighted inhabitants. A superficial acquaintance with the political and literary feuds behind the *Epistle to Dr. Arbuthnot* and *The Dunciad* may enable one to appreciate the broad swipes of Pope's satirical weapon, but only a much closer knowledge of the personalities and the petty gossip of Grub Street garrets and fashionable drawing rooms, at the very time Pope wrote, can make available the far more numerous, and subtle, dagger

62. Not that the political history of earlier or later epochs is irrelevant to the study of literature from those periods. See, for example, David Bevington, *Tudor Drama and Politics: A Critical Approach to Topical Meaning* (Cambridge, Mass., 1968), and Carl Woodring, *Politics in English Romantic Poetry* (Cambridge, Mass., 1970).

thrusts we find in these poems as well as in *The Rape of the Lock*.[63] In American literature, similarly, the humor of Irving's *History of New York* and Lowell's *Biglow Papers* is largely lost without an appreciation of the contemporary persons and events that called it forth.

Probably the most fundamental necessity, and the hardest to satisfy by any systematic means, is the mastery of an era's vocabulary. We have to learn the language of the past before we can accurately grasp its ideas. Denotations offer little trouble: we can quickly find out what obsolete or otherwise puzzling words meant, at a given time, by going to the *Oxford English Dictionary*, the *Dictionary of American English*, or more specialized lexicons such as those of slang and trade argot. But much more vital to understanding are the intellectual implications and the emotional connotations borne by words that epitomize dominant ideas and strains of opinion in various epochs. In the literary criticism of the sixteenth, seventeenth, and eighteenth centuries, key words like *wit, imagination, fancy, imitation, genius, irony, sublime, picturesque*, and *invention* had complex and unstable significance, and much research has gone into examining their histories and reinterpreting the critical documents accordingly. A substantial volume could be assembled of articles dealing with the word *romantic* alone. *Nature*, a word that for centuries was one of the main links between metaphysics and esthetics, has had an even more complicated, and by now intensively examined, career.

Terms with political or religious references—*Papist, Puritan, Tory, Jacobin*—usually are laden with feeling, the nature of which depends on the period, the user, the immediate circumstance. Whether he is examining a literary text or a historical record, the scholar is obliged to determine and take into account the aura of connotation surrounding such a word (mere description or heavily charged epithet?) wherever it occurs. In *Absalom and Achitophel* (lines 519–26), the succession of the words *cant, zealous*, and *inspiration* conveys to the alert

---

63. For a stimulating exposition, based on a wide variety of sources, of all that "Grub Street" meant, literally and figuratively, to Pope's readers, see Pat Rogers, *Grub Street: Studies in a Sub-Culture* (London, 1972).

student of Restoration attitudes, who recognizes their strongly derogatory implications, Dryden's feelings about Dissenters:

> Hot *Levites* Headed these; who pul'd before
> From th'*Ark*, which in the Judges days they bore,
> Resum'd their Cant, and with a Zealous Cry,
> Pursu'd their old belov'd Theocracy.
> Where Sanhedrin and Priest inslav'd the Nation,
> And justifi'd their Spoils by Inspiration;
> For who so fit for Reign as *Aaron*'s Race,
> If once Dominion they could found in Grace?

Dickens' intended effect in a passage in Chapter 16 of *Nicholas Nickleby* is preserved for us only if we realize that to his contemporary readers the word *serious*, which he uses with irony-filled iteration, designated the members of the Evangelical sect, whose sanctimonious attitudes and ways he detested.

The ability to hear the overtones in a document—not only what it says to us but what additional meanings its original readers found in it—is indispensable no matter in what way one is applying historical knowledge to the study of literature. But such an ability is particularly valuable in dealing with the materials of intellectual history, the discipline which until recently has had the longest common border with literary history. (Now the frontier is amicably and profitably shared by cultural and social history.) In recent decades so much interdisciplinary work has been done, in fact, that the dividing line has become quite obscured. The chief difference between the two fields is that the history of ideas utilizes a work of literature as an intellectual document rather than as an example of art; it is more interested in the substance of the work and in its relationship to other writings in the same philosophical current than in its literary characteristics. But the eventual gain to critical understanding is great, for when wisely and sensitively managed, the tools of intellectual history can dramatically enlarge, in fact can even transform, our interpretation of a poem or essay. Moreover, by combining a historically oriented analysis of a work's content with a close examination of its structure and idiom, we often realize how subtle and intricate is the interplay between statement and form. What a certain poem *is*, we discover, depends largely on what it *means* —and vice versa.

The diversity and fruitfulness of the branch of scholarship which examines the history of literature and of ideas through a single glass are exemplified in the work of three figures whose study of philosophical tendencies has had marked pertinence to literary history: A. O. Lovejoy, Basil Willey, and Marjorie Nicolson. Lovejoy's classic work, *The Great Chain of Being* (1936), traced a cluster of philosophical concepts, presided over by the religious-metaphysical-political idea of hierarchy, from Greek times down to the nineteenth century, both in literature and in non-literary works. Lovejoy's principal beneficiary has been the student of eighteenth-century philosophical prose and poetry, who has been enabled to view certain controlling ideas in, say, Pope, both as characteristic of Pope's age and as the product of two thousand years of evolution— thus, in effect, placing Pope's poetry more firmly in the eighteenth century and at the same time more expansively relating it to a long tradition. Basil Willey's major concern was to examine the interplay of epistemology and theology, on the one hand, and literature on the other, from Bacon to Tennyson. His series of volumes, beginning with *The Seventeenth Century Background* (1934), analyzes the way the poets of each age gave eloquent, and sometimes impassioned, utterance to the prevailing doctrines that were also set forth in learned treatise and sermon. Marjorie Nicolson's specialty was, to borrow the title of her 1956 volume, "science and imagination"—that is, the impact of seventeenth- and eighteenth-century natural science, theoretical and applied, upon the imaginative vision of poets and prose writers. By examining, side by side with the actual literature of the time, the voluminous writings of the scientific speculators and experimenters, Nicolson showed how manifold were the effects of the invention of the microscope and the telescope, of Newton's seminal treatise on optics, and of the insistent dreams of voyages to the moon, upon the language, imagery, and assumptions of contemporary literature.

These are but three of the many learned men and women who have demonstrated the relevance of intellectual history to the study of literature.[64] Specialists in medieval religion and philosophy have clarified the meaning of hundreds of passages in Chaucer; students of Renaissance theology have related *Paradise Lost* to the fervid religious climate of Milton's era; while in American studies, F. O. Matthiessen, for instance, interpreted the literature of Emerson's, Hawthorne's, and Thoreau's generation in terms of the derivative yet persistently adventurous New England mind, and Henry Nash Smith, drawing upon a fund of historical evidence that reached from poetry to political speeches and dime novels, described how the myth of the West as an earthly paradise and the settler as an ennobled yeoman—a theme that pervaded much nineteenth-century American literature—flourished, then faded.

Just as pertinent to literary study as intellectual history is social history, whose scope, as one of its greatest practitioners, G. M. Trevelyan, wrote in the introduction to his *English Social History* (1942), "may be defined as the daily life of the inhabitants of the land in past ages: this includes the human as well as the economic relation of different classes to one another, the character of family and household life, the conditions of labour and of leisure, the attitude of man to nature, the culture of each age as it arose out of these general conditions of life, and took ever-changing forms in religion, literature and music, architecture, learning and thought."

As Trevelyan implies, the three disciplines—the history of literature, of ideas, and of the conditions and habits that set the tone of everyday life in any given period—are inseparable. Social history to a great extent reports the way that ideas have been translated into attitudes, customary behavior, and physical environment. Much imaginative literature does essentially the same thing through the agency of art: it gives ideas a local habitation and a name, expressing them, illustrating them, working out their consequences through metaphor,

64. Another was Ronald S. Crane, who, in addition to his original research, was distinguished for his insistence on rigorous methodology in intellectual history and its application to literary studies. His searching reviews, in the earlier issues of the *PQ* annual bibliography of eighteenth-century studies and elsewhere, are required reading for every student who proposes to deal with the history of ideas.

character, situation, plot, setting, and whatever other devices serve to make them apprehensible to the writer's intended audience, who are people firmly rooted in place and time. Intellectual history explains the ideological themes of a literary work and relates it to other works in the same intellectual tradition; social history explains its temporal milieu, its reflection of the social attitudes, the manners, the visual surface of its age. All three kinds of history can be applied to a book like *Tom Jones*—literary history to reveal the meaning of its epic, picaresque, and theatrical qualities, the history of ideas to expose its embodiment of characteristic eighteenth-century philosophical assumptions, and social history to explicate it as a Hogarthian version of English life in the 1740's.

Like that of the source-student, the social historian's most important contribution to criticism is that he provides the data by which we can gauge the nature and extent of the artist's accomplishment. We do not read literature as authentic history; between the facts of experience and the substance of a poem or novel, a creative intelligence has intervened, to transmute the historically real, which is transitory, into the imaginatively real, which, once brought into being, is preserved through the centuries. By establishing the way people in general were feeling and acting at the precise juncture of time and in the precise locale that served as a matrix for a great book, the social historian reassembles the factual materials and the prevailing spirit which were poured into the alembic of the writer's imagination; with his aid, the critic is better able to describe and assess the distillate. Since the 1930's, for instance, much attention has been paid to Dickens' novels as incisive, often acidulous, criticism of the Victorian culture, with its pursuit of profit and its sacrifice of individual dignity to the demands of faceless institutions. A cluster of books and articles, typified by Humphry House's *The Dickens World* (1941), has studied the conditions and events that lay behind the novelist's growing disillusionment with contemporary society and, some feel, with the nature of mankind itself. From the bulky reports of parliamentary investigating committees that exposed some of the more dreadful social abuses, the journalistic and fictional literature of protest, and a host of other sources, researchers have brought evidence that makes it possible for us to compare Dickens' fictional vision with the actuality.[65]

At the same time, the social historian deepens our understanding of the artist himself. Whether he conformed to it or rebelled against it, every writer has inescapably been molded by his social environment, and to know what manner of man he was—and thus to account, in part, for the kind of literature he wrote—we need an accurate sense of what that environment was like and the impact it would likely have had on various kinds of temperament. In his *Mark Twain's America* (1932), Bernard DeVoto, a scholar extraordinarily knowledgeable about all that related to the history of the country west of the Mississippi, drew from the materials of social history a devastating counterblast to Van Wyck Brooks's psychoanalysis of Twain, in *The Ordeal of Mark Twain* (1920), as a potential Shelley nipped in the bud by the harsh American climate. From a great body of fugitive and obscure publications, such as travelers' narratives, old settlers' and rivermen's memoirs, crudely written and crudely printed weekly newspapers, and local histories, he evoked the flavor of Mark Twain's early milieu as it actually was: Hannibal, the River, the Nevada mines, the California newspaper offices—unsoftened America of mid-century, with its lynchings and sudden tendernesses, its physical hardships and occasional luxuries, its tall tales and practical jokes, its sporting houses and earnest but vague aspirations toward "culture." The upshot was both a less sentimental view of Twain the man and a more vivid sense of the social environment from which his art drew its sustenance.

Another important aspect of what is often called "the sociology of literature" is the history of the profession of authorship. Except for the hacks who fed the press at minimum rates from the sixteenth century onward, men seldom wrote for money from the public until Dr. Johnson's time. At that point, the patronage system, whereby authors were subsidized by the

65. Dickens has been particularly well served by research of this type. Excellent studies subsequent to House's, also dealing with the social reality behind the fiction, include Philip Collins' two volumes, *Dickens and Crime* (London, 1962) and *Dickens and Education* (London, 1963), and Norris Pope's *Dickens and Charity* (New York, 1978).

nobility, gradually gave way to the modern system in which literature is a commercial commodity, with authors deriving their living in the form of royalties from their publishers. Inseparable from the expansion of the reading public (or "market"), the emergence of authorship as a money-making profession worked profound changes in the aims and methods of literature. Increasingly, the people who paid the piper called the tune—and the piper, if he wished for a living wage, had to take into account their expectations and desires. The materials of social history, used in conjunction with authors' biographies and publishers' account books and editorial correspondence, document this vital relationship between authors and their public.[66]

Social history combines with intellectual history to open still another avenue by which a work may be interpreted and judged, because the two in conjunction help account for an era's taste. Taste, or fashion, emerges from the interaction of various intellectual tendencies and social conditions, and it manifests itself on many levels, from grave treatises on esthetics to popular demand for circulating-library novels, and in many fields of artistic expression, of which literature is but one. It is scarcely possible, for instance, to be at home in either the poetry or the criticism of the eighteenth century without a command both of contemporary literary theory and of the theory and practice of the other arts, from "Capability" Brown's gardening to Angelica Kauffmann's portraits, and without recognizing the reasons why, in landscape architecture, painting, and literature, the inclinations of artists and connoisseurs alike were increasingly divided between placid pastoralism and the romantically irregular and "sublime."

In late years, indeed, a growing number of literary scholars have been exploring hitherto neglected aspects of the many-sided relationship between literature and the visual arts, which have frequently adopted a common vocabulary and even similar techniques. Medievalists are expanding our appreciation of the literary art of Chaucer's time by studying the iconography and architecture which played a constant, if

66. For a general study of this subject in nineteenth-century England, see John Sutherland, *Victorian Novelists and Publishers* (London, 1976).

normally subliminal, role in men's everyday experience and thus colored their imagination. Specialists in the Renaissance are analyzing the "literary pictorialism" of poets like Spenser, and showing, too, how the manneristic fashion in painting had its reflections in poetry. A full-length study has revealed how deeply Keats's consciousness was permeated with memories of the paintings, prints, sculpture, and stained glass he had gazed upon with delight and awe.

In America, literary scholarship has profitably examined the interest that writers like Cooper and Bryant had in contemporary native painting, especially the Hudson River school, and it has laid bare the affinity and indebtedness that prevailed between certain writers and painters of that epoch. In a quite different vein, a whole new field of investigation has been opened by recent demonstrations that, far from being casually placed embellishments, the illustrations in the first editions of some nineteenth-century novels were meant to be closely integrated with the text, amplifying and giving finer point to what the novelist was himself attempting. Sometimes, notably in the case of Dickens, the novelist worked closely with the illustrator to make sure that the pictures, to be inserted at specified places in the text, would have a complementary rhetorical effect.[67]

The historical perspective toward which we strive includes, therefore, adequate realization of the role that prevailing taste and the coexistence of other arts play in determining the content and mode of literature. From intellectual and social history we learn not only how people thought and acted, but also how they responded to the various forms

67. For a full account of Dickens' collaborative relationship with his principal illustrator, Hablôt K. Browne, see Michael Steig, *Dickens and Phiz* (Bloomington, Indiana, 1978). Representative books which study the relationships between literature and the visual arts include John B. Bender, *Spenser and Literary Pictorialism* (Princeton, 1972); Roland M. Frye, *Milton's Imagery and the Visual Arts: Iconographic Tradition in the Epic Poems* (Princeton, 1978); Jean Hagstrum, *The Sister Arts: The Tradition of Literary Pictorialism and English Poetry from Dryden to Gray* (Chicago, 1958); Ian Jack, *Keats and the Mirror of Art* (Oxford, 1967); J. R. Harvey, *Victorian Novelists and Their Illustrators* (New York, 1971); and Hugh Witemeyer, *George Eliot and the Visual Arts* (New Haven, 1979).

of art that were available to them. With the best will in the world, we may find ourselves unable to participate in their enthusiasms: the contemporary fame of Gower's *Confessio Amantis* and of the American "magazinists" of Longfellow's time may strike us as virtually inexplicable. Sentimentality, exoticism, euphuism, melodrama, antiquarianism, devoted imitation of the classics—each of which made many a literary fortune at one time or another—are none of them very appealing to modern readers. But this is a place where the critic and scholar in us may legitimately part company. If we cannot share the taste we examine, we can do our best to grasp the motives that lay behind it, which is all that honest scholarship demands.

Inseparable from questions of taste are those of the attitudes and opinions on non-artistic matters held by the people to whom writers have addressed themselves. Criticism is coming more and more to recognize the advantage of considering literary works as implicit dialogues between writer and reader, their effect residing, to a greater or less degree, in the tension between the writer's purpose and his reader's preconceptions and expectations concerning the subject under discussion. For a full appreciation of Carlyle's rhetorical strategy in his social criticism, for example, we have to put ourselves inside his readers' minds, sharing their inherited complacency, prejudices, and fears regarding the "condition of England question." So ensconced, we are in a uniquely favorable position to understand why Carlyle felt it necessary to fire salvo after salvo from his amazing battery of rhetorical devices; only by such uninterrupted bombardment could he hope to overcome his readers' reluctance to dwell on such a disturbing subject and arouse them to understand the urgency of his message.

Comprehension of an author's purpose (to entertain? instruct? condemn? inspire? dissuade? soothe? . . .) and the means adopted to achieve it is increased if we can find out what conception of the prospective audience the artist held. But if this specific evidence is lacking, we still can discover much about the audience. Here again the diverse and often scattered and obscure data of social history are invaluable. Alfred Harbage's books, *Shakespeare's Audience* (1941) and *As They Liked It* (1947), have done much to clarify our hitherto hazy or misinformed notions of the social distribution of the clientele that attended the Shakespearean playhouse, the nature of its education and moral attitudes, and its expectations, whether of entertainment or of edification, as it paid its pennies at the entrance. The development of a mass reading audience, beginning in the eighteenth century, has been shown to be the result of many forces—educational, political, economic, religious—which combined, though often at cross purposes, to stimulate the reading habit among ordinary people.

Like so many topics bearing on, but not strictly belonging to, literary history, the size and makeup of the audience have to be studied through documents of a kind far different from those which ordinarily contribute to literary research: records of contemporary educational opportunity among the various social classes, literacy statistics, evidence bearing on the amount of available leisure and spending money, the cost of reading matter in comparison with other commodities, the attractions of other pastimes, the attitudes of dominant religious, political, and other groups toward the place of books in life. All the kinds of inquiry suggested in the present section require data lying off the usual path of literary investigation. One wishing to relate Spenser's poetry to events in courtly circles must consult the official and informal records of the Elizabethan nobility; if his interest is in comparing Dreiser's fictional version of Chicago politics and high finance with the actuality, he must dig out contemporary evidence in newspapers and in biographies of the city's mayors and bosses, such as Michael Kenna and Bath House John Coughlin. And a scholar intent on analyzing the art of De Quincey's "Dream-Fugue" in the light of what De Quincey's generation knew and speculated about dream psychology and opium addiction needs to find the relevant books and articles. For research purposes—the location of specific data—there are good guides to the materials of history, some of the most useful of which will be mentioned on pages 170–71.

But the surest way to acquire the *Zeitgefühl* that no scholar-specialist can be without is to read around in one's period, *ad lib:* in the diaries and letters, the newspapers and magazines, the political pamphlets and ponderous folios of divinity, natural science, political theory, exploration, and every other topic that engaged men's minds. Nor should one neglect the works of very minor literary figures, which often are more accurately indicative of the spirit of an age than the masterpieces, or such evidence as the age's painting and drawing, architecture, and music. By this kind of unrestricted exploration it is possible, in the course of time, to think approximately as the subjects of Charles II thought, with their unique equipment of information and habits of mind; or to re-create in one's imagination, by a coalescence of the slogans and shibboleths of the day, the tone of its popular literature, the brawling of its street gangs and politicians, the gutter smells, and the sight and sound of saloon and Methodist church, the atmosphere of the age which produced *Leaves of Grass*.

* * *

Apart from the information and vivid period-sense it provides, such free exploration of the sources is the surest means by which the scholar can build up relative immunity against the most common errors of literary-historical study. Some of these fallacies and oversights are peculiar to intellectual and social history; others, as we have seen, imperil the incautious in the various fields of specifically literary inquiry as well. They are:

1. *Unwarranted generalization.* This, probably the commonest of all perils, has the most varied origins. The instinctive preference most minds have for simplicity and uniformity when coping with large concepts or tendencies tempts us to make sweeping statements and unqualified assumptions where no such easy reductions are permissible. Generalizations cannot, of course, be avoided, but in adopting them, the scholar must ask himself, and satisfactorily answer, such questions as these:

(a) Have I taken adequate account of the complexity of the phenomenon I am describing or using as the basis of my argument? (The spread of the reading habit in the eighteenth and nineteenth centuries, for instance, was a cultural development with so many ramifications, limitations, and exceptions that every reference to it must be carefully qualified.)

(b) Have I allowed for opposing tendencies or doctrines? (The Renaissance was accompanied by a counter-Renaissance, and in every age that cherished the idea of progress there was a strong concurrent tendency to deny that very idea.)

(c) Were the attitudes, presuppositions, values in question prevalent *at the particular time* I am talking about? (A century is a hundred long years, during which minds are constantly changing. The intellectual orientation of an "Elizabethan" writing in 1570 was not the same as that of another "Elizabethan" writing in 1600.)

(d) Have I allowed for the variant forms a doctrine or concept may take (though it may be called by the same name) under the auspices of different writers or in different eras? (No two authors interpreted in precisely the same way the doctrine of "benevolence"—which, incidentally, was widespread before its reputed author, the third Earl of Shaftesbury, was born—and the doctrine itself was modified with the passage of time.)

(e) Is the body of evidence large enough to justify a general statement, or am I mistaking the unusual and the exceptional for the normal? (Remember Montesquieu's newspaper-reading slater.)

(f) Am I unconsciously accepting clichés and stereotypes handed down from previous writers who have failed to ask themselves the above questions? (It is an exaggeration to say flatly that the neo-classicists "distrusted" the imagination; the Middle Ages were no more characterized by serene and universal "faith" than the eighteenth century was unexceptionally an "age of reason"; and the notion of a once-existent "merrie England" where everybody, from lord to serf, gorged himself on plum pudding, wassail, and good fellowship, is a figment of sentimental sociology.)

2. (Vice-versa.) *Unwarranted specification.* The pitfall we have already noticed in connection with attribution and source-hunting also awaits the careless student of cultural history: that of mistaking for a novelty, a unique peculiarity at a given period, or in one author, what was in fact a commonplace of thought with a long previous history.

3. *Failure to allow for prejudice and emotional distortion in the sources.* Here is where close and sympathetic reading is important. Anyone can see at a glance that the Puritans' descriptions of the riotousness which they alleged typified both conditions in the playhouses and the private lives of the players are of dubious worth as sober history: the frenetic language gives them away. But unreliability is not always so apparent, and language that is notably judicious and restrained may muffle the sound of a grinding ax. It is the scholar's business to cultivate a knowledge of historical situation and person that will enable him to detect whatever partisanship or animosity, self-seeking or championship of a cause, lurks in a superficially objective document.

4. *Unhistorical or oversimplified reading of language.* The meaning of many of the key words used in the documents of intellectual and social history constantly shifted as discussion of the ideas they represented progressed, and some also possessed several meanings at once. Accurate interpretation of evidence and the making of a sound case require the scholar to determine the precise intended meaning of a word each time it occurs. As Raymond Williams showed in *Culture and Society 1780–1950* (1958), the key words *industry, art, culture, democracy,* and *class* either entered common usage or acquired new meanings in the late eighteenth and early nineteenth centuries, and all study of the discussion, dating from that period or later, of the role of culture and the arts in an industrial, democratic society must take account of these semantic shifts and their reflection of contemporary thought.

5. *The attribution of modern judgments to another age.* In reconstructing the attitudes and responses an event (or a poem) would likely have evoked in its time, we must exclude any reaction of our own insofar as it is conditioned by the time and place in which we live. To a certain extent, of course, human nature is changeless, and we react to the elementary situations of life—love and hope and grief and fear—as members of every other generation have. If this were not so, the literature of past ages would say nothing to us. But we must recognize the historical differential that sets each generation apart from every other: the ethical, religious, political, and other attitudes that

are not for all time but of an age. Nothing that is identifiably twentieth-century must be allowed to affect our conception of an Elizabethan's or a Victorian's frame of mind.[68] But once we have successfully eliminated the modern bias, there remains the task of deciding, so far as we can, which of several historically possible attitudes or responses would have been most probable in the circumstances.

These fundamental rules can be found, amply illustrated, expanded, and supplemented, in various treatises on historical method. But what they amount to, for the purposes of literary study, is very simply expressed. They are among the empirical lessons learned by many generations of inquirers after truth. With their aid, the historian, including the historian of literature, reads more accurately the record of human life; they enable him to determine with increased confidence what really happened, and why. And to this inherited realism of approach the scholar adds what is at least as valuable, the intelligence he personally brings to his task: an intelligence sharpened by his own direct experience and observation. No textbook, no long shelf lined with textbooks, offers any substitute for the intellectual keenness gained from living and watching. In the last analysis, it is this combination of received and privately cultivated wisdom that makes literary research an effective instrument of learning. It is the application of the testimony of life to literary assumptions—not only to what a work seems to assert, but to what its author's purposes and achievement are reputed to be.

68. Of course, critics are free to interpret pre-twentieth-century literature in Marxist, existential, or whatever other terms they find congenial, and sometimes insights are attained by this method which give the works under scrutiny fresh and immediate relevance to the present moment. The danger lies in the anachronistic assumption, often present even if not explicitly stated, that such systems of thought affected authors who could not possibly have known of them.

CHAPTER FOUR

The Task

~~~~~~

Who has ever tasted the powerful wine of absorbing labor
without finding that in comparison with it, all other pleasures, except, perhaps, those of love, are flat and insipid?
—Preserved Smith, *A History of Modern Culture*
(New York, 1930), I, 377.

Most literary research projects, whether as modestly scaled as
an undergraduate term paper or as ambitious as a 500-page book
by a seasoned scholar, are demonstrations which begin with a
question and end with an answer. The answer may be conclusive enough to warrant the Q.E.D. the author implicitly
inscribes on his last page, or it may, if some clinching information is not to be had, be candidly tentative—offered as a step
toward the solution but not as the solution itself. The only
papers and books that are exceptions to this general statement
are those which are purely descriptive or enumerative, but even
in these, incidental snags—errors, discrepancies, incomplete data
—turn up which must be disposed of by the method now to be
outlined.

The question with which an inquiry starts is generated by facts, found in a literary text itself or in the surrounding circumstances of history and biography, or, quite possibly, in both places. These facts may range from a series of seemingly related and psychologically meaningful symbols in a romantic ode to typographical differences between two impressions of a first edition. Whatever their nature, they excite curiosity: was the poet haunted by the fear of death by drowning? why were there two distinct printings of that volume, apparently separated by some months? To such questions, the inquirer's mind responds by attempting to arrange the scattered iron-filings of fact into the neat patterning of a magnetic field. This patterning is a hypothesis, a line of relationship which may or may not prove true but which is plausible enough to serve as a basis for further investigation.

If "hypothesis" smacks a bit too forcibly of the laboratory, substitute "critical interpretation," or "ordering of events," or whatever other term seems more suitable to the library. The method, in any case, remains the same: the setting up and test-ing of a conjectural explanation for certain observed or re-corded phenomena. And so does the goal: the discovery of truth through a confirmation of this or a substituted theory. We begin with known quantities; the unknown is their rela-tionship and the meaning of that relationship. The critic's un-known normally is the correct interpretation of the text. The literary historian's unknown takes many forms: the truth about a controversial episode in the life of a poet, the most authentic text of a novel, the authorship of an anonymous essay, the source of an unusual poetic image, the impact of a satirist upon his contemporaries, the prevalence of an intel-lectual concept in one era, the extent to which a literary con-vention dominated practice in another.

Commencing with the facts that stirred the question in the first place, the investigator proposes an answer which he con-siders, in his present state of imperfect knowledge, to be the most reasonable. This is the hypothesis, X:

> Beowulf as we know it was composed as a literary (i.e., written) rather than an oral poetic work.

William Langland (born 1332 at Ledbury, Shropshire, educated at the priory of Great Malvern, the holder of
minor orders, mendicant singer, died 1400) wrote all
three versions of *Piers Plowman.*

The 1640 and 1660 folios of Donne's sermons print the
texts found in the manuscripts from which Donne actually preached and many of which he revised late in life.

Bunyan's method in *Pilgrim's Progress* was directly responsible for the casting of much subsequent popular
religious and didactic literature into dialogue form.

Many Restoration and eighteenth-century dramas remained popular in the nineteenth century but in versions so bowdlerized that critical elements of plot, characterization, and theme often were garbled or wholly
destroyed.

The faithful minuteness of Tennyson's description of small
objects in nature was due to his nearsightedness.

Women writers in nineteenth-century England and America faced substantial pressure from their editors and
publishers to limit themselves to domestic subjects in
which the complications of plot found resolution in a
system of reward and punishment exemplifying conventional religious, social, and economic maxims.

The reception of Hemingway's *A Farewell to Arms* in the
popular press concentrated on the love story and dramatic action and virtually ignored those experiences in
the author's own life which especially qualified him to
write such a book.

Each of these statements may or may not be true, but each
serves as a working assumption, to which, however, the researcher must resolve from the outset not to become emo-
tionally attached. A hypothesis is a tool to be used, not a cause
to be advanced. True inquiry is an exercise of cool reason, not
advocacy, and the moment the supposed explanation becomes
clearly untenable, it has to be dropped.

Once it has been carefully formulated, the hypothesis is
tested against all the discoverable facts which pertain to it.
The more that can be gathered in behalf of the supposition,
the stronger (as we saw in connection with authorship- and

source-study) is the likelihood of its being true. The likelihood increases in proportion not only to the sheer quantity of supporting evidence but also to its variety and to the diversity of independent sources from which it comes. But even the most imposingly buttressed structure of data and argument falls short of absolute certainty, and it can collapse when confronted with a single hard fact that cannot be reconciled with the rest. Lewis Mumford, in his influential biography of Melville (1929), argued at length that the tragic quality of Melville's life was due largely to the cold unresponsiveness of his friend Hawthorne; witness, said Mumford, the way Hawthorne portrayed Melville in "Ethan Brand." But, as Randall Stewart quickly pointed out (*Saturday Review of Literature*, April 27, 1929), when "Ethan Brand" was published, Hawthorne had not yet met Melville, hence could hardly have used him as a model.[1]

If the hypothesis is based on a reading of the text (a fresh interpretation of a symbolic motif, the significance of a reiterated allusion), the internal evidence that tends to support it must be brought face to face with whatever internal evidence may contradict it, and the author's other work, where it is reasonable to expect further instances of the motif or allusion, must be subjected to the same dispassionate scrutiny; and, of course, all the arguments mustered from the text alone must then be confronted with external evidence. The obligation of every honest scholar is to look as hard for—and at—the inconvenient facts as those which suit his theory.

At the same time, he must give equal consideration to other

1. Some years ago the actor Felix Aylmer, in the course of unearthing new information about Dickens' liaison with Ellen Ternan, asserted —with a combination of demonstrable facts and ingenious conjecture— that in 1867 Ellen had had a child at the York Road hospital whom Dickens registered, by prenatal arrangement, as the son of a London housepainter named Tringham and his wife. It is known that Dickens used "Charles Tringham" as his alias where Ellen Ternan was involved, and the real Mrs. Tringham, according to Aylmer, bore no baby at that time (*Dickens Incognito* [London, 1959]). But this elaborate hocus-pocus, so suitable to the dénouement of a Dickens novel, turned out to have no foundation in fact, for another Dickens student, Graham Storey, discovered in a hospital record, which Aylmer had overlooked, proof of the birth of a child to—Mrs. Tringham herself.

hypotheses (Y and Z) which, while not initially as persuasive as X, may gain in probability as the evidence mounts. Was it not Goethe, rather than Tennyson, whom Matthew Arnold had in mind when he wrote of "one,/ Who most has suffer'd" in "The Scholar Gypsy"? Or might it not have been Leopardi? (All three have been nominated.) Which of the several theories offered best explains what really occurred that stormy night at Tanyrallt when the hyperexcitable Shelley saw a face—the devil's?—at the window? How well supported is the argument that the main source of Chaucer's *Troilus and Criseyde* was not Boccaccio's *Il Filostrato* but *Le Roman de Troyle et de Criseida*, by Beauvau, Seneschal of Anjou? It may well be that X, the odds-on favorite, will fade in the stretch, and Z, the thirty-to-one dark horse, will nose out Y at the finish. Many a piece of research, like a horse race, is a process of elimination, and the strength of one's scholarly character is measured both by refusing to bet on the winner and by being prepared to concede a dead heat when it occurs. Literary scholarship is replete with questions which, after being canvassed for many years, still can be answered in two or more ways with equal persuasiveness.

The method boils down, then, to a pair of elementary principles: (1) collect all the evidence, internal and external, that has any connection with your hypothesis, and (2) give as much consideration to evidence that weighs against the hypothesis, or that tends to support an alternative one, as to the substantiating kind. And maintain the critical attitude to the very end; the collapsible premise and the spurious fact are always lurking in the path of the unwary. Every received generalization, every piece of data, should be examined afresh, regardless of the authority behind them. T. S. Eliot's assumption that a momentous "dissociation of sensibility" occurred in seventeenth-century literature has been vigorously contested; the theory of the communal origin of ballads, so stoutly maintained in older books on the subject, is now discredited; the notion that Donne's poetry was known to few readers in the nineteenth century and had little influence (except on Browning) until it was "rediscovered" through Herbert Grierson's edition in 1912, is now pretty well exploded.

All of which amounts to a recapitulation of what was said, more discursively, in Chapters Two and Three. Now that we have the method more or less in hand, to what uses shall we put it?

No scholar ever has to peer around for something to do. His unquenchable curiosity of mind guarantees that. As Uncle Pumblechook says in *Great Expectations*, "Plenty of subjects going about, for them that know how to put salt upon their tails. That's what's wanted. A man needn't go far to find a subject, if he's ready with his salt-box." So long as one studies literature with an alert, creative, and critical intelligence, research subjects, far from blushing unseen, swim unbidden into one's ken. They are problems that refuse to take "no" for an answer, and once recognized, they jostle one another for the scholar's immediate attention. The big decision he has to make is not *what* to write about, but which of several enticing leads he should, in his circumstances, pursue.

Most of us, I imagine, incline toward the large subject rather than the small—perhaps because, with so many cautionary examples before us in the files of the learned journals, we are afraid of being trivial. Some people, however, are more prone than others to bite off more than they can chew. It is they in particular who must temper their enthusiasm and ambition with practical considerations. One immediate question to be answered is, Is there world enough and time for all that I propose to accomplish?

A student doing research as part of an undergraduate or graduate program has a deadline to meet. Deadlines are nuisances—they will continue to be so throughout his scholarly career, if he reviews books or signs publishers' contracts—but they do have the advantage of limiting a project's scope. Ordinarily a senior thesis, a master's thesis, or a graduate term paper must be completed within six months or less. Some of this time must be allotted to preliminary background reading, and some more set aside for the work required in other courses. Hence a modest proposal that can be realized with distinction is far preferable to a grandiose scheme which can be achieved only partially and superficially, if at all.

Then comes the doctoral dissertation. No longer, except in

the unworldly phraseology of graduate-school regulations, are dissertations expected to be true "contributions to knowledge." Of course they must be more than uninspired rehashes of existing information or ideas, but they are nowadays regarded less as the first product of the certified scholar than as the final performance of the novice. As such, they are designed to test the writer's command of the techniques of scholarship and of a limited portion of subject matter. A good dissertation is proof that the student is well qualified to enter the scholarly profession. Some dissertations ultimately get published, though seldom in the form in which they are accepted for the degree. Even the best require revision, if not complete re-casting, and the months and years a young scholar devotes to this task, once he has got used to being called "Doctor," can be among the most profitable of his career. At last he is entirely on his own. From the supervised dissertation emerges an unsupervised book, and in the process the graduate student is metamorphosed into a professional scholar.

What kind of topic, then, should this prospective scholar—you, for instance—select for the diploma exercise? The choice is, in the first instance, your own. Once you have settled on the general field in which you want to specialize and contracted with a favorite professor to serve as your adviser, it is up to you to propose a topic about which you are genuinely curious and which you are eager to explore. Nothing makes a worse impression on an adviser than a student's asking *him* for a dissertation subject. Actually, if one has done the required homework and surveyed the present state of scholarship and criticism in the specific field where one wishes to work, he will be aware of numerous topics that cry out for investigation.

And so, turn up at that first conference well armed—with, if possible, more than one topic, so that if your adviser sees some disadvantages to the first, you can fall back on another. Be sure you have already prospected the field intelligently. Having conducted a preliminary bibliographical survey, by use of the tools to be discussed in the next chapter, you will know what has already been published on your proposed subject. If someone has anticipated you in a completed dissertation, there is no law against your plowing the same ground, but duplication of effort would seem to be rather pointless. The same remark applies in the case of a dissertation currently being written on what appears to be the very subject you propose. The trouble here is that there is no easy means of finding out what dissertations are under way; the only major exception is the admittedly incomplete quarterly announcement, in *American Literature*, of the dissertations being written in that field. However, since the chance of close duplication is small, and in any event the world will not end if you and Mr. Casaubon at a university two thousand miles away prove to be writing on the same topic, there undoubtedly are better-grounded anxieties you can cultivate.

When you and your adviser are satisfied that there is both reason and room for investigation of your suggested subject, a whole series of fresh questions turns up. Is enough material available, in print or in accessible manuscripts, to make the investigation worthwhile? Plenty of important scholarly topics would have been dealt with long ago if adequate data existed. Next: where will you be doing your research—on the university campus, or somewhere else, perhaps teaching at another institution? Whatever the answer, will the library resources at your disposal be sufficient? Your own university library may be one of the best for most purposes, but it still may lack some of the books that you will need continually to consult for your dissertation on medieval sermons. Or you may find yourself teaching at a college remote from such research centers as Boston, New York, Washington, Chicago, and Berkeley: what then? Inter-library loan and microfilm may help, but there are obvious drawbacks to having to rely too heavily on them. And if most of your primary sources are abroad, scattered, say, through the British Library, the Bodleian, and the lumber rooms of several private families from Sussex to Yorkshire, will you be able to afford the time and expense of travel? A first-rate topic is useless if circumstances prevent you from working on it.

Again, that matter of size. Realism is the better part of ambition. No matter how consuming your zeal, stay away from the subject that is too big. Presumably you will want to take your Ph.D. before you are eligible for retirement. The blind mouths of a doctoral candidate's family are not fed by an ever-mounting pile of dissertation notes. And in every candidate's path lie many unforeseeable delays—illness, the pressure of teaching duties, change of residence, the arrival of another child. These may make even a fairly short dissertation hard to finish; how much longer would it take to complete one conceived on the grand scale? Save that subject for your first, or fifth, post-doctoral book. You will be better qualified to write it then, anyway.

But avoid, also, the subject that is too small. Your master's thesis and graduate term papers have shown your quality in the short dash; now can you show the same form in the middle distance? In composing a dissertation, say of two or three hundred pages, you face problems of organization and management of emphasis that were absent from the earlier, shorter exercises. And can you sustain a vigorous prose style through chapter after chapter? Only a topic large enough for monograph-length treatment will enable you to answer such questions to your own, as well as your severest critics', satisfaction.

Let us assume, then, that the topic you contemplate is practicable. But is it of the kind you, personally, can handle? You have a wonderful idea for a dissertation on Angus Wilson—but your graduate training has centered in the eighteenth century, and you haven't read nearly as widely as you should have in modern British fiction. You want to do a critical study—but your best work, as attested by your grades, has consistently been done in papers embodying straight historical research. Attractive though a subject may appear, it just may not be for you. It is far better to realize this before you commit yourself than to waste a year finding out the hard way.

In settling on a topic that suits your personal abilities and tastes, you are taking out insurance against that most dreadful destiny of the Ph.D. candidate—acute incompatibility of topic and person. A question much debated in academic circles is, Which decision is more critical: choosing a spouse or choosing a dissertation topic? In either case, the governing consideration is wearability. Of course, given luck and determination, you will keep house with your dissertation for only one or two years. But those few years can seem an eternity if they are spent in uncongenial company. There are times in every scholar's life when he cannot bear even to think of his current project, let alone do any of the reading or writing it requires. Even the most burning passion for one's work has its limits. But underlying the normal fluctuations of enthusiasm we all experience should be an unfeigned respect for the importance of what we do. If, at the very outset, you fear that you will not be able to maintain that respect when the going is rough and familiarity threatens to breed contempt, it is best to look for another topic.

* * *

And now you are a Doctor of Philosophy. Your dissertation is microfilmed, and you've revised three chapters and published them, with pardonable pride, in *ELH, Modern Fiction Studies*, and (flourish of trumpets) the *Hudson Review*. What now? Research and writing, it has turned out, are in your blood; the exhilarating experience of reading proofs has confirmed your vocation beyond reasonable doubt. Relieved of term-paper deadlines, freed from the nudging necessity of producing an acceptable dissertation for the sake of some honorific initials after your name, you are now at liberty to follow your own bent and work at your chosen pace. The sole determinant of what should engage your talents from now on is the nature of your intellectual interests.

It is necessary, if only because academic minds work that way, to be a "specialist" in one field or another. There is no harm in that. Indeed, everyone should have a subject—a period, a genre, a major author—about which he is exceptionally well informed; otherwise he is more dilettante than scholar. But genuine scholarly specialization is not narrow. It implies, rather, a command that is both broad and profound—and continually growing—of a considerable tract of humane knowledge. A scholar may be ticketed, conveniently, as "a Jacobean drama expert" or "a Carlyle specialist," but a true scholar is reasonably at home everywhere in the Renaissance or the nineteenth century and several other places besides.

This breadth of interest, this aversion from the intellectual myopia that "specialization" often connotes, characterizes the scholar from the beginning of his career. He ceaselessly strives for the command that is derived from simultaneous saturation and perspective. The linking of the two seems paradoxical, but it is not. As he works on his chosen subject, the researcher not only reads and re-reads the literary texts, seeking a profounder insight into their author's habits of thought and art, but sees them from without, as they were typical of, or perhaps in remarkable variance from, the spirit of their age. And at the same time that he achieves perspective within the framework of an historical era, he tries to enlarge it by viewing both the work of art and its matrix-epoch from greater distances of time.

It is this dual vision which gives validity to both the highly specialized printed products of research—the journal articles, the monographs—and the grand syntheses that the ripest and most gifted scholars create from them. No student who knows the manner in which knowledge advances hesitates to publish his findings in notes and articles. So long as they add to our comprehension of a specific literary work, or, more generally, of the ways in which the consciousness of the race has found literary expression through the various genres and traditions, they are necessary and honorable goals of scholarly activity. Some of these may be complete and final in themselves; others may serve as interim reports, which eventually will find their place in the books toward which most scholars' ambition urges them. For the final proof of the scholar's maturity, as it is the ultimate justification of the profession to which he has dedicated himself, is the book that contains the essence of a thousand books and articles and reveals in bold outline the patterns of art and thought that hitherto were hidden under the weight of detail. Although few of us can hope to produce an *Allegory of Love*, a *Road to Xanadu*, a *Mythology and the Renaissance Tradition*, or a *Great Chain of Being*, such monuments of learning can well guide our own endeavors. If we cannot match their erudition and brilliance, we can draw from them the sense of high purpose that informs all good literary scholarship, however modest our individual tasks.

CHAPTER FIVE

Finding Materials

~~~~~~

Knowledge is of two kinds. We know a subject ourselves,
or we know where we can find information upon it. When
we enquire into any subject, the first thing we have to
do is know what books have treated of it.
—Dr. Johnson, before dinner at
Mr. Cambridge's house, 1775.

It is said that there once was a time when a scholar could
carry all the bibliographical information he needed under his
hat. But the good old days ended at least half a century ago.
The gross (inter)national product of English and American
literary scholarship has reached staggering proportions. Between 1940 and 1970 alone, some 2,300 books, articles, and
notes on Charles Dickens were published in the English language; in the final year of that period, the centenary of Dickens'
death, the total exceeded 165. In the three years preceding the
preparation of this revised edition, the average annual count of
books and articles on Chaucer and Milton was approximately

120 each; on Shakespeare, the undisputed leader, 441; on Faulkner, 127; on Joyce, 170; on Virginia Woolf, 43. The *MLA International Bibliography* currently lists an annual total of more than 12,000 items of possible interest to students of English and American literature. To find one's way through this ever-thickening jungle of print in pursuit of a topic becomes a steadily more formidable task.

How much of the work heretofore done by hand can be taken over by electronic brains? The most prudent answer probably is, In some fields, very much; in the rest, not as much as was envisaged a decade or so ago. Two fundamental truths shape and qualify the role of storage-and-retrieval systems—familiarly called computers—in literary research: (1) the material to be stored and classified must be of a homogeneous nature, adaptable to mechanical handling (in other words, not a mass of discrete data); (2) the computer can handle data only in ways for which it is specifically and precisely programmed, and no matter how sophisticated its operation, it must initially be programmed by trained human labor. The cost of a programmer's expertise and of time on the computer can be substantial; it, too, may be an important limitation on the size a particular project may assume.

The computer excels in lexical tasks, storing great quantities of words and phrases, organizing them, and giving them back in any combination desired, in the form of dictionaries, indexes, phrase books, and, especially important for literary purposes, concordances to the whole corpus of an author and to individual works. The list of concordances, produced with far less labor than previously and with great gains in accuracy and flexibility, grows year by year. Already in existence, with many more to come, are exhaustive concordances or word indexes to *Beowulf*, Shakespeare, Sidney, Milton, Herbert, Vaughan's *Silex Scintillans*, Swift, Dr. Johnson's poems, Blake, Byron's *Don Juan*, Arnold, Hopkins, D. H. Lawrence's poetry and short stories, Emily Dickinson, Stephen Crane, Robert Frost, Dylan Thomas, Faulkner's *As I Lay Dying*, Ezra Pound, Joyce's *Portrait of the Artist as a Young Man*, and Shaw's, Yeats's, and O'Neill's plays.

Investigations of literary style are assisted by the computer's ability to analyze and classify, in whatever ways are desired, such elements as word frequency, sentence length and structure, rhetorical and grammatical forms, images, metrical patterns, and special techniques such as Chaucer's alliteration. Applied at times to provide a statistical profile of a given author's stylistic habits—a noteworthy pioneering instance is Louis Milic's work on Swift—computer techniques are also brought into play for comparative purposes, such as re-studying problems of disputed or obscure authorship. The basis of the attempted discrimination or identification is the old one of vocabulary, rhetorical and metrical habits, and other characteristics which together differentiate one author's style from that of others, but the method is infinitely faster and considerably more sophisticated, and perhaps most important of all, it reduces the element of impressionism. Experiments are also being made in machine-aided studies of literary influence and indebtedness; the computer is called upon to determine the extent to which a given literary work, such as *Prometheus Unbound*, bears significant resemblance in style and idea to a preceding one, such as *Paradise Lost*. Perhaps the fairest verdict to be made on the results of these kinds of computer projects is that they are, at best, subject to moderate criticism and, at worst, sharply controversial.

A scholar at the University of Munich is now using a sophisticated computer technique to solve one of the most difficult problems in the history of textual scholarship, the establishment of a "pure text" for Joyce's *Ulysses*. The first edition of that work was set in a French printing house, only one of whose employees knew any English (this in itself was a mixed blessing, because he, like other printers to come, took it upon himself to "correct" Joyce's idiosyncratic language, replete with word plays and other kinds of subtle linguistic games). Joyce, nearly blind, was unable to proofread carefully, and in addition he continued to write even as his manuscript was flowing to the printers. Thus Joyce was engaged simultaneously in composing new matter (adding a third to the book's total length) and rewriting old matter time after time as fresh sets of proofs came from the printer. That was bad enough, but worse was to come. The first legitimate American edition, that of Random House, was not set from a copy of the original Dijon edition, but from one that was still worse, a totally unproofread forgery produced for the American pornography trade. It had over eight thousand textual errors. While some of these were subsequently corrected, new ones inevitably crept in. Fortunately, an abundance of pre-printing material—manuscripts, typescripts, proofs—survives. But these successive fragmentary versions of the text were so heavily altered by Joyce (see the photoreprint *Joyce Archive*, 1977–79, sixteen of whose sixty-three volumes are devoted to *Ulysses*) that no amount of unaided human labor ever could be equal to the task of relating them. Only a computer is capable of arriving—for the first time—at the text Joyce intended his readers to hold in their hands.

In textual studies, computers speed up the process of collation, especially in cases where, because the editions to be compared are from different settings of type, the Hinman Collator is not useful. They have been employed to reveal variants in the several versions of Henry James's *Daisy Miller* and are being utilized in the preparation of elaborate definitive editions like the California *Dryden*. Sometimes they can be put to the task of sorting out and organizing a mass of variants in the interests of creating a "textual tree" (called a *stammbaum* earlier in these pages)—the genealogy of a literary work, involving a multiplicity of intricately related manuscripts and perhaps printed versions as well.

Computers also have their bibliographical and informational functions. They can compile and cross-reference great lists, such as those of the first lines of some 45,000 manuscript poems in the British Library, the Bodleian and Huntington Libraries, and similar repositories (a project advocated by the late James M. Osborn, but not yet realized). They can compile bibliographies of books and articles on any topic as well as break down, under any desired system of classification, the contents not only of the bibliographies themselves but of the individual books and articles they list. Computers can also add new dimensions to an existing reference work. Thus *Poole's Index to Periodical Literature*, which originally was a subject index only, now has been provided with a computer-printed author index as well.

Less has been done, as yet, with raw data found outside literary works and bibliographies. Perhaps the most ambitious enterprise involving this kind of material is the "information bank" at Lawrence University, Wisconsin, in which are stored the hundreds of thousands of tiny individual facts contained in the eleven-volume *London Stage 1660–1800* (1960–68)—box office receipts, dates of performances, casts, lists of actors' roles, authors' payments, details of scene design, musical accompaniment, advertising—and which can sort out and assemble them in whatever categories and combinations are necessary for a particular line of research. Every similar hoard of information (Chambers' *Elizabethan Stage*, Bentley's *Jacobean and Caroline Stage*, Allardyce Nicoll's handlists of English plays) might be stored in computers in the same way.

But the great obstacle to much wider application of storage and retrieval technology in literary research is the necessity for initial programming, which, as has been said, requires much money and highly qualified personnel. It is this consideration that, more than any other, tends to scale down extravagant reliance upon the future use of the computer in our field. To cite a few random examples, it would be highly desirable to have on tape the complete file of English parish registers and of London street directories; the complete records of English and American publishing houses, with their editorial correspondence and accounts; subject breakdowns of all articles in a given periodical; an instantly available list of all allusions to a certain author in books and essays published over a long span of time; complete analyses, by author, title, date, printer, publisher, subject-matter (etc.) of all books listed in the Pollard–Redgrave and Wing *Short Title Catalogues*, the *English Catalogue*, and Evans' *American Bibliography*; a master list of all the books and authors referred to in the correspondences of major American authors . . . The list of worthwhile tasks to be entrusted to the tireless computer is literally endless.[1] But pending a financial millennium that lies beyond the horizon, every reader of these pages will have to continue to master the traditional way of finding his facts. There is no discernible prospect of the pad of note slips being superseded by the instantaneous printout. Fortunately, we are well supplied with bibliographical guides. These tools, efficiently used, enable us to take the utmost advantage of all existing printed or unprinted source material.

This, of course, the standards of our profession obligate us to do. We must always lead, as the diplomatic jargon has it, from a position of maximum strength; our statements must rest on a sure knowledge of all the relevant facts. And only thoroughness can insure us against one of the most painful blunders a researcher can commit—trumpeting as a fresh "discovery" some information that was scholarly news when we were in grade school. Apart from the time we have wasted, we suffer the acute embarrassment of being proved not to have done our bibliographical homework satisfactorily. Listen again to Dr. Johnson's trenchant words:

By the Means of Catalogues only can it be known, what has been written on every Part of Learning, and the Hazard avoided of encountering Difficulties which have already been cleared, discussion of Questions which have already been decided, and digging in

---

1. Probably the best way to keep up with the rapid developments in computer-assisted literary research is to consult the articles and bibliographies in the journal *Computers and the Humanities* (1966–   ). Articles in this periodical which can serve as introductions to the subject include: Louis T. Milic, "Winged Words: Varieties of Computer Applications to Literature," 2 (1967), 24–31; William Ingram, "Concordances in the Seventies," 8 (1974), 273–77; R. L. Widmann, "Computers and Literary Scholarship," 6 (1971), 3–14 and "Trends in Computer Applications to Literature," 9 (1975), 231–35; Todd K. Bender, "Literary Texts in Electronic Storage: The Editorial Potential," 10 (1976), 193–99; and Simone Reagor and W. S. Brown, "The Application of Advanced Technology to Scholarly Communication in the Humanities," 12 (1978), 237–46. See also Miriam J. Shillingsburg, "Computer Assistance to Scholarly Editing," *Bulletin of Research in the Humanities*, 81 (1978), 448–63; *The Computer in Literary and Linguistic Research*, ed. Roy Albert Wisbey (Cambridge, 1971); *The Computer and Literary Studies*, ed. A. J. Aitken et al. (Edinburgh, 1973); and Robert L. Oakman, *Computer Methods for Literary Research* (Columbia, S.C., 1980).

Mines of Literature which former Ages have exhausted.

How often this has been the Fate of Students, every Man of Letters can declare, and, perhaps, there are very few who have not sometimes valued as new Discoveries, made by themselves, those Observations, which have long since been published, and of which the World therefore will refuse them the Praise; nor can that Refusal be censured as any enormous Violation of Justice; for, why should they not forfeit by their Ignorance, what they might claim by their Sagacity? [2]

A *gaffe* that was more comic than anything else occurred when Alan Clutton-Brock noted in the *Times Literary Supplement* (January 19, 1951) that in *Murder in the Cathedral,* T. S. Eliot borrowed fragments of Conan Doyle's story, "The Musgrave Ritual." In the next issue, J. Isaacs commented that this was nothing new: Grover Smith, of Yale, had pointed out the borrowing in *Notes and Queries* for October 2, 1948. A month later (*TLS*, February 23), Smith declined credit for the "discovery," because Elizabeth Jackson had made it still earlier, in the *Saturday Review of Literature* for January 25, 1941. Here was a clear case of two scholars independently publishing a fact that each honestly thought he had been the first to come upon, whereas actually a third person had beaten both of them to it. Although this *TLS* correspondence was promptly listed in the standard annual bibliography of research in Victorian literature, four years later (*MLN*, 70 [1955], 269–71) still another scholar, observing that "apparently attention has never been called to the fact that ten lines of *Murder in the Cathedral* are taken with very little alteration from the Sherlock Holmes adventure 'The Musgrave Ritual', " proceeded to dish up the parallel once again. We can expect it to be rediscovered any day now.

The exact procedure to be followed in using bibliographies, and the number of bibliographies that have to be consulted, differs with every problem.[3] If only a single fact or cluster

2. "An Account of the Harleian Library," reprinted in *Gentleman's Magazine*, 12 (1742), 637.

3. Except in a very few great libraries, which contain virtually everything printed on a topic, and for special limited problems, a library catalogue is not a tool of scholarly bibliography. Since it is only a location-directory to a particular stock of books and analyzes the contents of relatively few of these, it should never be resorted to for the guidance that thorough research requires.

of facts is needed, one bibliography may suffice, and with luck and good judgment it may be the first one consulted. Ordinarily the most direct way to find what you need to know about a strictly limited topic (the boar in *Venus and Adonis*, the game of ombre in *The Rape of the Lock*, the influence of Persian poetry on Emerson's work, a biographical fact about George Washington Cable) is to go to the appropriate one of the two basic bibliographies in our field: the *New Cambridge Bibliography of English Literature* (with the caution noted below, page 158) or Volume II of the latest edition of the *Literary History of the United States (LHUS)*, edited by Robert E. Spiller and others. In one or the other of these tools you may find references to the precise books or articles that will give you the information you want, or, failing that, it may direct you to a specialized bibliography on the subject, which will contain the desired references. In either case, once you have obtained your information, you are finished—almost. For one precaution is necessary. There is a good chance that the information you have found has subsequently been modified, amplified, or challenged. By consulting more recent bibliographical sources (to be mentioned on pages 158–59), you can make sure that you are abreast of the very latest discoveries.

Many research projects, however, are of larger scope, requiring the use of not one but several, perhaps a dozen or more bibliographies. Since we want to enjoy a fairly wide view of the bibliographical landscape, in the rest of this chapter we shall assume a topic of quite ambitious dimensions, always with the understanding that no two projects are ever conducted in exactly the same manner and that very few call into play all the kinds of bibliographies we shall be looking at. Every researcher has to decide for himself which reference tools have possible relevance to his work, and in what order it would be most efficient to use them.

Usually it is best to break the ground of a large-sized enterprise with one of the two "first-help" guides already mentioned —the *NCBEL* or *LHUS*, supplemented, in the former case, by T. H. Howard-Hill's *Bibliography of British Literary Bibliographies* (Volume I of his *Index to British Bibliography*). From there the next move is to the specialized bibliographies. A paper on the medieval lyric, for instance, would call for Carleton Brown's *Register of Middle English Religious and Didactic Verse*, the later Brown and Robbins *Index of Middle English Verse*, and John Edwin Wells's *Manual of the Writings in Middle English*, now appearing in a revised and enlarged edition by J. Burke Severs and others. Other specialized bibliographies—literally thousands of them, including compilations relating to very recent and contemporary writers such as Gwendolyn Brooks, Flannery O'Connor, Sylvia Plath, Anne Sexton, John Osborne—are devoted to individual authors. Some of these bibliographies are limited to works *by* the author, often with minute details of publication, subsequent editions, and so forth. Some are devoted instead to lengthy lists of the secondary (i.e., factual and critical) material that has been published about the author—for example, the series of guides to Chaucer scholarship by Eleanor P. Hammond, Dudley D. Griffith, and W. R. Crawford; the similar series on Spenser studies by Frederic I. Carpenter, Dorothy F. Atkinson, and Waldo F. McNeir and Foster Provost; those on Milton by H. F. Fletcher, D. H. Stevens, and Calvin Huckabay; those on Wordsworth by James V. Logan, Jr., Elton F. Henley, and David H. Stam. Some cover both of these major areas. Collectively, they are uneven in quality. At their best, they are so full as to obviate the need to consult other bibliographical sources, except to bring the record up to date. But relatively few are so gratifyingly exhaustive; most simply provide the easiest starting-point for further investigation.

What if the topic is a literary theme (the Danaë myth in English poetry), the history of a technique (stream-of-consciousness before Joyce), the relation of a genre to the thought of a given period (the familiar essay and the concept of "romanticism"), or some other general subject? The *NCBEL*, Howard-Hill, and *LHUS* are again the best starting places, though some time and patience are required to round up the needed references; the researcher may find what he wants under "General," "Literary Movements," "Social Background," "Intellectual Relations"—it all depends on the classifications and headings the editor has adopted. Beyond these specifically literary guides, there is a wide range of general "subject bibliographies" which will be glanced at on pages 170–73.

In addition to these formal lists, many standard histories of periods and types of literature are rich in bibliographical apparatus. Not only are they sometimes fuller on a given topic than the lists in the *NCBEL* and the *LHUS*, which are necessarily selective, but also they may contain references to out-of-the-way items. The volumes so far published of the *Oxford History of English Literature* have copious references; so too do the histories of the various periods of the English drama by Karl Young, E. K. Chambers, and G. E. Bentley.

Several groups of the Modern Language Association have sponsored extremely useful "guides to research" in the English romantic poets and essayists (two volumes, one edited in the current edition by Frank Jordan, Jr., and the other by Carolyn W. and Lawrence H. Houtchens), the Victorian poets (Frederic E. Faverty), Victorian fiction (two volumes, the earlier edited by Lionel Stevenson, the more recent by George H. Ford), the major Victorian writers of non-fictional prose (David J. De Laura), Victorian periodicals (J. Don Vann and Rosemary T. Van Arsdel), and Anglo-Irish literature (Richard J. Finneran). In the same series are three volumes on American writers: eight major nineteenth-century ones (current edition by James Woodress), twelve additional nineteenth-century ones as well as Edward Taylor, Jonathan Edwards, and Benjamin Franklin (Robert A. Rees and Earl N. Harbert), and sixteen twentieth-century authors (Jackson R. Bryer). These eleven volumes are composed of bibliographical essays, each written by a specialist, surveying and evaluating the bibliographical, editorial, biographical, and critical work that has been done on the authors treated. The experts, by calling attention to topics that have hitherto been neglected, often provide suggestions for fruitful research.

As you work through one bibliography after another, the law of diminishing returns is bound to set in. Most of the references found have already been noted. But there is always that "plaguy hundredth chance," as Bishop Blougram put it, that in the next bibliography you open, an obscure item, overlooked by all the others, will change the whole direction or complexion of your project. Time-consuming though the chore may be, there is really no alternative to canvassing every bibliography that shows even the faintest promise of having something for you.

To this all-important survey of the existing books and articles on a given topic must be brought not only a fine-tooth comb but a constant awareness that bibliographies and reference works vary greatly in authority. If you are working on Swift's Irish pamphlets, you should know that H. Teerink's Swift bibliography, erudite as it is, cannot always be depended upon (it has subsequently been revised by A. H. Scouten); if your project involves the Gothic novel, it is well to handle two of the more obvious tools, Andrew Block's *The English Novel* and Montague Summers' *A Gothic Bibliography*, with great caution, for Block's is compiled uncritically from secondary sources and omits a great deal, while Summers' is extremely careless in regard to titles and dates. Never trust appearances or the assurances of the compiler; the façade of a bibliography may be noble and its dimensions imposing, but closer inspection may well reveal serious defects of bibliographical workmanship. The accuracy and thoroughness of every such guide can be determined only by reference to authoritative reviews and practical experience in using it.

The number of absolutely complete bibliographies is negligible, if, indeed, any such exists. The compilers may have deliberately been selective or otherwise limited their range of coverage; or they may not have had access to libraries in which they could have discovered many more titles; or they may simply have overlooked some items. One old vellum-bound folio owned by the Bodleian Library is not entered in its printed catalogue for the sufficient reason that during the whole process of compilation, the editor was sitting on it.[4]

Seldom do bibliographies adequately "analyze" (distribute under all relevant subject-headings) the contents of a book that has numerous distinct topics. At best, they provide a certain number of cross-references to the main entry. Normally a book or article is listed, as it should be, under the topic announced in its title. It may, however, contain valuable material on another topic—the very one you are investigating. Hence

4. William Dunn Macray, *Annals of the Bodleian Library Oxford* (2nd ed., Oxford, 1890), p. 388n.

it is prudent not to limit yourself to the most directly relevant subject-heading but to look also under related headings that might harbor items of tangential value. The more you read around in bibliographies, the more you discover.

Most bibliographies compiled by groups of contributors are bound to be uneven and to some extent inconsistent. The *NCBEL*, whatever its considerable virtues, is notorious for the unequal treatment it apportions to various authors; some sections are thorough, others are superficial. Although in most cases the *NCBEL* is the best place to begin research into a topic in English literature, it should never be relied upon for complete lists either of an author's works or of the scholarly and critical work that has been done on them, or for accurate titles, dates, or lists of editions. Similarly, though they are indispensable to research, the various serial bibliographies to be mentioned in the next paragraph, also the products of collaborative effort, must not be regarded as the last word on recent scholarly publication. Because each contributor has his personal standards of pertinence and importance—and in addition sometimes nods—a few items of possible usefulness are inevitably omitted from these annual records.

Bibliographies are prime examples of inherent obsolescence. Even when they are confined to the works of an author published, say, in his lifetime and the first century after his death, they are subject to revision in the light of newly found editions or new data on editions already recorded. If they list secondary material, the progress of scholarship renders them incomplete from the moment the editor sends his copy to the printer. Therefore, it is essential to continue the search down to the present minute, beginning not with the actual year when the bibliography was issued but two or three years earlier, which may be nearer the time when the manuscript was finished. For this vital purpose, among others, serial bibliographies have been established, the oldest dating from the time of the First World War. Three annual lists cover English literary study: the *MLA International Bibliography*, which is also strong on linguistics; the *Annual Bibliography of English Language and Literature*, published by the Modern Humanities Research

Association, the British-based counterpart of the MLA; and *The Year's Work in English Studies*, which makes no attempt to be exhaustive but whose chapters conveniently review, with summaries and rather bland critical comments, the more important books and articles published during the year.

In addition, specialized bibliographies appear in the pages of various learned journals.[5] The major ones in English literature, published annually, cover the Restoration and eighteenth century (formerly in *PQ*, now published as a monograph with the title *The Eighteenth Century: A Current Bibliography* under the auspices of the American Society for Eighteenth Century Studies), the romantic movement (formerly in *ELH* and *PQ*, now in *English Language Notes*), the Victorian age (formerly in *MP*, now in *Victorian Studies*), and the twentieth century (in *Twentieth Century Literature*). A similar current list of articles—not books—on American literature appears in each quarterly issue of *American Literature*. This can be supplemented, especially in respect to books, by the annual *American Literary Scholarship*, which is analogous to *The Year's Work in English Studies* but more authoritative.[6] Other serial bibliographies list work in such areas as Old English studies, folklore, Shakespeare, the Keats-Shelley circle, Afro-American literature, literature and psychology, literature and science, film, short fiction, popular culture, fantasy, science fiction, women's studies, prose style, bibliographical studies, and modern drama. All of these inevitably overlap; a book or article with wide ramifications may be listed in as many as half a dozen bibliographies. But that is all to the good, because such duplication reduces by just so much the chance that a scholar

5. This moment is as appropriate as any to point out that it is a *faux pas*, no less deplorable than eating peas with a knife, to speak of our professional publications as "magazines." Magazines are publications of miscellaneous content for the lay reader: *Time* and the *Smithsonian* are magazines. The proper generic term to use is *periodicals;* if the periodicals are devoted mainly to research, they are *journals;* if to criticism, *reviews.* But never "magazines."

6. The very first of these specialized period-bibliographies, the Renaissance one in *Studies in Philology*, was concluded with the issue for 1969, but its file of course remains useful.

will miss the very item he most needs to know about.[7]

Not the least important of the services rendered by some of these compilations (among the general ones, the MHRA *Annual Bibliography*, which in this respect is clearly superior to the *MLA International*) is their practice of listing the reviews of new scholarly and critical books in their respective fields. Whether one is using a book in direct connection with a research project or reading it to broaden his knowledge of a subject, e.g., in preparing for an M.A. or a Ph.D. general examination or a thesis or a dissertation, it is always good to find out what reception it has had among the experts. Acquaintance with the scholarly notices may save one from trusting what is actually an unreliable book. Thus the register of reviews in the annual bibliographies (which should be consulted for at least three years after the book's publication because reviews of scholarly books are often late in appearing), supplemented by the list of reviews included in each issue of the *Humanities Index*, constitutes our professional equivalent of the index of more popular reviews contained in the *Book Review Digest*.

An ideally thorough survey of all that has been written on a topic includes dissertations. "Like all scholarly productions," to plagiarize a few sentences I have uttered elsewhere, "dissertations are of extremely variable quality. By no stretch of the charitable imagination can some of them be regarded as having any value for research. On the other hand, hundreds of unpublished dissertations contain factual [and bibliographical] material that is not found elsewhere or critical interpretations that fully deserve to be absorbed into the main stream of literary study." The essential guide here is Lawrence F.

7. Scanning a whole run of a serial bibliography, as is sometimes necessary, is a tiring business, but the publication of collected and indexed volumes has minimized the toil in several cases. The *PQ* bibliography of Restoration and eighteenth-century studies is collected through 1970 (six volumes, edited by Louis A. Landa and others); the *ELH-PQ-ELN* romantic, through 1970 (seven volumes, edited by A. C. Elkins, Jr., and L. J. Forstner); the Victorian, through 1974 (four volumes, edited respectively by William D. Templeman, Austin Wright, Robert C. Slack, and Ronald E. Freeman); the twentieth century, through 1970 (with thousands of additional items, seven volumes, edited by David E. Pownall); and American literature, through 1975 (articles only, but with many additions, three volumes, edited by Lewis Leary).

McNamee's *Dissertations in English and American Literature*, which brings the record down to 1973. This computer-produced listing of dissertations accepted at American, English, and German universities is limited in general to those written in departments of English. Since dissertations of substantial importance to literary studies are also occasionally written in other disciplines such as drama, philosophy, and history, it is sometimes necessary to go beyond McNamee to the lists, covering all fields, in the *Comprehensive Dissertation Index 1861–1972* (1973), with its ongoing supplements.

Now comes the question of how to locate printed material that is not in your headquarters library. Thanks to the highly developed services and guidebooks of American librarianship, this task is not difficult. One basic tool to refer to, once you have ascertained that the book you need is not in your library, is the 685-volume *National Union Catalog: Pre-1956 Imprints*, which indexes the holdings of over two thousand libraries in the United States and Canada. The largest single publishing enterprise ever undertaken,[8] it has rendered obsolete the older Library of Congress Catalog,[9] which listed the books on the LC shelves down to 1956 and gave locations for some books in one other library as well. Along with its open-ended continuation, which lists titles acquired by all participating libraries since 1956, the *NUC* provides a master key to the contents of most American libraries having research importance. It is supplemented, especially for books published very recently, by the OCLC (Online Computer Library Center), a nationwide computerized network which stores over 6.2 million titles of books and other materials in 2,300 American libraries, including the LC. It may be searched by using terminals at any of the subscribing libraries.

Another aid to locating books is Robert B. Downs's *American Library Resources*, a bibliography of printed catalogues, inventories, exhibition lists, and other guides to individual library collections. By referring to the local lists cited by

8. For sheer number of volumes, the prize may go in a few years to the New York Public Library, whose ten million deteriorating catalogue cards are being published in a projected 800 volumes as well as on microfilm.

9. The spelling is American library usage. But *catalogue* is still preferred everywhere else; hence the curtailed spelling should be used only when you are reproducing a title in which it appears.

Downs, you can often locate nearby copies of the books you need. Particularly useful in this search are the general catalogues that various American libraries—the Boston Athenaeum, the Peabody in Baltimore, and so on—issued in the nineteenth century before card indexing replaced the former system of cataloguing a library's whole collection in printed volumes.

In addition, many scholarly bibliographies give at least one, and as many as five or ten, locations for each book they list. Among the multivolume standard works, the *Short-Title Catalogue* (of English books printed through 1640) locates copies, as do Donald Wing's continuation of the same catalogue to 1700, Joseph Sabin's *Bibliotheca Americana*, and Charles Evans' *American Bibliography*. So do many more specialized bibliographies, such as Carl J. Stratman's *Bibliography of Medieval Drama*, W. W. Greg's *Bibliography of the English Printed Drama*, Cyrus L. Day and Eleanore Murrie's *English Song Books*, and William H. McBurney's *Check List of English Prose Fiction*.

Winifred Gregory's *Union List of Serials*, although not absolutely complete or up to date, serves the same purpose for periodicals. Once you become accustomed to the abbreviated system of entry, which is not difficult, you can discover which American libraries have files of the periodical you need to examine and exactly how extensive those files are—beginning when, ending when, and lacking which volumes.

Before going to the trouble of borrowing the books or periodical volumes you need, however, it is well to make sure that they have not already been reproduced in microform (a generic term that includes microfilm, microcard, microprint, and microfiche). In recent decades the development of the several different microreproduction processes has enabled even libraries of fairly modest proportions to acquire immense quantities of rare books and periodicals. Every pre-1641 English book (called, for short, an "STC" book), and a large selection of those from 1641 to 1700; thousands of English and American plays; complete files of hundreds of literary periodicals and of newspapers, ranging from the London *Times* to small-town Iowa weeklies; every American imprint listed in Evans' *American Bibliography*, beginning with the "Bay Psalm

Book" of 1640 and reaching down to 1800; thousands of the nineteenth-century English and American novels listed in the bibliographies of Michael Sadleir and Lyle H. Wright; doctoral dissertations written since the Second World War; and many other kinds of source material, totaling tens of millions of pages, are available in the library of nearly every institution that offers graduate degrees in the humanities. Cards for certain classes of microtext, such as the *STC* books, files of periodicals, and pre-1800 American imprints, usually are found in their alphabetical places in the library's main catalogue. But some other classes are not so catalogued, and in any event, practice differs from library to library. Furthermore, because of budgetary limitations not all libraries receive all the microtexts that are issued. If you are in doubt whether the books you want are available in your library in microform, ask a librarian.

Microtext series are projects to which many cooperating libraries subscribe, just as they do to periodicals and other kinds of serials. Numerous firms now prepare and sell microforms of books, journals, and other materials; their stocks are listed in three annual publications: *Guide to Microforms in Print, International Microforms in Print: A Guide to Microforms of Non-United States Micropublications*, and *Micropublishers' Trade List Annual*. Much additional material, such as miscellaneous out-of-the-way books, pamphlets, newspapers of local interest, and obscure journals, has been reproduced by individual libraries and other agencies on special order. The masters from which prints can be made are located in the serial *National Register of Microform Masters*.

Thus no scholar nowadays has to be limited to what he finds in the book stacks; the thousands of little boxes filed in another part of the library building contain material whose originals would otherwise occupy miles of shelf space, and would cost the library, if they could be obtained at all, the price of several late-model cruise missiles. Infinite riches in a little room, indeed! And modern technology has given the researcher one more boon. If he must work constantly with a certain rare item, and convenience [10] and concern for his eyesight make it

10. Notwithstanding their advantages, the various kinds of microreproductions cannot be read with the physical comfort associated with the

undesirable for him to spend many hours at a microtext reader, he can have a full-sized Xerox copy made for him.

Sometimes a research task involves a particular copy of a book—one that contains, for example, annotations by its author or by a subsequent reader, such as Keats's copy of Shakespeare or Melville's copy of Arnold's poems. Leads to the present whereabouts of such books can be found in certain author bibliographies and the catalogues and other guides to special collections listed in Downs's *American Library Resources*. If these prove of no help, results can often be obtained by tracing the movements of the book from the time it left its owner's library. Uncounted annotated books and "association" copies, prized because of their unique literary and sentimental interest, have passed from collector to collector, frequently by way of a bookseller's auction. For reconstructing this pedigree of successive ownership, which can, with reasonable luck, reveal the book's present location, the basic tools are the printed catalogues of various private collections (Ashley, Britwell Court, Huth, Newton, etc.) in the nineteenth and early twentieth centuries; two histories of book collecting, Seymour De Ricci's *English Collectors of Books and Manuscripts (1530–1930)* [11] and Carl L. Cannon's *American Book Collectors and Collecting;* and the files of the several annual records of book sales, such as *Book-Prices Current*. If the book you are looking for appears to have turned up last in a bookseller's or auction house catalogue, write the seller. Although some firms are reluctant to divulge the names of purchasers, you may succeed in learning who bought the volume. Often the trail will end at a library, where, ordinarily, the book will be made available to you; if it ends at the doorstep of a private collector, there is no harm in writing to ask whether, in the interests of research, you might be allowed to examine it.[12] Many collectors willingly

---

old-fashioned printed book. As Louis B. Wright, the former director of the Folger Shakespeare Library, once observed, reading a literary work through an optical device is as unsatisfactory as kissing a girl through a plate-glass window.

11. On the incredible De Ricci, a walking data processing machine whose brain held the exact history of ownership and present location of several million books and *objets d'art*, see E. Ph. Goldschmidt's obituary article in *The Library*, 4th series, 24 (1944), 187–94.

cooperate, but some regard their literary treasures as chattels whose main value resides in their prospective sale price or in their uniqueness. (It is reported that when the political scientist Harold Laski tried to see one of the manuscripts of John Stuart Mill's *Autobiography*, the owner, reputedly Lord Rosebery, "sent an unsigned note saying the pleasure of possessing a manuscript consisted in the fact that nobody else could see it."[13])

Locating manuscripts calls for the same general techniques and, sometimes, the same bibliographical tools. Although some authors' personal archives, like their libraries, have been kept intact down through the years, dispersal has been much commoner, with the result that their books and papers are now scattered in scores of British and American libraries and private collections. To locate a particular item requires knowledge, ingenuity, patience, and persistence, in approximately equal, and generous, parts.[14] Until recently, the task has been more difficult as a rule than that of finding books, but good new highways have now been opened and others are under construction. The three years 1960–62 saw the publication of three major location-tools—Philip M. Hamer's *Guide to Archives and Manuscripts in the United States* (now largely superseded by a

12. A good illustration of the technique of running down a particular copy of a book, in this case Browning's copy of Shelley's *Miscellaneous Poems*, is found in Frederick A. Pottle, *Shelley and Browning* (privately printed, Chicago, 1923). Two narratives by Sir Geoffrey Keynes (*TLS*, March 8, 1957, p. 152, and May 3, 1957, p. 277) describe his protracted but eventually successful search for Blake's annotated copies of Bacon and of Dante's *Inferno*.

13. Jack Stillinger, "The Text of John Stuart Mill's *Autobiography*," *Bulletin of the John Rylands Library*, 43 (1960), 224n.

14. For several copious examples of how widely a body of manuscripts may be dispersed, see Mary C. Hyde, "The History of the Johnson Papers," *PBSA*, 40 (1951), 103–16; Kenneth N. Cameron (ed.), *Shelley and His Circle* (Cambridge, Mass., 1961), II, 892–913; and D. Anthony Bischoff, "The Manuscripts of Gerard Manley Hopkins," *Thought*, 26 (1951), 551–80, supplemented by the Preface to *The Journals and Papers of Gerard Manley Hopkins*, ed. Humphry House, completed by Graham Storey (London, 1959). An exciting narrative of the patient regathering of the manuscript of Frank Norris' *McTeague*, which had been broken up, page by page, to adorn sets of an expensive edition of Norris' works, is given in James D. Hart, "Search and Research: The Librarian and the Scholar," *College and Research Libraries*, 19 (1958), 365–74.

publication of the National Historical Publications and Records Commission, *Directory of Archives and Manuscript Repositories in the United States*, 1978), the Library of Congress' *National Union Catalog of Manuscript Collections* (a continuing series, also available in many libraries on alphabetically arranged cards), and *American Literary Manuscripts: A Checklist of Holdings in Academic, Historical and Public Libraries in the United States* (a project of the Modern Language Association's American literature group; revised edition, 1977). These have made it possible to discover in a few minutes which United States libraries have collections of individual American and English writers' personal papers, annotated books, and manuscripts of their published and unpublished works. It is also advisable to look into Downs's *American Library Resources;* there you can learn if a library has issued some sort of description or catalogue of its special collection of an author in whom you are interested. If it has, by tracking down the catalogue you can often discover the extent of the manuscript holdings. Additional valuable suggestions for tracing manuscript material in the United States are contained in the introduction to *American Literary Manuscripts*, just mentioned.

Finding a specific manuscript, as distinguished from broad collections, requires additional tools. The ones mentioned in the preceding paragraph, naturally, are first steps: there is a good chance that the document you seek may be found among the collections listed there. If it is not listed in the printed guides to the collections which you suspect might contain it, bear in mind that most libraries have unpublished calendars (inventories) of their manuscripts, and a letter to the librarian or curator of the collection would settle the matter. For older manuscripts there is Seymour De Ricci's and W. J. Wilson's *Census of Medieval and Renaissance Manuscripts in the United States and Canada.* For later manuscripts especially, follow the procedures outlined above in connection with finding specific copies of books.[15]

15. Lewis Carroll is known to have written nearly 103,000 letters. For the strategies used in a comprehensive effort to locate as many of these as possible, see Morton N. Cohen and Roger Lancelyn Green, "The Search for Lewis Carroll's Letters," *Manuscripts*, 20 (Spring 1968), 4–15. The product of this search was Cohen's two-volume collection, *The Letters of Lewis Carroll* (New York, 1979).

Exhausting all the leads provided by printed sources takes a long time, but only after this has been done, with no results, is a public appeal advisable. This usually takes the form of a brief note to the *TLS* or the editor of the appropriate informal publication that is circulated among scholars in your field of interest, such as the *Johnsonian News Letter*. Quite often, these requests for help are successful; some other scholar may just happen to have the clue that will guide you to the volume or manuscript needed. But do not ask for aid until you have yourself done all that a resourceful scholar, surrounded by reference books and making the utmost use of them, can do.

This is not to say, however, that public appeals for aid must *always* wait for the last moment. It is accepted practice for a biographer undertaking the life of a recently deceased, or hitherto unwritten about, figure to announce his intention quite early in the game; equally so for a scholar editing an author's correspondence. A public appeal is especially legitimate and necessary when a writer's papers are scattered in private hands and when people are alive who can contribute personal reminiscences of him. The *TLS* and the *New York Times Book Review* are the standard places to send such a note, with the customary (and sincere) assurance that all documents received will be promptly copied and returned. (If you are lent such documents, guard them from every conceivable source of harm, and return them, securely packaged, by *registered* mail.)

Especially if his interest is in English literature, a scholar needs to be equally at home among guides to British resources. Robert B. Downs's *British Library Resources* is useful for orientation. But since the British Library [16] is the richest research center in the United Kingdom (see below, pages 187–88), its *General Catalogue of Printed Books*, with five million entries, is the supreme everyday tool—not only for locating books but for many bibliographical purposes. (It is currently being absorbed and supplemented by the *British Library Catalogue of Printed Books to 1975*, which is scheduled to be completed, in some 360 volumes, by 1985.) There are also many printed catalogues of special collections and classes of

16. The new name (1973) of the former British Museum Library. Obviously, the old title occurs in all pre-1973 books and articles which refer to materials in that vast collection.

books in the library, such as incunabula, romances, seventeenth-century controversial pamphlets (the famous Thomason tracts), and pre-1641 books.

In respect to periodicals, the British are as well served as we are; their *British Union-Catalogue of Periodicals* is the equivalent of our *Union List of Serials* and often supplements the *ULS* by locating files of extremely rare or obscure periodicals which are not to be found in the United States.

There are hundreds of printed catalogues of manuscript collections in the British Isles. The British Library has a number of "named" collections (Sloane, Egerton, Harleian, Cottonian, Stowe, Arundel, Lansdowne, etc.), most of which are richest in medieval and Renaissance material, and for which there are printed catalogues, though some are both ancient and inaccurate. But by far the biggest British Library collection is the so-called "Additional Manuscripts," into which have been funneled all the miscellaneous bequests and purchases of the past century and a half. The "Additionals" are most important to literary students because of the great masses of papers they contain relating to British literary figures of the eighteenth, nineteenth, and twentieth centuries. The MS of Hawthorne's *The Marble Faun*, acquired in 1936, has the numbers Add. 44,889–44,890; the several MSS of *Finnegans Wake* are Add. 47,471–47,489. In all, counting the named collections and the Additionals, the library possessed in 1974 (the last year for which figures are available) well over 70,000 volumes of manuscripts. A series of printed catalogues exists, but its compilation has fallen far behind the pace of acquisitions. A consolidated index, assembling into one sequence all acquisitions down to 1950, has been promised. For acquisitions after 1950, preliminary descriptions are available in the manuscript room of the library itself.

Outside the British Library, the greatest concentrations of manuscripts are at the two old universities. The Bodleian at Oxford has a seven-volume *Summary Catalogue* of manuscripts, completed in 1953—a not wholly satisfactory compilation, but better than none at all. At Cambridge, the manuscripts owned by the various colleges have been catalogued in many volumes by Montague Rhodes James, provost of Eton and well-known author of ghost stories.[17]

Then there are the catalogues of manuscripts held at other ecclesiastical and educational centers—Lambeth Palace, Westminster Abbey, cathedrals (Durham, Lincoln, Hereford, etc.), and the ancient public schools. Most of these manuscripts date from the Middle Ages and represent but a pathetic fragment of the wealth the religious foundations contained before the depredations of Henry VIII. Of frequent usefulness to literary scholars, also, are the many volumes of reports of the Royal Historical Manuscripts Commission, established in 1870 to make inventories of all archives in institutional and private hands to which access could be gained. Through the ensuing decades, inspectors of the Commission labored in the muniment rooms of old castles, the archives of municipal corporations, and the libraries of noble families. The results of these canvasses were printed in the capacious, small-type reports, which are in part simply calendars but which also contain great expanses of summaries and direct quotations from the documents examined. The long series is a rich mine of primary material for students working in any period down to the beginning of the nineteenth century. As Allan Nevins once pointed out, "Many of the searches of the Commission were made in the nick of time. . . . Numerous collections of family papers, especially those containing autographs of value, have been sold piecemeal; others have been bought in bulk and transported abroad" (i.e., to America), and others have been destroyed.[18] Thus the series often contains the only available excerpts and summaries from important historical documents which are now lost.

Supplementing the services of the HMC is the National Register of Archives, founded in 1945 and housed in Chancery Lane, London. It is a kind of union catalogue-*cum*-information clearing house for the contents of the various county record offices, which have grown more numerous and active in recent years, as well as of the private collections that have been inventoried by agencies other than the HMC. The so-called

17. See Richard William Pfaff, *Montague Rhodes James* (London, 1980).
18. *The Gateway to History* (Boston, 1938), p. 106.

NRA Reports—manuscript, mimeographed, or printed indexes, analyses, excerpts, and summaries—facilitate access to the holdings of over 13,000 archives. All this information is joined with similar data from the (American) *National Union Catalog of Manuscripts* and the catalogues of such major archives as the Folger and Huntington Libraries to form a master file which indicates at a glance where the papers of a given person or family are located.

With the HMC and NRA reports we cross the boundary between the tools designed for the student of literary history and those that serve more specifically historical research. As we saw in the final section of Chapter Three, the literary investigator often needs information which lies within the province of the general historian. To find that information he must usually consult the general historian's tools. But his specialized bibliographies are still of frequent assistance. For subjects immediately adjacent to literary history, such as the history of English education, printing and publishing, and the social backgrounds of some periods, the lists in the *NCBEL* are invaluable. So too are those on "Literature and Culture" and "Movements and Influences" which occupy half of the bibliographical volume of the *LHUS*. For very recent books and articles on historical subjects, the sections headed "Economic, Political, Religious, and Social Backgrounds" (or something similar) in the serial bibliographies devoted to particular periods of English and American literature (see above, pages 158–59) are the best place to go. In some of these serials, to be sure, the coverage of non-literary history is skimpy, but others, notably that for 1660–1800 in *The Eighteenth Century: A Current Bibliography* and that for the Victorian era in *Victorian Studies*, are so full that they are as useful to professional historians as to literary students.

For topics in British history there is a series of period bibliographies which begins with Wilfrid Bonser's *Anglo-Saxon and Celtic Bibliography* and Edgar B. Graves' *A Bibliography of English History to 1485*. The ensuing centuries are well covered in five relatively up-to-date bibliographies, compiled by Conyers Read (for 1485–1603), Godfrey Davies (1603–1714), Stanley Pargellis and D. J. Medley (1714–1789), Lucy

M. Brown and Ian R. Christie (1789–1851), and H. J. Hanham (1851–1914). The record can be brought virtually down to date through Alfred F. Havighurst's *Modern England 1901–1970* and the annual bibliography on British and Irish history of the Royal Historical Society.

On American historical subjects, there is Henry P. Beers's list of *Bibliographies in American History* (1942), which can be easily supplemented for more recent material by the *Harvard Guide to American History* and by the American sections of the *American Historical Association's Guide to Historical Literature*, which is worldwide in scope.

Indispensable to historical research, less for their bibliographies (which are outdated, though often useful for leads to older sources) than for their factual information, are the two fullest ready-reference sources of biographical data: the *Dictionary of National Biography* (for Great Britain) and the *Dictionary of American Biography*, published in 1885–1900 and 1928–37, respectively. Each now has several supplementary volumes listing people who died after completion of the main alphabet. Though works of such magnitude are bound to have some errors, both the *DNB* and the *DAB* have a well-deserved reputation for accuracy. However, since the former is now almost a century old, a thoroughgoing revision, including subsequently discovered information about the persons included as well as correcting errors, is much to be desired; but there seems little prospect of such a formidable undertaking.

But when the scholar must go beyond history into other areas of human interest that bear on literature, such as the fine arts, psychology, philosophy, religion, sociology—what then? There are no standard procedures; every problem must be attacked in its own terms. Where he begins depends partly on the thoroughness with which he wants to acquaint himself with the topic. If he simply wishes to orient himself in a general way, or find a fact that might reasonably be expected to appear in a standard reference work, the best thing to do is consult the American librarian's bible, Eugene P. Sheehy's *Guide to Reference Books*, and its British counterpart, A. J. Walford's *Guide to Reference Material*. These contain authoritatively selected, well classified, and annotated lists of the best bibliographies, histories, manuals, and encyclopedias in every field of learning. The lists are, naturally, not exhaustive for any one field, but somewhere among the half-dozen books to which one is referred may well be all the material needed. In addition, the researcher might consult the concise bibliographies appended to the longer articles on his topic in the *Encyclopaedia Britannica* and, even better, in specialized encyclopedias such as the *New Catholic Encyclopedia*, the *International Encyclopedia of the Social Sciences*, the *Encyclopedia of Philosophy*, and the monumental *New Grove Dictionary of Music and Musicians*. Some of the other specialized encyclopedias, among them Baldwin's *Dictionary of Philosophy and Psychology* and Hastings' *Encyclopaedia of Religion and Ethics*, are useful for finding older treatments of a subject, but their bibliographies are seriously out of date.

For more intensive study, requiring as many books as can be located, it is best to begin either with subject indexes (bibliographies that classify books under topic) or with bibliographies of bibliographies. Here again the choice is determined by the nature of the individual project; the former are more convenient, in that they involve one less step, but the latter (bibliographies raised to the second power!) offer better insurance against missing anything. The main subject indexes are those of the British Museum, which classify the books the Museum received between 1881 and 1950 (for books received before 1881, see R. A. Peddie's *Subject Index*, uneven but sometimes helpful), and the Library of Congress' subject catalogue of newly published books, begun in 1950. This last tool, along with the several weekly or monthly British and American trade lists of new publications, can bring one down to the present moment.

These guides, however, are restricted to books, and much specialized material is published in periodicals, finding its way into books, if at all, in synthesized or fragmentary form. The bibliographies in some of the volumes found by the procedure just described enumerate at least a scattering of articles but seldom can be relied on for full coverage. To supplement them, use the *Humanities Index*, which since 1916, under other titles, has efficiently analyzed the contents of many scholarly journals in areas related to literature. For older material that the bibliographies in standard works may have overlooked, *Poole's Index* to nineteenth-century English and American periodicals should be consulted.

Maximum thoroughness, however, requires using the fourth edition (1965–66) of Theodore Besterman's *World Bibliography of Bibliographies,* which lists about 117,000 bibliographies on every conceivable subject. (Note that Besterman cites only bibliographies which have been separately issued; he omits those that appeared as parts of larger works, as well as some other classes of bibliographies, such as booksellers' catalogues and general library catalogues. Hence, even with 117,000 entries, his work is by no means exhaustive.) The scholar should copy Besterman's list for the topic in which he is interested; then find the individual bibliographies mentioned therein; then, as a final step, find the books *they* list—and he is within sight of his desired information. The easiest way of bringing Besterman down to date is to consult the *Bibliographic Index,* a continuing publication, begun in 1938, which records newly published bibliographies, both those appearing separately and those included in larger works.

Using these and similar tools in whatever combination and sequence seems most feasible, you soon will amass a list of books and articles that will be adequate for your purposes. It is true that when you find yourself adrift for the first time on strange seas of learning, you will feel somewhat bewildered and helpless. But the scholarly intelligence and resourcefulness that serve you well in your home waters, assisted by bibliographical charts of the kind just touched upon, may be depended upon to bring you safely to port. The fundamental techniques of finding material are the same, no matter what the subject-matter may be, and exploring unfamiliar reaches of knowledge is not the least adventurous part of research.

CHAPTER SIX

Libraries

~~~~~~

Assiduus sis in bibliotheca, quae tibi Paradisi loco est.
            —Erasmus, letter to Bishop Fisher,
    1524.

A knowledge of the history, strengths, and facilities of major research libraries is as indispensable as a command of the bibliographical tools that are the primary keys to their contents. "Houghton," "Berg," "Huntington," "Folger," and "the British Library" are terms that figure in the shop talk of scholars wherever they gather. What, and where, are these libraries? What do their major collections contain? Above all, which have the greatest wealth of books and manuscripts relating to one's particular field of interest?

Unfortunately, there is no such convenience as a literary scholar's Baedeker. Printed information on the growth and holdings of research libraries, though fairly abundant, is scattered through various kinds of books and periodicals. Important new acquisitions are announced in the annual reports of the various libraries' directors and in the periodicals issued by some libraries (Yale, New York Public, Princeton, Library of Congress, Texas, Newberry, Huntington, etc.).[1] These sources are often supplemented by the grapevine that connects the librarian's world with the scholar's. The way to locate your own bibliothecal paradises, apart from consulting the printed sources, is to note where the leading researchers in your field go to do their work, and as you read their books, observe, in the prefatory acknowledgments and footnotes, where the material was gathered. Make a habit (it is easily cultivated, and a pleasant one) of storing away information about the history of book collecting, because most of the contents of the fabulous collections that were amassed and sold in the past century or so (Church, Hoe, Devonshire, Halsey, Quinn, Kern, Bixby) have by now found their permanent homes in institutional libraries. You can trace their migrations, down to recent decades, with the aid of De Ricci's and Cannon's books mentioned on page 164. Moreover, a little knowledge of academic history comes in handy. It is no accident, for example, that the Yale Library is supreme in eighteenth-century literature; the university's English Department has been famous for its eighteenth-century specialists, typified in an older generation by Chauncey Brewster Tinker and Wilbur Lucius Cross. The University of Texas traces its Pope collection to the long presence on the faculty of the poet's bibliographer, R. H. Griffith. University library strengths are frequently memorials to the ambition, tenacity, and resourcefulness of scholars; to the same qualities in librarians, who found the money and knew how to spend it; and, far from least, to the generosity of wealthy alumni and other friends of libraries, who signed the checks.

Thanks to all these people, American literary scholars are in an extraordinarily fortunate position. It is only to be expected that most of the documentary materials for the study of any aspect of American literature are to be found in the continental

1. Some useful sources of information on American and British libraries are listed in Richard D. Altick and Andrew Wright, *Selective Bibliography for the Study of English and American Literature* (6th ed., New York, 1979), pp. 39–47. Most of the data in the present chapter are drawn from the books and articles cited there, with occasional supplementation from Hamer's *Guide to Archives and Manuscripts in the United States.*

United States. But it is much more remarkable that America possesses so large a portion of the books and manuscripts needed for research in English literature. Ever since the late nineteenth century, the virtually unlimited buying power of certain great American fortunes, exerting itself during years when the British purse was steadily shrinking, resulted in a massive movement of literary treasures across the Atlantic. Today, by an irony that a few of them understandably fail to relish, English scholars sometimes must come to American libraries to study their own country's great authors.

Only in a large book could even moderate justice be done to the incalculable wealth of rare books and manuscripts that American scholars have at their disposal in their large research libraries. In these few pages, all that is possible is to single out a handful of the Meccas to which scholars gravitate. Our tour of the pleasure domes and gold mines of research will take us from Massachusetts to California.

Harvard's is the undisputed monarch of academic libraries. The Widener Library, built as a memorial to the scion of a wealthy Philadelphia family who at twenty-eight, when he went down on the *Titanic*, was already known as "the Marcellus of the race of book collectors," houses Harvard's vast general collection. In addition, it contains certain specialized ones, such as the folklore material gathered by Francis James Child and his students, the poetry collection (a pioneer in the recording of poets reading their own works), and the theater collection, whose hundreds of thousands of playbills, programs, prompt-books, photographs, manuscripts, and books associated with the history of the stage make it one of the Big Three in this field, the other pre-eminent American collections being at the New York Public and Folger Libraries.

Most of Harvard's rarities, however, are housed in the adjacent Houghton Library, a Georgian structure with sumptuous furnishings, electrically controlled doors, quiet, and every other amenity. Its ever-increasing wealth ranges over the whole of English and American literature, but one of its particular glories is its collection of seventeenth-century English books. The 300 stack sections devoted to manuscripts house, among other treasures, the largest single parcel of papers by and associated with Keats (the merging of collections formerly owned by the Marquess of Crewe and Amy Lowell). More recently, the Houghton bought from Sir Charles Tennyson a large portion of the extant papers of his grandfather, including many unpublished drafts of the Laureate's poems. Among the manuscripts of other English authors, there are the holographs of novels by Conrad, Disraeli, Hardy, George Moore, Trollope, and D. H. Lawrence, and quantities of letters and manuscript literary works of such diverse figures as De Quincey, Max Beerbohm, Kipling, Ruskin, and Thackeray. The roster of American authors whose papers are concentrated in the Houghton's vaults is as long as it is lustrous; the names range from Melville to J. P. Marquand. Thomas Wolfe's famous packing cases, crammed with the interminable, chaotic products of his creative seizures as well as his college lecture notebooks, exam papers, checkbooks, and royalty statements—for Wolfe never destroyed anything—came to Harvard, where he took his M.A. Henry James's papers are there, as are those of Emerson (10,000 letters to him, and 140 volumes of journals), Lowell, Longfellow, Holmes, Howells; and in the Houghton a large portion of Emily Dickinson's manuscripts, so long the subject of bitter dispute among her survivors, has found a final home.

Yale's Sterling Library is the headquarters of a whole complex of literary industries, among them the "Boswell factory" (producing complete editions of Boswell and Johnson), a branch of the "Walpole factory" (main plant at Farmington, Connecticut, where the late Wilmarth Lewis pursued his lifework of issuing the complete correspondence of Horace Walpole), the "Franklin factory," and, most recently established, "the More factory," from which the definitive edition of St. Thomas More is emerging. The storehouse from which these editorial enterprises derive the multitude of facts they need is Yale's book collection. Annotating Boswell's journals or Walpole's letters, for example, requires a huge array of printed aids that will supply dates, identify allusions, provide biographical sketches of obscure persons, and perform the thousand other services that such work requires. County and local histories, maps, town directories, biographies and memoirs without number, files of contemporary magazines and newspapers—nothing that is germane to the English eighteenth century is foreign to the Yale Library. In the nineteenth century, Yale is especially strong in first editions and manuscripts, some of them still unpublished, of Carlyle, Ruskin, Mill, Arnold, George Eliot, Meredith, and Stevenson, and the library's lively interest in preserving the papers of twentieth-century authors is symbolized by its possession of Gertrude Stein's manuscripts (11,500 pieces), Edith Wharton's (5,000), and Sinclair Lewis' (1,000). It also holds the largest collections extant of Eugene O'Neill and Ezra Pound materials. The Yale rarities are housed in the Beinecke Library, a building of great architectural distinction.

At Fifth Avenue and Forty-Second Street, New York City, stands the nation's second largest library. The heart of the "New York Public" is its research collection of over four million volumes, covering with amazing thoroughness all but a few fields of humanistic and scientific interest. Its several specialized collections are of great scholarly importance. The manuscript division, which owns more than 9.1 million pieces, is especially rich in the papers of writers associated with New York (Walt Whitman and Washington Irving, for instance), and the theater collection, housed separately in the Lincoln Center for the Performing Arts, is, as noted above, one of the largest in the nation.

But the library's jewel, as far as literary research is concerned, is the Berg Collection. Its creation, little more than four decades ago, gave the New York Public Library the added distinction of being one of the three or four richest rare-book treasuries in the United States. Henry W. and Albert A. Berg were two New York physicians, under whose care, happily for the future of literary study, came some of the nation's most eminent supermillionaires. When Doctor Henry died in 1938, his brother gave to the library, in his memory, 3,500 rare books and manuscripts, a nucleus that was especially strong in nineteenth-century English and American writers. A little later, two larger collections came up for sale: those of W. T. H. Howe, president of the American Book Company (16,000 volumes, also concentrated in the nineteenth century) and Owen D. Young, the head of General Electric (over 10,000 items, ranging from the fifteenth to the twentieth centuries, and rich not only in first editions but in association copies, autograph letters, and manuscripts of literary works). Dr. Albert Berg forthwith bought them for the library, too, with the result that in a span of only fifteen months the Berg Collection increased tenfold. Upon his death in 1950 he left a large endowment which permits the constant enlargement of the collection. Though the representation of eighteenth-century English literature is imposing enough by any ordinary standards (Pope's draft of the first three books of the *Essay on Man*, fifty letters each by Gray and Dr. Johnson, a huge mass of Burney papers), the Berg Collection's supreme strength resides in its first editions of all major nineteenth-century American and English authors, including such rarities as Browning's *Pauline*, Poe's *Tamerlaine*, and the Bristol edition of *Lyrical Ballads*, and thousands upon thousands of letters and literary manuscripts by such writers as Coleridge, Thackeray, Dickens, Kipling, Hawthorne, and Whitman. Many of these prizes, among them Thoreau's nature studies (1,700 manuscript pages) and some of the fifty Mark Twain manuscripts, are as yet unpublished. In recent years much Berg money has gone into the purchase of the first editions and personal papers of twentieth-century English authors, most notably Arnold Bennett, Joseph Conrad, John Masefield, Bernard Shaw, and Virginia Woolf, the great bulk of whose manuscripts are here. T. S. Eliot is another star of the collection; the surfacing in the Berg of the long-lost typescript of *The Waste Land*, dense with comments and alterations by Ezra Pound, was a headline event some years ago. (Published in facsimile in 1971, this is one of the most fascinating documents of modern literature.)

Walking a few blocks down Fifth Avenue and then east on Thirty-Sixth Street, one comes to the Pierpont Morgan Library (given to the public in 1924), which is dedicated exclusively to rarities. Its founders, the elder and younger J. P. Morgan, were among the most redoubtable bidders in auction rooms during the decades when the transatlantic cables pulsed with carte blanche orders from American collectors to their London agents. As a consequence of one of their hobbies, the library has an array, unmatched in this country and rivaled by few in Europe, of ancient and medieval manuscripts, especially masterpieces of the illuminator's art, as well as of finely bound books. It has over 1,800 incunabula, including the richest collection of Caxtons in America (some seventy, one of which is the only known perfect copy of the first edition of Malory's *Morte Darthur*). The library's first editions, especially of authors like Dickens, who were fashionable in collecting circles during the peak of the Morgans' buying, are superb. But for literary researchers, probably the heart of the collection lies in the almost bewildering range of authors' manuscripts: the first book of *Paradise Lost* (in the hand of Milton's amanuensis), Keats's *Endymion* and his sonnet on Chapman's *Homer*, Lamb's "Dissertation upon Roast Pig," one hundred poems of Burns, ten novels of Scott, Rossetti's "The Blessed Damozel," many Byron poems (including Cantos I–V of *Don Juan*, *The Corsair*, and *Manfred*), Thackeray's *The Virginians* and a portion of *Vanity Fair*, Dickens' *A Christmas Carol* and *Our Mutual Friend*, Ruskin's *The Stones of Venice* and *Modern Painters*, Meredith's *Diana of the Crossways*, Browning's *Dramatis Personae*, Mrs. Browning's *Sonnets from the Portuguese*, Stevenson's *Dr. Jekyll and Mr. Hyde*, Mark Twain's *Life on the Mississippi*. To say nothing of personal papers: thirty-eight volumes of Thoreau's journals, ninety letters of Pope, over 1,300 of Dickens, hundreds by Burns, Byron, Carlyle, and scores of other celebrated authors. Perhaps the inclusiveness of "the Morgan's" interests is best suggested by the fact that under the same roof are cherished one of the most magnificent collections in existence of William Blake's illustrations and the nation's largest mass of scores, programs, manuscripts, and other memorabilia relating to Gilbert and Sullivan.[2]

What the New York Public and the Morgan are to New York, the Library of Congress and the Folger are to Washington. The Library of Congress, appropriately, as the national library, is the possessor of more books than any other in America. Late in 1978, it owned some 18.5 million books and pamphlets. In addition, it had 70,585 bound volumes and 368,096 film reels of newspapers, 3.2 million pieces or reels of

2. For a fuller description see Israel Shenker, "J. Pierpont Morgan and the Princely Library He Founded," *Smithsonian Magazine*, 10 (September 1979), 77–83.

microforms, and 8.5 million photographic negatives, slides, and prints. The rare-book division alone has more than 300,000 volumes on its shelves. Since the passage of the first effective copyright law in 1870, the library has received two copies of every new American publication, be it a book, periodical, piece of sheet music, photograph, motion picture, phonograph record, or a copyrighted advertisement for a dictionary.[3] But these acquisitions are responsible for only a few of its many strengths. It is one of the very first places to go for any piece of Americana regardless of date; its holdings in numerous areas of English literature are extensive; and it has over 32.8 million pieces of manuscript. The latter are, for the most part, the papers of public men, the "makers of the nation": presidents, congressmen, diplomats, cabinet members, generals, scientists, explorers. Although comparatively few of its author-archives are as extensive or as important for the study of literature as those in several other libraries, hundreds of American writers and journalists, including some still living, are represented by at least a few boxes of papers.

Across the street from the Library of Congress since 1932 has been the Folger Shakespeare Library, the amazing monument to the lifelong hobby of a shy, almost reclusive Standard Oil executive, Henry Clay Folger. As a youth—he graduated from Amherst in 1879, and under the terms of his will the library is administered by the college—he read Emerson's eulogy of Shakespeare in the essayist's "Saturday Club address" and forthwith dedicated all his leisure and his (prospective) fortune to collecting Shakespeareana. For decade after decade, Folger and his wife devoted their evenings to poring over sale catalogues and sending off purchase orders to dealers and the special agents they had stationed in the principal bookselling centers abroad. When Folger died in 1930, he owned what was unquestionably the greatest hoard of Shakespeare material in the world. Ironically, he never saw most of it, because as soon

3. Before 1870, the Library of Congress was one of several copyright depositories designated by law and as such received many new publications, but loopholes in the earlier acts, widened by languid enforcement, prevented it from receiving all publications automatically, as it did after that year.

as the boxes arrived, he had them carted, unopened, to bank vaults and Brooklyn warehouses, where they remained until the library building in Washington was finished. Then a heavily guarded procession of trucks, loaded with three thousand of the most precious packing cases in literary history, moved down U. S. Route 1 to Washington, and the Folger was in business.

"Here," wrote the first librarian, Joseph Quincy Adams, "in almost unbelievable fulness and richness, are assembled books, pamphlets, documents, manuscripts, relics, curios, oil-paintings, original drawings, water colors, prints, statues, busts, medals, coins, miscellaneous objects of art, furniture, tapestries, play-bills, prompt-books, stage-properties, actors' costumes, and other material designed to illustrate the poet and his times. The Library is thus more than a mere library; it is also a museum of the Golden Age of Elizabeth, and a memorial to the influence that Shakespeare has exerted upon the world's culture."

The subsequent growth of the Folger has turned Adams' exuberant claim, which may have seemed slightly hyperbolic at the time, into something approaching understatement. Thanks to the income from the well-invested endowment and the vision and energy of the library's staff, the Folger's scope has steadily widened. Its center, of course, remains Shakespeare: out of some 240 known copies of the First Folio, the Folger has seventy-nine (compared with the British Library's five); over two hundred copies of the quartos, including several unique ones, such as the 1594 *Titus Andronicus* that surfaced in Sweden in 1904, was sold at auction, and then submerged again—in one of Henry Clay Folger's warehouses; thousands of association copies of Shakespeare's works, and scores of thousands of books in which Shakespeare is simply alluded to; and virtually all the collected editions and editions of separate plays, in whatever language and from whatever period.

The Folger Library's Shakespeareana, then, is almost boundless; but Shakespeare was a man of the theater, and so the library is, as well, a treasure house of stage history, with prompt-books, playbills (over a quarter million), manuscripts, and other memorabilia of thousands of actors and producers, reaching from Elizabethan times to the present. And Shakespeare was a man of the Renaissance, so the Folger has also built up a magnificent collection of books and manuscripts from, and relating to, that resplendent era. Every year hundreds of Renaissance and drama specialists from all over the world, working on subjects that have nothing to do with Shakespeare, come to the Folger for material they could find elsewhere with great difficulty, if at all.

At the University of Virginia in Charlottesville is the Clifton Waller Barrett Library covering American literature from 1775 to 1950: a collection of well over a quarter-million first editions and manuscripts which aims at completeness down to 1875 and thereafter concentrates upon the major writers. All told, some five hundred authors are "collected in depth"—that is, everything by them or relating to them, whether in manuscript or print, is sought and preserved. Here, for example, are letters, counted in the hundreds for each author, of Irving, Longfellow, Hawthorne, Whitman, Mark Twain, Edwin Arlington Robinson, and Theodore Dreiser, as well as the largest collection of Willa Cather's; four hundred pieces of the manuscript of *Leaves of Grass;* a large portion of the Alcott family papers; the largest Robert Frost collection in existence; and the manuscripts of Hemingway's *Green Hills of Africa* and Steinbeck's *The Grapes of Wrath.* At Virginia also, though not in the Barrett Library, are the papers of William Faulkner.

Although the Eastern seaboard possesses the greatest concentration of literary research facilities (both general collections and assemblages of rarities), the nation's interior, once known as a cultural wasteland, is dotted with a number of splendid libraries. Only a few can be cited here, and inadequately at that. Because it is perhaps the least famous of the major American research libraries, the Newberry, on Chicago's near north side, has a special claim to mention. Though the library contains fewer of the classic, headline-making rarities than its sister institutions on the East and West Coasts, and its holdings of literary manuscripts are not especially noteworthy (though the papers of Sherwood Anderson, for instance, are here), its general collections in literature, history, biography, philosophy, folklore, music, and allied fields make it as useful to scholars in the Midwest as Harvard and the New York Public are to their Eastern colleagues. Its periodical files are especially extensive. In addition, the Newberry has many special collections, among the most notable being the Wing Collection relating to the history of printing, which is a gorgeous gallery for the student of typography, illustration, and similar arts, and the Ayer Collection of books and other material dealing with the American Indian. In English literature, the Newberry's greatest strength lies in books of the sixteenth and seventeenth centuries, but in recent years it has been purchasing heavily in the later periods.

Two other university libraries cannot be omitted from even the briefest survey of the Midwest and Southwest. In 1960 Indiana University dedicated the beautiful building that houses the Lilly Library, a private collection amassed and given to the university by an Indianapolis pharmaceutical manufacturer, Josiah K. Lilly, Jr. In addition to a wealth of Greek and Latin classics, books on the history of science and thought, and the literature of Europe, the Lilly collection of first editions and manuscripts runs the entire gamut of English and American literary history from the introduction of printing (two Caxtons) through Shakespeare (all four folios), Walton (all five editions of *The Compleat Angler* printed during his lifetime), and Burns (a remarkably extensive array) down to the manuscripts of Bennett's *The Old Wives' Tale* and Barrie's *Peter Pan*. For many first-rank American authors, from Poe to Hemingway, there are complete sets of first editions. And the library is constantly being added to. Among other noteworthy purchases made since it was transferred to the university have been eight tons of Upton Sinclair's papers, Louis Untermeyer's comprehensive collection of modern English and American poetry, and 900 titles of rare early American fiction. The research potentialities residing in the Lilly's 75,000 rare volumes and 1,500,000 pieces of manuscript will not soon be exhausted.

At the University of Texas, the rare book library, built up over many years by the indefatigable Miss Fannie Ratchford and liberally supplied with books and purchase funds from oil, grain, and other fortunes, is richest in English literature of the past three centuries. Because of its holdings of Dryden, Defoe, Swift, Fielding, and Pope, as well as of its files of periodicals from the era, it serves students of the Queen Anne and early Hanoverian period as adequately as Yale serves those concentrating in the second half of the eighteenth century. Moreover, it is one of the country's leading places for the study of the

English romantic poets. Its Byroniana rivals that in the Morgan Library (one of the principal scholarly works based on Texas' Byron manuscripts is the variorum edition of *Don Juan*). Another pronounced strength is in the late nineteenth and early twentieth centuries; among other authors of whom Texas has extensive collections are Lawrence, Hemingway, Shaw, Joyce, Beckett, O'Neill, and Henry Miller.

In recent years Texas has devoted untold amounts of money to purchasing manuscripts of contemporary writers, of both major and minor rank. It now possesses rough notes, first drafts, and finished manuscripts and printer's proofs of such writers as Arthur Miller, Tennessee Williams, Lillian Hellman, Jack Kerouac, Allen Ginsberg, Graham Greene, and Vladimir Nabokov. Texas' voracity has become something of a cynical joke in England, where even minimally famous writers have known they could always get a grub stake by selling off the contents of their desk drawers to Austin.[4] Most of this material has not been intensively used, and indeed much is not yet fully catalogued. So wide and deep is its scope that among students of twentieth-century literature a working axiom is that the two most likely places to find primary sources for authors in whom they are interested are the Humanities Research Center at Texas and the Berg Collection in New York.

The golden years of American book collecting centered in the epoch before and just after the First World War, when the Morgans and Folger, among others, were reaping the harvest of London auctions and of sale (as the delectable English expression goes) "by private treaty." A monarch even among such titans was Henry E. Huntington, who built much of southern California's transit system and at one time sat on no fewer than sixty boards of directors. A story, possibly apocryphal, has it that he acquired the collecting mania one day in New York, when a sudden shower forced him to take shelter in a doorway of a building where an art auction was being held. He sauntered inside and came out, a little while later, the owner of a Rembrandt. The nucleus of Huntington's library was the collections of three other bibliophiles, E. Dwight Church, Robert

---

4. See Jenny Stratford, "The Market in Authors' Manuscripts," *TLS*, July 24, 1969, and Stewart McBride, "Austin, Texas: Storehouse of British Culture," *Christian Science Monitor*, February 5, 1981.

Hoe, and Beverly Chew, which he bought in 1911–12 and which were particularly noteworthy for their early editions of Shakespeare, Spenser, Milton, and other seventeenth-century poets. To these he soon added the Kemble-Devonshire collection of 7,500 English plays (the library now contains a printed copy, film, or photostat of every known pre-1800 play), the Frederic R. Halsey library of 20,000 rare volumes, including twenty Shelley first editions, and the Bridgewater House Library of sixteenth- and seventeenth-century literature, which contained numerous literary manuscripts of the period. When the library that Huntington built at San Marino, adjacent to Pasadena, was completed in 1920, the collection was already especially strong in the earlier centuries of English literature, and it has remained so through subsequent purchases. It owns more incunabula than any other library in the western hemisphere, and its assemblage of *STC* books is exceeded only by the British Library's. Surrounded by over 200 acres of botanical gardens and groves, and having as near neighbor a gallery with a rich collection of British paintings, this library has an ambiance unmatched by any other major research center.

The Huntington's manuscripts, contained in some 450 collections, number over 1,500,000 leaves, and range from 230 Middle English literary texts (including the Ellesmere Chaucer, the Towneley Plays, the Chester Cycle, and four manuscripts of *Piers Plowman*) to rich assemblages of the manuscripts and correspondences of nineteenth-century English authors: Lamb (228 pieces), Southey (over 1,300), Ruskin (626), Thackeray (316), Dickens (1,250), the Rossetti circle. . . . Nor are American history and literature neglected. One of the founder's special interests was Americana, from the New England of Cotton and Increase Mather to the exploration of the Pacific Northwest. The representation of first editions and manuscripts by celebrated American authors is the most extensive west of the Alleghenies: there are some 45,000 pieces of manuscript by 330 authors. Their scope includes the papers of James T. Fields, the Boston editor and publisher (among them 5,300 letters to and from luminaries like Whittier, Longfellow, Lowell, Holmes, Emerson, and Hawthorne) and the Jack

London collection of 60,000 pieces. The Huntington also has several thousand copies of Beadle's Dime Novels, and—to further illustrate its diversity—it has recently acquired many papers of Conrad Aiken and Wallace Stevens.

A more comprehensive survey of American libraries that are of constant, and sometimes prime, usefulness to literary scholars would include the Boston Public Library ("New Englandana" and rare books, especially of the Renaissance, collected by properly wealthy Bostonians a century ago); Cornell University (a magnificent Wordsworth library, now complemented by an equally important James Joyce collection); the Lockwood Library at Buffalo, which specializes in the working drafts of modern writers—"poetry in process"; and the William Andrews Clark Library of the University of California at Los Angeles, which is most famous for its 3,000 manuscripts relating to Oscar Wilde and the *Yellow Book* nineties and for its English literature from the Commonwealth to the mid-eighteenth century—a period in which the neighboring Huntington Library is (relatively!) weak.

As has been noted in the preceding chapter, the British Library, in the Bloomsbury section of central London, is the British equivalent of our Library of Congress and one of the two or three greatest libraries in the world. In its circular reading room (headquarters of the Department of Printed Books), countless books have been prepared for, or in some cases, such as *Das Kapital* and Samuel Butler's *The Way of All Flesh*, actually written; and in the adjoining Department of Manuscripts scholars have, for generations, pored over the papers of hundreds of famous authors.

One reason, among many, for the library's pre-eminence is that it is the principal British copyright depository. Like America, Great Britain long had laws making copyright contingent upon the sending of copies of all newly published matter to several libraries. But only little more than a century ago, at the very time the American law began to be rigorously enforced, did the energetic librarian, Sir Anthony Panizzi, take similar measures. The result is that the British Library has the most comprehensive collection of books and periodicals published in Britain in the last century.[5] But, again like the LC, the BL is just as capacious a storehouse of older material. Ever since it was founded in 1753, it has acquired, by gift or purchase, books, pamphlets, periodicals, and manuscripts relating to every conceivable subject, literary or non-literary. Its collection of material by and about most British authors is the richest in the world, and its holdings in peripheral areas—history, art, philosophy—make available to the literary student all the tools he needs to elucidate incidental allusions and supply whatever background information he lacks. From the fabled *Beowulf* manuscript fragment down to the latest issue of a paper for schoolboys, it is all there.[6] That is why every serious researcher, even if he has no immediate prospect of going to the library, should acquaint himself with the institution's history and holdings by reading Arundell Esdaile's flavorful book, *The British Museum Library*. Lists of the printed catalogues that guide searchers through the many special collections of books and manuscripts have been printed by F. C. Francis and T. C. Skeat respectively (*Journal of Documentation*, 1948; 1951, revised 1962).

Second in importance to the British Library is Oxford's Bodleian Library, founded in the seventeenth century, and today a fascinating medley, in both outward appearance and contents, of the old and the new. The original portion, "Duke Humphrey's Library," is the very exemplification of the pursuit of knowledge under difficulties: dark aisles of shelves, ponderous folios, some of them chained to the desks, cold readers' cubicles that obviously were modeled after monastic scriptoria; and at the entrance, the charming admonition, which every library should copy,

5. Although most of the material necessary for research in American literature is obtainable in major American libraries, even in this sphere the British Library sometimes proves indispensable. It has been pointed out that whereas the Library of Congress lists 384 editions of Longfellow, the BL holds 531.

6. The library's loss of about 150,000 volumes in the Second World War did not seriously affect its strength in literary and related subjects. But the bombing of its newspaper warehouse in a northern suburb, followed by a week of heavy rain, turned some 30,000 bound volumes of irreplaceable newspapers into sodden pulp.

Tread Lightly and Speak Softly

But the reading rooms in both the "old" Bodleian and its modern "extension," a block away, are spacious, light, uncluttered; and in the new building, the storage areas, most of them underground, are thoroughly Americanized with their concrete and steel stacks, adequate lighting, and air conditioning. On the open shelves in the stacks, unguarded by grills and marked by no other special distinction, are the priceless "named" collections—the tall brown folios and squat quartos redolent of pioneer English antiquarianism, philosophy, and other learning that figure in countless volumes of literary scholarship.

Because the Bodleian's one catalogue of its book holdings, unlike the British Library's *General Catalogue*, is for internal use only and is not available elsewhere, it is often hard for the researcher to decide whether he could work more profitably at Oxford than in London. The published works on the topic in which he is interested often give some indication of the degree to which his predecessors have relied on the Bodleian. In general, it is well to remember that the book collection, while smaller than that of the British Library (it could scarcely be bigger), has the particular value of greater age; the Bodleian, after all, was a hundred and fifty years old, and well stocked even then, when the British Museum was founded. Moreover, it too is a copyright depository, though it now receives only the newly published books it specifically requests; and its manuscripts are multitudinous, ranging from treasures from the Middle Ages to, for instance, papers of such relatively modern figures as Shelley. Many scholars discover that they need to use both the British Library and the Bodleian, which is not difficult, since Oxford is only an hour's train ride from London.

For the literary scholar, Cambridge offers somewhat smaller opportunity, partly because she has traditionally been the seat of the sciences rather than of humane learning. But the University Library contains well over a million and a half volumes and some 10,000 manuscripts. The Trinity College Library, a gem of Wren architecture, is rich in English literary manuscripts, including, for example, many of Tennyson's and

Macaulay's. And at Magdalene College is housed Samuel Pepys's private library (including the incomparable diary), preserved in exact accordance with the provisions of his will.[7]

In Manchester is the John Rylands Library, founded by a widow as a memorial to her husband, a pious Victorian businessman who seldom had time to read. In accordance with Mrs. Rylands' own tastes, theology is a chief interest in the library. But the Rylands, now a part of the University of Manchester, has much else besides, including the Althorp Library of 40,000 early printed books, which Mrs. Rylands bought from Lord Spencer for over £200,000, the largest sum paid up to that time (1892) for a single collection. In Edinburgh, the National Library of Scotland is the natural *pied-à-terre* of anyone working on a topic with Scottish bearings, such as Boswell or Sir Walter Scott.

Though its contents—some fifty million pieces of manuscript —are primarily of interest to specialists in English history, the Public Record Office in London's Chancery Lane (always called the "PRO") claims a place in even the briefest account of British institutions the literary student must know. The PRO houses about three-quarters of the nation's surviving official archives, the products of eight hundred years of government and the administration of justice. Among these thousands of tons of documents are many of great importance to literary history: deeds and depositions signed by Shakespeare; the coroner's report which, when discovered by Leslie Hotson, revealed the circumstances of Marlowe's murder; Shelley's letters to Harriet Westbrook; official documents throwing light on "Silas Tomkyn Comberback's" (i.e., Samuel Taylor Coleridge's) discharge from the British Army, in which he had ill-advisedly enlisted in 1793. The very diversity of the Public Records is guarantee enough that they often repay

7. American students should perhaps be reminded that, because the two ancient English universities are composed of autonomous colleges (Trinity, Corpus Christi, All Souls, Balliol, Pembroke, Gonville and Caius, Peterhouse, St. John's, and the rest), many of the most precious books and manuscripts in Oxford and Cambridge are found not in what we would call the "main library" (the Bodleian or the Cambridge University Library) but in the dim religious light of the individual college libraries.

searching by biographers and other literary historians.[8] The
Revels Accounts and other classes of documents have provided
a great deal of information on the history of the Elizabethan
and Restoration drama.[9] The records of the Admiralty may
throw light on the careers of seagoing authors like Smollett and
Marryat (and, as we have seen, they have provided a valuable
check on Trelawny's incurable romancing); the archives of the
various courts of justice and the so-called "state papers domestic and foreign" contain the answers to nobody knows how
many literary puzzles—because they are so extensive, and so
complicated in their arrangement, that many sections have
never been explored.

The PRO is no place for a novice. To find his way among
these documents one needs specialized knowledge that can be
obtained only by years of experience and a firm understanding
of English law and administrative organization and procedure
as they existed in the period in which he is interested. He can,
however, profit by reading V. H. Galbraith's *Introduction to
the Use of the Public Records*, based on a series of lectures
delivered before Oxford students contemplating original research. And it is comforting to know that in London one can
hire, for a modest hourly fee, expert record searchers who have
had many years of experience at the PRO, the British Library,
and other libraries and archives.

The libraries mentioned throughout this chapter differ considerably in their admission policies. Some, such as the Library
of Congress, the New York Public (reference collection), and
the Newberry, are freely open to all serious students, from
undergraduates on up. Others, like the Berg and the Humanities
Research Center in Austin, are more restrictive. Some will ad-

8. The bulk of the so-called "modern" records have been moved to an
ultra-modern facility in the London suburb of Kew, but most of the papers
of potential value to literary scholars remain in Chancery Lane.

9. Among all the scholars who have seined the Public Records for data
bearing on theatrical history, C. J. Sisson has probably drawn up the
fullest nets. For an absorbing account of the way in which records of
early seventeenth-century lawsuits enabled him to reconstruct the plots
of two lost plays, Chapman's *The Old Joiner of Aldgate* and the Dekker-
Rowley-Ford-Webster collaboration, *The Late Murder in Whitechapel,
or Keep the Widow Waking*, see Sisson's *Lost Plays of Shakespeare's
Age* (Cambridge, 1936).

mit graduate students equipped with good credentials, and the Folger, Newberry, and Huntington, for example, make a special point of welcoming such readers, who are, after all, the mature scholars of the next generation. At the British Library, admission to the reading room is only by "ticket," a card which can be obtained without trouble by presenting a letter of introduction, accompanied by a more or less *pro forma* assurance that the work one proposes to accomplish there cannot be done in any other, less crowded, library in the city. The Bodleian is less restrictive than the Cambridge University Library, which requires an introduction from a don or other university dignitary. When in doubt whether you would be allowed to work in a certain American or British library, it is always advisable to write ahead or to consult a scholar who knows the ropes. It is well to remember, also, that several major research libraries, among them again the Folger, Huntington, and Newberry, offer fellowships to post-doctoral scholars (and in some cases dissertation writers as well) whose projects require extensive use of those libraries' specialized collections. The chief sources of research subsidies are listed in the annual Directory Number of *PMLA*.

The researcher leaves every library he visits with more than his sheaf of notes. For libraries, in addition to the wealth they possess on vellum, paper, and film, are physical and personal presences, and each has an atmosphere of its own. The old ladies at their tables in the genealogical divisions of the large public libraries and historical societies, engrossed in their seemingly endless pursuit of ancestors; the papery redolence of an old library's stacks; the air-conditioned immaculateness and ease of the Houghton and Folger and Huntington reading rooms, where scholarship is made to seem not only a dignified but almost a luxurious way of life; the somnolent attendants in soiled jackets who bring you your books at one library, and the extraordinary courtesy and helpfulness of the staff at another; the noble dimensions of the King's Library in the British Museum, its walls lined with folios in the richest of bindings; the tourists peering into the display cases containing great documents of history in the exhibition room at the Public Record Office. . . . These general sensations of place mingle, in retrospect, with closer, more personal ones: the comeliness of a well-printed book, its type still black, its margins still ample, its rag-content pages still crisp, strong, and white after the passage of three centuries; your own expectancy as you open a cardboard file-box and undo, for the first time since his widow tied it very long ago, the ribbon that binds a stout bundle of a famous author's private letters. These are elements of the scholar's experience which do not ordinarily suffuse the books and articles he writes after he goes home, but they leave ineffaceable traces in his memory, and they are not the least of the personal satisfactions afforded by the profession he has chosen.

CHAPTER SEVEN

Making Notes

He walked much and contemplated, and he had in the head of his Staffe a pen and inke-horne, carried always a Note-Book in his pocket, and as soon as a notion darted, he presently entred it into his Booke, or els he should perhaps have lost it. He had drawne the Designe of the Booke [*Leviathan*] into Chapters, etc. so he knew where-about it would come in. Thus that booke was made.
—John Aubrey, "Thomas Hobbes" (*Brief Lives*).

No two persons make research notes in exactly the same way, and there is, in fact, no absolutely "right" or "wrong" way to do so. The two goals are efficiency and accuracy, and whatever methods achieve them for the individual scholar are wholly legitimate. The prescriptive portions of what follows will be clear enough. The rest I offer simply as the fruit of my own experience: these are the techniques that have served me best. In general, I shall be talking about taking notes for a large project, such as a book. But my suggestions can readily be scaled down to be useful in collecting data for a term paper or article.

If you know how to type, by all means do so, both at home and in whatever sections of the library allow typing. You save an incalculable amount of time, and what is even more important, your notes will be legible. No matter if your handwriting is itself utterly clear, at least to you; typing is faster and better.

Slips are preferable to cards, because they take up less space, a fact which makes an important difference both in portability and in convenience of filing if the amount of data you accumulate proves to be considerable. Furthermore, if slips are made of high-quality bond paper, they are just as durable as cards. No other kind of paper is satisfactory. Avoid particularly the sort on which typing smudges and over which a ballpoint pen infuriatingly skips.

Now enters a touch of heresy. All the chapters of advice on note-taking I have seen stress that cards or slips should be of uniform size. I recommend two sizes, each for a very specific purpose: three-by-fives for bibliographical references *only*, five-by-eights for the notes themselves. The former are as large as necessary for the amount of information they will have to contain, but they are not large enough for comfortable recording of facts, ideas, and quotations, especially when you have no idea how many more related notes you will eventually want to enter, for convenience, on the same slip. In addition, they are easily distinguishable and can be filed separately.

For every book and article you consult, make out a bibliographical (three-by-five) slip. If your project is a fairly modest one, to be finished in one or two months' time, before your memory starts to fail, this point is not so important; in such a case, modify the rule to read "for every book and article in which you find information." But if you are working on a dissertation or book, it is extremely useful to keep a record of every source you examine, whether or not you take anything from it. A few months later, running across a reference to a certain article that sounds as if it might be valuable, you may forget whether or not you looked at it. Quick recourse to your file of bibliographical slips may save you, at the very least, the labor of hunting it down again in the library and, often, the trouble of re-reading it.

On the face of the bibliographical slip, copy the author, title, edition (if any is specified), place and date of publication, and (if it is a fairly recent book) the publisher. Or, if it is an article you are recording, note the author, title, periodical, volume number, year, and pagination. *Always take this information from the source itself* as it lies before you, never from any reference in a bibliography or someone else's footnote. Authors' initials and the exact spelling of their names, the titles of books and articles, and dates have a way of getting twisted in secondary sources. Play safe by getting your data from the original, and doubly safe by re-checking once you have copied down the information. On the face of the same slip—I use the bottom lefthand corner—record the call number of the book or periodical, and if it is shelved anywhere but in the main stacks of the library, add its location. If you have used the item at a library other than your headquarters, record that fact too ("Harvard," "Newberry," "Stanford"). These are small devices, seemingly unimportant, but in the aggregate they are tremendous time-savers if you are dealing with hundreds of sources and the storage space in your brain is reserved, as it should be, for more vital matters.

On the back of the bibliographical slip, I usually write a phrase or even a short paragraph of description and evaluation, again to refresh my memory two or three years after I have used the book. Since nobody sees these slips but me, I am as candid, peevish, scornful, or downright slanderous as I wish; if a book is bad, I record exactly what its defects are, so that I will not refer to it again or, if I have to do so, in order that I will remember to use it with extreme caution. If, on the other hand, it is a valuable book, I note its outstanding features. And I also record just what, if anything, it has contributed to the study on which I am engaged. Perhaps I also leave a memo to myself to re-read or re-check certain portions of it at a later stage of research, when conceivably it will provide me with further data that at this point I do not anticipate I shall need. Finally—and this is particularly recommended to students whose research requires them to scan large quantities of dull material, such as rambling four-volume Victorian literary reminiscences—I note the degree of exhaustiveness with which I inspected the item, by some such phrase as "read page by page" or "thoroughly checked index." Similarly, I recommend that you make a slip for every bibliography you have consulted, so that you can be sure you have not inadvertently overlooked it. If it is one of the serial bibliographies of literary scholarship, such as the annual bibliography of studies in romanticism, record the precise span of years you've covered. If it is a subject bibliography, such as *Poole's Index*, list the individual entries under which you have looked ("Education," "Literature," "Reading") in case other possibilities occur to you later on. Once again, the whole idea is to save wasteful duplication of effort. Three or four minutes spent in making such a slip can save a whole day's work a year or two later.

So much for the three-by-five slips. Now for the larger ones, which can accommodate enough material to minimize the nuisance of riffling through a whole sheaf in search of one elusive piece of information. Every slip should be devoted to a single topic, perhaps a very small sub-topic; you must be the judge of that. It should therefore bear, at the top, a readily intelligible caption. And it should be strictly confined to that single topic. That means that when you have finished with a certain book or article—and don't take any notes until you have finished; simply jot down page references on a piece of paper until you have come to the very end—the data it contains may have to be distributed among a dozen or more slips. That may take a bit more work, but in the end it's worth it, because you will have all related material where it should be—in the same place. As your slips on the same topic multiply, use the same heading and add consecutive numbers.

A definite skill is attached to note-taking. Most novices write far too much. There is no inherent advantage in putting down whole sentences when compressed phrases are just as meaningful ("Percy Bysshe Shelley was born on August 4, 1792, at Field Place, near Horsham, Sussex": why not "PBS b. Aug. 4, 1792, Field Place, nr. Horsham, Sussex"?). Definite and indefinite articles and other such amenities can be dispensed with. And if you can devise a consistent personal system of abbreviations, which will be absolutely clear and incapable of later misinterpretation, you will save more time and space than you can easily conceive. In note-taking I automatically type *shd* and *wd* for *should* and *would*, *bg* for *biography* and *bgr* for *biographer*, *edn* for *education* or *edition* (I fear no ambiguity: the context always makes it clear), *pbd* for *published*, *ptr* for *printer*, and so on. In addition, I have a whole stock of abbreviations for the names of authors I am making notes on: RB, MA, ACS, DGR, CD, WMT, HWL, WW (William Wordsworth or Walt Whitman?), STC, TC, MT, RWE.

It follows that in note-taking, verbatim quotations should be kept to a minimum. If you are simply extracting facts or ideas from your source, reproduce them in as small a compass as accuracy permits; it is substance, not wordage, that you want for your slips. Thus, you can boil down a *DNB* sketch of a minor eighteenth-century writer just by eliminating all the prose in which it is embodied and confining yourself to the hard facts—names, places, dates; and you can handily summarize a critic's four-page interpretation of *The Turn of the Screw* in a paragraph, by disregarding both the complete sentences and (if it is not essential for your purposes) the step-by-step construction of the argument. One thing, however, you must always do: whenever you take a phrase or a sentence directly from your source, enclose it in quotation marks, to remind you, infallibly, that you have borrowed it and thus must retain the quotation marks if it appears, intact, in your finished product. Failure to do this often results in embarrassment, if nothing worse. No scholar is less to be envied than the one who, having neglected to use quotation marks in his original notes, embodies in his finished article phraseology which he honestly now regards as his own but which a perceptive reader spots as someone else's.

There are many occasions, of course, when direct quotations must be copied into your notes. Any hitherto unpublished documentary material, such as a record of marriage or a holograph letter, should be transcribed word for word. Even if only the substance is desired, it is useful, and what is more, a valuable safeguard, to have the exact text, rather than a summary, in your possession. Later developments may make desirable its literal reproduction. Again, when dealing with crucial points of biographical or critical opinion, you should have at your fingertips the author's exact words, so that you can re-examine them. Often after a lapse of months, and with the advantage of further knowledge and longer thought, his position proves not to be what you first assumed, or has implications of which you were earlier unaware. Word-for-word copying unquestionably is a weariness of the flesh (the author of Ecclesiastes may have had it especially in mind when he complained of study and the making of books), but it often cannot be avoided.

When occasion requires you to transcribe verbatim, do so with clear head, patience, and devotion to absolute accuracy: not a comma omitted, not a phrase accidentally skipped. Recognizing the vicissitudes a quotation can undergo in successive drafts of a manuscript, most scholars as a matter of routine compare the version in their final draft with the original. This is good practice, but it is time-consuming, and in any event some of the originals may not again be accessible, having been seen at other libraries or having in the interim mysteriously disappeared from the shelves of one's own. An even better practice, therefore, is to certify the accuracy of your initial transcription on the note-slip itself. Having quoted a paragraph from Northrop Frye, take the time—even though it is a nuisance, the hour is late, and your eyes are tired—to collate your note-slip, word by word, with the page before you. When you have corrected your transcription (and the odds are that you will have to—the capacity for faithful copying is one of man's rarest talents), put along the margin some private sign of approval—my own is "Text $\sqrt{}$d"—which will bear eternal, unequivocal witness to the fact that the passage as copied is, *is*, IS accurate. Five minutes spent re-checking in January are an hour in the pocket in necessitous May.[1]

1. I have let these paragraphs stand essentially as they were originally printed, because despite the ubiquity of the copying machine, the point is still important. The "Xerox" has unquestionably made it easier to accumulate the documentary data one needs, even to the extent that the reckless feeding of coins into a slot sometimes becomes a means by which a student postpones having to apply his powers of discrimination to the raw material he unearths. But photocopying is not always available or practicable—some materials cannot be photocopied because of the nature or age of their bindings, and some may not because of copyright restrictions—and at such times the necessity for manual transcription with mechanical fidelity remains undiminished.

One more word about quotations, again having to do with the changes that affect them as they pass from one writer to another. A cardinal rule of scholarship requires that quotations be made from the source that is closest to the author—the book in which the passage first appeared or, in the case of manuscripts which are themselves unavailable, the most authoritative printed text. If for any reason you are unable to use these original sources, and must rely instead on the passage *as quoted by* someone else, always state that fact in your footnote reference. This is a means of self-protection. If the quotation is inaccurate in the source you have used, you show that the fault lies there, and not with you. Nevertheless, quote secondhand only when absolutely necessary. It is worth much trouble to get the words precisely as they came from their author's pen. The same caution applies to facts derived from a secondary source. No matter how reputable the book, it is always advisable to go back to the place where its author or compiler got his information; a typographical error, a careless transcription, or an omission of important qualifications may make his account in some respect inaccurate or misleading. And the bibliographical reference may itself turn out to be wrong.

But to return to the actual process of note-taking. After every statement of fact, every condensed or paraphrased generalization, and every direct quotation, write the source. Here is where the system of separate bibliographical slips comes in especially handy, for it enables you to use the shortest reference form possible. If you are borrowing from an author represented in your file by only one slip, you need to write after your note only "Loomis, 133"; the bibliographical slip will provide you with all the further information you need for your documentary footnote and for re-checking if that is necessary. And if you have consulted more than one book or article by the same author, or anticipate doing so before you are finished, you still can abbreviate without any danger of misunderstanding: "Loomis, *Arthurian Tradition*," or "Loomis in *Romanic Review* 1941"—each of which is clue enough to the full bibliographical information on your three-by-five slip. It thus becomes unnecessary to repeat the full reference after every substantive note; all you need do is specify the page. If, in a single note, you take material from several successive pages of your source, the best practice is to put page references along the lefthand margin, indicating by a slash or two (//) in the body of the note exactly where your use of one page ends and the next begins.

In addition to being a repository of factual data and ideas drawn from your sources, substantive slips provide a way of storing your own ideas, fresh from the mint. Often, as you read, your mind goes a step or two beyond your author's, extending an argument that he left incomplete, or generalizing, as he does not, from a body of data; or, on the other hand, you may disagree with some of his statements. In order that these quick flashes of inspiration be not lost, record them as they come, no matter how fragmentary or tentative they may be. You can organize, criticize, and amplify them later on; the big thing is to preserve them. But to keep them entirely separate from ideas that are already present in your source, make plain to your future self that these are genuinely your own by initialing them. In the course of most scholarly projects, as opinions and interpretations churn around inside the writer's head, there is eventually bound to be some confusion as to which were acquired from his predecessors and which originated with him. The scholar can clarify matters (including his own conscience) by maintaining this simple record of his independent thought processes.

Write on only one side of each slip—at the outset. Save the other side for incidental addenda, corrections, and queries directly relating to the notes contained on the face of the slip. To ensure that these later accretions are not overlooked, write a big red "OVER" in the margin alongside each item to which they refer.[2]

But fresh notes, as distinct from brief commentary and added details on previous points, call for fresh slips. And these, in any major program of research, mount up at a surprising

2. This is another point on which I happen to differ with the authorities; cf. the stern capitals of Barzun and Graff, *The Modern Researcher,* p. 26: "NEVER WRITE ON BOTH SIDES OF ANYTHING." All I can say is that I don't think I have ever overlooked anything on the other side.

rate. To keep them well classified and accessible with the least trouble, use dividers, and arrange them in some logical order; roughly, perhaps, in the succession in which you anticipate dealing with them in the prospective book. When, as is inevitable, a fact or remark on one slip has a bearing on a fact or remark on a slip further down the line, enter some sort of cross-reference on the margin of both, so that you will know where each is. At a fairly late point in your research, after your major ideas have fallen into a reasonable sequence and you consequently have a guide for arranging your various groups of slips, it is worthwhile to number them. I followed this procedure with the data-slips for a book on the mass reading public in nineteenth-century England. First I divided the notes into fifteen major topics and gave each slip the number of the category to which it belonged; then I sub-divided them, and sub-sub-divided them; and to each sub- and sub-subdivision I also gave numbers. This scheme sounds rather complicated, and I admit that it was at least Linnean. But, just as in a library every book has its own unduplicated call-number, every slip received a distinctive designation (12.3.6.1), which meant that it had its own inalienable—and fairly logical—place in my file; furthermore, the number provided the easiest conceivable way of cross-referencing, and any later slips that had to be interfiled could simply be given a higher terminal number (after 12.3.6.1 there was room for 12.3.6.2. et seq.). In short, the system worked, and I used it again when gathering data for a book on *The Shows of London*. I recommend it unreservedly to anyone confronted by the chaos of hundreds of five-by-eight slips.

The particular method of note-taking one adopts depends partly on the nature of the material involved. For a book on the history of literary biography, the material comprised not so much a myriad of tiny facts that had to be conveniently assembled as large quantities of longish notes on individual books and articles. Here the five-by-eight system would have been too dispersive. Instead, I wrote my notes on ordinary typewriter paper and organized the numbered sheets in a succession of spring binders. Preparation of a simple page index enabled me to have quick access to their contents. Given the special character of the materials involved, this proved as efficient a way of proceeding as had the slip system.

It remains only to say a little about the habits that mark responsible researchers when they are in libraries. For one thing, they *never* bring bottles of ink anywhere near books or manuscripts; and many rare-book libraries, bearing traumatic memories of awful accidents, forbid even the use of fountain pens. Scholars come to work with a good supply of well-sharpened pencils, which are the safest tools to use if typewriters are unavailable. But they *never* place the paper on which they are writing on top of the manuscript or opened book; pencil points or ballpoint pens leave embossings on the receptively soft paper beneath the note-slip. Scholars *always* keep the manuscript or book from which they are taking notes safely away from any possible source of damage, and if they prop a book up for easier reading, they make sure it can't fall. (Most libraries have stout book racks to help prevent this.) And scholars *always* handle their materials with the utmost care; they turn pages carefully; they treat manuscripts, which are often extremely frail, with the delicacy connoisseurs always accord to fragile *objets d'art*, opening folds slowly and cautiously, lifting their leaves—depending on their form and condition—either by the margins or in the flattened hand. (Rare books and manuscripts deserve at least as much care as one lavishes on his most precious stereo records!) Although perspiration mingled with the dust acquired from old books may coat their fingers with a species of mud, scholars *never* leave a trace of smudging, even the faintest thumbprint, on a document or book they have been using.

I wish I did not have to write this final paragraph, because it is incredible that anyone interested in the subject of this book would need to read it. But the bitter truth is that a few of the very people whom one would expect to know better are, to put it bluntly, book vandals. Ask any librarian, or, for that matter, consult your own experience. How many times have you been annoyed by the marginalia left by some idiot—huge and redoubled exclamation points, uncomplimentary expressions ("absurd," "oh, come now," "for God's sake!!!!"), and long, scrawled explanations of what seems perfectly clear in the printed text? The critical points may be well taken, but the margin is no place to utter them. Pencilings of this sort—and I include compulsive underlining, a sophomoric affliction if there ever was one—are bad enough; even worse is marking with ink. And worst of all is that indefensible sin, outright mutilation: the removal of whole pages or sequences of pages. Every library has penalties for such misdemeanors, which, in many cities and states, is what they are in the eyes of the law, but the penalties are not severe enough. At least they do not discourage either the vandal-by-momentary-impulse or the vandal-by-habit. The result is that everybody else suffers; for who can read with comfort an ink-glossed book, or contemplate with equanimity a volume from which some essential pages have been rudely sliced out? Our indignation can be all the freer, our execrations the more profane, if our own consciences are perfectly at ease.

The Philosophy of Composition

The idea that histories which are delightful to read must be the work of superficial temperaments, and that a crabbed style betokens a deep thinker or conscientious worker, is the reverse of the truth. What is easy to read has been difficult to write. The labour of writing and rewriting, correcting and recorrecting, is the due exacted by every good book from its author, even if he know from the beginning exactly what he wants to say. A limpid style is invariably the result of hard labour, and the easily flowing connection of sentence with sentence and paragraph with paragraph has always been won by the sweat of the brow.
—G. M. Trevelyan, "Clio, A Muse."

There was a time, within the memory of senior professors yet in service, when the chief reproach laid against literary scholarship was that it was sterile, unimaginative, divorced from both life and literature, and preoccupied with absurd trivialities —"the date of Hegetor, swan maidens, Celtic cauldrons of plenty, the priority of the A or B versions of the prologue to the *Legend of Good Women*, medieval lives of Judas Iscariot, Vegetius in English, or Caiaphas as a Palm Sunday prophet."[1] It would be less than candid to assert that present-day scholarship has purged itself in that respect, though the tendency in recent years, for better or worse, has been toward the other extreme—a kind of scholarship, often brilliantly imaginative, that leaves hard facts far behind in its sweep toward broad generalization.

But oftener heard today, and with all too good reason, is the complaint that scholars can't write decent English. For years, trade publishers have been telling our profession at every opportunity, "Give us a manuscript on a reasonably important subject *that is well written*, and we'll give it every serious consideration for publication." The seventy-odd American university presses, which are devoted to publishing the results of research, echo the plea. They know that if their authors wrote more attractively they could sell more books and thus, by plowing the profits back into the business, give more scholars a chance to be read.

The relation between prose style and economics is less crucial among the scholarly journals, because they have a captive subscription list (mostly libraries) and in any event are subsidized by the institutions where they are published. But their editors and the consultants who read manuscripts for them make the same complaint. Even the articles selected for publication are more than seldom flawed by a style that is, at best, pedestrian and, at worst, leaden, uncouth, obscure, and repetitious.

We, of all people, should know and do better. Presumably we are dedicated to the proposition that the English language is not merely a communication tool (a repulsive phrase to which some English teachers, alas, are addicted) but the medium

---

1. This particular indictment dates from 1913 (Stuart Pratt Sherman in *The Nation*, September 11; reprinted in his *Shaping Men and Women* [Garden City, 1928], p. 66), but it was echoed for the next thirty years at least.

of a fine art. In the classroom we may delight in analyzing the skills of great English prose writers, but when we sit down at our desks and draw upon our private resources of language, we seem to have learned nothing useful from the masters we praise. No one expects a person reporting on his or her research to be a brilliant stylist. Writers with so pronounced a gift for language and form that they can make a ten-page paper a work of art are as rare inside the profession as they are outside. But though scholarly writing is not meant to offer an aesthetic experience, it does not have to be either dull or unnecessarily complicated.

This is nothing more than what has been urged by numerous scholars depressed by the stylistic apathy or pretentiousness of so much of our professional literature.[2] Actually, though there unquestionably is such a thing as "academese" or "dissertation style," it has no reason to exist, and every scholarly writer should avoid it as assiduously as he wars on the comma splice in his students' themes. There is no difference between a good scholarly style and a good English style addressed to the intelligent layman.

The hallmark of good scholarly prose is lucidity. It is not easy to achieve. It never has been—the old adage about hard writing being the prerequisite to easy reading is a sound one—but it has become even less so in an age when too much of the critical writing on which the young scholar is nurtured is opaque, tortuous, and jargon-laden. Consider the following two-sentence paragraph:

To get the proper "mix" of factors in the instance of *Kaddish* (Ginsberg's lament on the death of his mother), we need an addresser-context ratio, for the biographies of both Allen (addresser) and his mother (context) determine the message to a great extent—which is not to say that other factors do not influence the message.

2. I am thinking especially of R. B. McKerrow, "Form and Matter in the Publication of Research," *RES*, 16 (1940), 116–21, reprinted in *PMLA*, 65 (1950), No. 3, pp. 3–8; Samuel Eliot Morison, "History as a Literary Art" in his *By Land and by Sea* (New York, 1953), pp. 289–98; and—a much more extensive treatment, which relentlessly comes down to brass tacks—Barzun and Graff, *The Modern Researcher*, Part Three. I make no attempt here to repeat their sage and urgent counsel; hence they should be read in conjunction with this chapter.

What I am saying, in effect, is that once the framework has been exhausted as a series of compartmentalized factors used to generate information (although the model is necessarily simplified for heuristic purposes), then the factors can be combined in ratios, and the investigator can begin to work back toward the holistic view that was so unmanageable originally.

The style of influential modern critics, heavily tinctured with borrowings from the vocabulary and ponderous mannerisms of sociologists, psychologists, anthropologists, and linguists, gets into the blood.[3] It has insidiously osmotic properties; too extended a course of reading in the books and periodicals of contemporary criticism, and you are almost bound to write the same way. Admittedly, present-day literary theory sometimes is concerned with subtle concepts that can be discussed only with the aid of esoteric terminology. But while such language (which often strikes one as sheer gobbledygook) may have its place, that place is in a very restricted area of discourse, and only there.

Another symptom of the pretentiousness syndrome is what might be called pseudo-erudition, or learned name-dropping. Novices in the profession, troubled by a sense of inadequacy, often seek to add weight to their arguments by making calculatedly offhand references to whoever happen to be the big names in critical fashion at the moment—Barthes, Harold Bloom, Derrida, Lévi-Strauss. Thus, the preceding paragraphs might have acquired a certain grandeur by citing Ludwig Wittgenstein (*Tractatus Logico-Philosophicus*): "Anything that can be said can be said clearly." But, apart from whatever benefit might have accrued from reiterating, in self-illustrating language, a point already made, there would have been no reason for invoking Wittgenstein. Whether or not one is justified in using such a device hinges upon the twin issues of pertinence and necessity: Is it appropriate to my level of discourse and vital to my argument? Often, of course, the considered answer turns out to be Yes. But the question nevertheless should be asked whenever the temptation arises.

To return to the matter of style itself. One of the most

3. See Wallace W. Douglas, "Souls Among Masterpieces: the Solemn Style of Modern Critics," *American Scholar*, 23 (1954), 43–55.

deplorable characteristics of "academese" is the sentence that, like a wounded snake, drags its slow length along.[4] All I need by way of example are three such sentences, written by respected present-day scholars:

The whole Prologue [John Fletcher's to his play *The False One*] is worth comparing with the corresponding section of Shaw's Preface to *Caesar and Cleopatra* (where, in his own characteristic way, he says very much the same thing) and appears to have escaped the notice of those scholars who maintain that *Antony and Cleopatra* was never produced in its author's lifetime, but the general impression it gives is that the play, and *Julius Caesar,* were sufficiently well established in common knowledge for some such disclaimer to be necessary if another play about the principal characters were to get a hearing.

* * *

In "Tennyson's 'Palace of Art'—an Interpretation" (*SP*, 1936), A. C. Howell first reviews the various explanations of the poem, those supplied by the poet himself and those offered by others, together with some account of this "curse of Tennyson's poetry," allegory; these are followed by Howell's own interpretation— worked out with great fullness as one of the "lesser meanings" (Tennyson's phrase), but as so developed appearing larger— namely, that the Palace is Trinity College, Cambridge, "the cloistered life, the life of the scholar, surrounded with art and knowledge, but ignorant of the active life of the common world," and the whole poem represents obliquely Tennyson's disappointment at being forced to leave without a degree and his protest against the College's "deadening influence upon the development of the artist, the genius."

* * *

Believing firmly, as his son later, that the artist's subject matter is inextricably knotted to his life ("A man can only paint the life he has lived!") and that the greatest artist is a man passionately devoted to his friends (Shakespeare, he once wrote Yeats, must have been "very lovable and fond of his friends," and then, underlining the words, added, ". . . *he couldn't have been otherwise. How else could he have written his dramas?*"), Yeats's father drummed into his young son aesthetic principles which, at first rejecting, Yeats eventually modified into some of the most basic structural elements in his own system of aesthetics.

4. When you embody in your prose a familiar phrase that most of your readers can be depended on to recognize as a borrowing, it is pedantic to use quotation marks. Quoted phrases that border on the cliché, such as the one from which this note hangs, had better not be used at all.

Nor is length any more virtuous when it is the result of verbosity. The inviolable rule of good scholarly writing is: Say what you have to say, and when you've said it, quit. Longwindedness, repetitions, digressions are as out of place in a research article or book as they are anywhere else. The scholarly writer is never in the position of an undergraduate who must turn in a two thousand-word theme but has material only for fifteen hundred words. He should think of himself instead as a welterweight striving to lose enough poundage to box a featherweight. Just as a few ounces here, a few ounces there, day by day, will eventually put the fighter in shape, so will trimming away a redundant phrase in one sentence, an unnecessary word in another produce that spareness which marks a good research article. Rare is the paper that cannot be cut by at least 15 percent by deleting verbose locutions and substituting single words that are just as accurate and often more emphatic. So long as neither clarity nor *necessary* substance is sacrificed, the shorter the article, the better.

Undergraduate theme writers have a tendency to add weight by loading their pages with quotations. Serious researchers seldom deliberately do so, but sheer indolence—copying being, on the whole, easier than original composition—sometimes tempts them to "lard their lean books," as Robert Burton put it, "with the fat of others' works." The truth is that another writer's exact words are not sacrosanct if you can convey the same point more succinctly in your own language. You can do it oftener than you may think. When you are about to quote more than a sentence or two from a secondary source, pause a moment. Couldn't you adequately summarize the idea in half the space? If you can, why burden the page with the superfluous wordage that direct quotation would entail?

On the other hand (to return to a point made earlier), if by condensing or paraphrasing your author's statements you risk distorting his position, then you have no choice but to quote him verbatim. Nuances of meaning are as important in learned writing as they are in poetry, and no scholar wants to appear to misrepresent someone else's assertion or position. To ensure that its author's intention is faithfully conveyed, the quotation must not only be absolutely accurate but must incorporate all pertinent qualifications and details. It may not make much difference, perhaps, that Katharine Anthony (*The Lambs* [New York, 1945], p. 136) writes, "The celebrated painter Benjamin Hayden [*sic*] complained that Hazlitt's infant 'put his fingers into the gravy,'" whereas what Haydon really recorded (*Life of Benjamin Robert Haydon . . . from His Autobiography and Journals,* ed. Tom Taylor [New York, 1853], I, 204–5) was that "the boy, half clean and obstinate, kept squalling to put his fingers into the gravy." The effect on the onlookers no doubt would have been the same in either case. But careless or inadequate quoting can seriously distort meaning, as this example shows: [5]

The next paragraph, indeed, calmly begins by saying that what this news caused at the time was "a melancholy slackening". But they hurry on down the gorge and see

> The immeasurable height
> Of woods decaying, never to be decayed . . .
> Winds thwarting winds, bewildered and forlorn . . .
> The rocks that muttered close upon our ears,
> Black drizzling crags that spake by the way-side
> As if a voice were in them; the sick sight
> And giddy prospect of the raving stream . . .

Nature is a ghastly threat in this fine description; he might well, as in his childhood, have clasped a tree to see if it was real. But what all this is *like*, when the long sentence arrives at its peroration, is "workings of one mind" (presumably God's or Nature's, so it is not merely *like*),

> Characters of the great Apocalypse,
> The types and symbols of Eternity,
> Of first, and last, and midst, and without end.

The actual horror and the eventual exultation are quite blankly identified by this form of grammar. . . . No doubt some kind of pantheism is implied, because Wordsworth feels that Eternity is turbulent like the Alps and not calm like the Christian God. But the last line of the passage contradicts this idea by putting the calm

---

5. I owe the example to Professor M. H. Abrams. Another instance of distortion through selective quotation, pointed out by Gordon S. Haight in his Riverside edition of *Middlemarch* (pp. xii–xiii), is F. R. Leavis' treatment of that novel in *The Great Tradition.* Compare Leavis' quotations (pp. 61–79) with George Eliot's full text.

back, and in any case the metaphysics would be a deduction only; what he sets out to do is to describe the whole development of his feelings about crossing the Alps, and he asserts it as a unity.

(William Empson, *The Structure of Complex Words* [London, 1951], p. 303)

Compare, now, Wordsworth's actual lines (*The Prelude* [1850 text], VI, 624–40; the passages omitted by Empson are italicized).

> The immeasurable height
> Of woods decaying, never to be decayed,
> *The stationary blasts of waterfalls,*
> *And in the narrow rent at every turn*
> Winds thwarting winds, bewildered and forlorn,
> *The torrents shooting from the clear blue sky,*
> The rocks that muttered close upon our ears,
> Black drizzling crags that spake by the way-side
> As if a voice were in them, the sick sight
> And giddy prospect of the raving stream,
> *The unfettered clouds and region of the Heavens,*
> *Tumult and peace, the darkness and the light—*
> *Were all like* workings of one mind, *the features*
> *Of the same face, blossoms upon one tree;*
> Characters of the great Apocalypse,
> The types and symbols of Eternity,
> Of first, and last, and midst, and without end.

Many an exciting "discovery" has proved to rest on the false premise of a quotation that is incomplete, misread, or divorced from its context. As Geoffrey Tillotson once wrote, it is a sobering but prudent practice to re-check one's quotations against their source before using them in any argument:

There are occasions when the checker finds his transcript so badly wrong that it could only serve the present occasion if kept wrong. . . . To check the transcript of a quotation is sometimes to discard the quotation. Further, even if the transcript is accurate, turning it up may lead the checker to find that he has so far forgotten its context as to have come to misunderstand what the writer of the quotation intended it to mean. To re-examine the context of a quotation is sometimes to discard the quotation. [6]

---

6. *Criticism and the Nineteenth Century* (London, 1952), p. ix.

And organize, organize, organize—but without ever seeming to do so. Construct your paper as coherently as your resources of thought and language allow. Never leave the reader uncertain as to your—and his—destination or the relevance of each statement to your purpose. Keep your direction sure and steady and the pace as brisk as the amount of pertinent material and the complexity of the argument permit. The sentences and paragraphs should fit as tightly as the teeth of a zipper. The familiar cohesive fragments of language—*thus, therefore, again, on the other hand,* and the rest—may be used, but sparingly. And the finished structure should contain no trace of the rough scaffolding that went into its erection. Such self-conscious locutions, so redolent of a high-school classroom "presentation," as "Up to this point, my intention has been . . ." or "Now let us turn to . . ." merely distract the reader, calling untimely attention to the author sweating to sort things out for himself. Your chief dependence should be upon the forward thrust and clarity of the argument: upon the tenon and mortise of rigorous thinking, not the easily available hot glue of methodical rhetoric.[7]

While the pains we take to increase logical coherence are amply justified by their service to our intended reader, they are still more valuable as stimulus and safeguard to our own thought. By the time most of us sit down at our typewriter, we bask in the illusion that we have our material and our ideas well under control: all we have to do now is let flow on paper the close-knit sequence of our argument—or so we regard it—that we have already formed in our mind. Ordinarily, things just do not work out that way. We need first to outline and then to write; and after that, we re-write.

An outline, including abbreviated cues to all the data and logical relationships to be covered in the proposed paper, may be as informal and scrawled as we like. Nobody else will ever see it. But the simple act of making it forces us to collect, review, and systematize our thoughts before starting the first paragraph and provides at least a tentative itinerary for the whole trip. A preliminary chart in black and white affords an

7. Reasonable consistency of metaphor within a short compass also helps.

invaluable overview of everything that is to be said and often, by exposing gaps or non-sequiturs, may forestall time-wasting digressions that prove to lead either nowhere or in the wrong direction. It is much more economical to discover weaknesses at this stage than after a first (freehand) draft has been toiled over, read and groaned over, and thrown into the wastebasket.

But even the most conscientious preliminary outlining and sentence-by-sentence writing seldom results in a first draft that can also stand as the final one. Some writers, in fact, confess that their hardest and most profitable thinking is done in the very act of composition. Only when they are compelled to lay out their argument in sentences and paragraphs, scrupulously designed to lead the prospective reader from point to point, do they finally see it as a logical whole, and only then do remaining deficiencies of evidence and reasoning become apparent. Re-thinking calls for rearrangement, and rearrangement means re-writing; perhaps a paragraph here, a whole page there—or the whole article or chapter. But one can find a positive gain in necessity. For if the process of writing is in part destructive, exposing as it does the flaws of one's thinking, it can also be creative, because by forcing reconsideration of what has been said, it sharpens insight into the meaning of one's material, suggests new sources of data, perhaps makes it possible to extend the argument a further step.

Such, in any case, has been my experience, and I know it is that of others as well. Each chapter of the present book has gone through at least four drafts; a previous book went through six. The successive drafts are messes to behold. Some pages are montages pasted together from the salvage of earlier versions, and all are full of interlineations, impatient black deletions, and red-penciled lines transferring a sequence of sentences from one paragraph to a later one. But, like every writer, I seek solace in the hope that each fresh version is a little easier to read, a little more tautly constructed, a little more vigorous than the preceding one.

Completion of an outline and the ceremonious insertion into the typewriter of a clean sheet of paper, radiant with expectancy, is far, then, from marking the end of thought and the beginning of art. The two will proceed simultaneously, each nourishing the other. But that very first page may remain immaculate (or else hideously besmirched with x-ed out sentences) for some time; for a well-known neurotic symptom, called First Paragraph Block, often attends the beginning of composition. Its causes, amateur psychiatrists say, are a subconscious awareness of one's incomplete state of preparation and fear of what lies ahead. The best way to break the impasse is to write that first paragraph, even if, in the very act of setting it down, you know it will never do. In that fashion you will arrive at the second paragraph, and writing will become slightly easier; you will be getting into the swing of things. From there on, following your outline of I, II (a), (b), (c), and so forth, you will have comparatively little trouble. Then, still despising that first paragraph, put the completed paper away for a time, and when you take it up for revision, re-write Paragraph One in the light of all that follows. The very fact that it no longer stands alone, but serves as an introduction to a whole argument, will help you improve it.

In any event, don't discourage your reader with the point-blank announcement in Sentence One that "The purpose of the following article is to . . ." This is as feeble a gambit as that favorite among freshman theme writers, the quoting of a dictionary definition. Nor is much to be said for a plodding initial Review of Previous Knowledge (or Opinion) on the Subject at the gateway of an article that promises either to add to the knowledge or reverse the opinion. Some better way can be found of enlisting the reader's attention, such as a terse, question-raising statement of the problem, a pertinent anecdote, or an apt quotation from the literary text under discussion which will serve as a springboard into the paper itself. (The previous history of the topic, if it needs to be reviewed, may be summarized unobtrusively in a footnote or the relevant material recalled as you go along.)

I consider these, in their respective ways, attractive openings:

Comedy deals in stereotypes rather than fully rounded, three-dimensional, living characters, just as much of social life is conducted by stereotypes rather than by fresh, objective appraisal of each situation as it arises. It is possible for those who habitually deal in stereotypes to break loose from their moorings and to engage in fresh appraisals, but the latter is counterpointed against the former. That is, we are conscious of making a special effort for a special case, different from the customary ebb and flow of daily existence. These rules (or rules of thumb) also apply in comedy, where there is continual skirmishing between originality and convention, between the demands of live persons and the easy familiarity of stock types. Great comic characters like Falstaff are both highly original and highly traditional, depending upon what aspect of the character we choose to consider, but the originality is especially striking because of (and not in spite of) the basis in convention.[8]

* * *

A seldom discussed resource for literary and cultural studies of colonial America is the genre that I shall comprehensively label "early American gallows literature." Included under this label are sermons, moral discourses, narratives, last words and dying sayings, and poems written for, by, and about persons executed for criminal activity in America before 1800. Although the genre accounts for only a very small percent of the 50,424 titles listed in Charles Evans's *The American Bibliography* and Roger Bristol's *Supplement* to that work, the genre clearly had a hold on the American imagination from the earliest days of New England's Puritan settlements through the last decades of the eighteenth century. Unlike some of the literary types introduced to the colonies by Puritan settlers, this genre, with its several forms, survived the disintegration of Puritan faith during the mid-eighteenth century, and during the period from 1750 to 1800, the genre actually continued to develop and to exceed in numbers and variety the forms of gallows literature initially developed by New England Puritans.[9]

* * *

When I first began teaching courses in women's literature, my students gently complained that I seemed obsessed with madness and suicide. I glanced over the syllabus: first, *The Awakening* (Edna drowns herself); second, *The House of Mirth* (Lily takes an overdose); third, *The Bell Jar* (Esther tries both of these, compounded by wrist-slashing and hanging). Clearly my students had a point, though I eventually diagnosed the obsession as not really being mine but as belonging to the delicate relationship between women and literary art, out of which suicide blooms like one of Rappaccini's flowers. We expect suicide both of women writers and their crea-

---

8. Maurice Charney, *Comedy High and Low: An Introduction to the Experience of Comedy* (New York, 1978), pp. 50–51.

9. Ronald A. Bosco, "Early American Gallows Literature: An Annotated Checklist," *Resources for American Literary Study*, 8 (1978), 81.

tive heroines and are no more surprised than when salmon batter their way upstream to spawn and to die. Yet we should remember that the correlation between creation and death in women writers, unlike that in salmon, is not natural but cultural. Historically speaking, women have lacked money, experience, education, privacy, and often leisure. They have been taught that writing—or at least serious writing—is really a male vocation.[10]

* * *

The predominant theme in the works of Ralph Ellison is the quest for cultural identity. Although he does not realize this himself, the protagonist of *Invisible Man* seeks identity, not as an individual, but as a black man in a white society. He encounters and combats the problem Ellison identified in an interview with three young black writers in 1965: "Our lives, since slavery, have been described mainly in terms of our political, economic, and social conditions as measured by outside norms, seldom in terms of our *own* sense of life or our *own* sense of values gained from our *own* unique American experience." The invisible man searches for self-definition in terms of the sense of life and values gained from the unique black-American experience. His quest, however—like that of almost every other Ellison protagonist—ends in the conviction that the black experience is not so unique: "Who knows but that, on the lower frequencies, I speak for you?" Cultural identity becomes indistinguishable from the human condition.[11]

* * *

Popular culture is often defined as the widely shared practice or experience of a social group. However, in the academic study of the history of popular culture, the least explored area is that of the experience of culture by ordinary individuals. A large number of major historical studies have been made of popular art, entertainment, material culture and ideas. Similarly, there has been a lesser, but still conspicuous, effort by historians to explore the means of transmission or communication of popular arts and ideas. But the question of how ordinary individuals experience their culture is a topic which has been largely ignored. Several valid reasons can be given for this ignorance: the dearth of written sources and especially of unmediated written sources, the methodological problems of critically analyzing and evaluating idiosyncratic sources for emotional as well

10. Sheila Ortiz Taylor, "Women in a Double-Bind: Hazards of the Argumentative Edge," *College Composition and Communication*, 29 (1978), 385.
11. Susan L. Blake, "Ritual and Rationalization: Black Folklore in the Works of Ralph Ellison," *PMLA*, 94 (1979), 121.

as intellectual and aesthetic content, and the lack of the requisite multi-disciplinary training which an historian would need to explore such a topic. Certainly, the exploration of individual consciousness of popular culture is no easy task. But a difficult task is not the same as an impossible task; there are a number of possible approaches or methods available for such study.[12]

The final paragraph offers a cognate problem, which, however, can be solved more easily. Conventionally the last paragraph should summarize all that has preceded it and point up the ultimate significance of the discovery or argument. This is good sense. But the writer cannot say, in so many words, that "the purpose of the foregoing article has been . . .": that is a privilege reserved for the scientists. Instead, it should sum up without seeming to do so; it should be a coda, not an abstract, and it should leave the reader with a satisfying sense of gain —new information acquired, an enlarged historical apprehension, a stimulating critical perception:

I do not wish to overemphasize the "modern" historical approach in Chaucer at the expense of the "medieval." In history things happen slowly. In an artistic sense, Chaucer is always modern; but he is also partially a creature of history and in him are to be seen the various conflicting ideas of the fourteenth century, some destined to wax and others to wane, perhaps only temporarily if we take a point of view long range enough. For today we may see, I think, a turning away from the historic again. But the sense of history which we find in Chaucer, however undeveloped, is one element which was destined to play a very important part in the succeeding centuries; perhaps even more important, however, it is an element which gives us some clue to the heart of the mystery of Chaucer's art. Chaucer may be studied as a figure in the history of ideas as well as an artist, and in isolating at least his sense of the historic, we must eventually turn back to his art with a new awareness and a new understanding of his aims and methods.[13]

* * *

Although Herrick's epigrams on commoners are not all masterpieces of the genre, the percentage of failures among them is probably no

12. Susan S. Tamke, "Oral History and Popular Culture: A Method for the Study of the Experience of Culture," *Journal of Popular Culture*, 11 (1977), 267.

13. Morton W. Bloomfield, "Chaucer's Sense of History," *JEGP*, 51 (1952), 312-13.

higher than it is among his other poetic types. There is no indication that he spent more time on a lyric line than on one in an epigram, and Herrick is surely the most accomplished English writer of such pieces before Walter Savage Landor in the nineteenth century. Though we have been concerned wholly with scurrility, we should remember that many of Herrick's most beautiful short poems also belong to the genre, as do his delicately sad epitaphs, the sententious couplets and quatrains in *Hesperides,* and most of the didactic poems in *Noble Numbers.* When we hear Herrick's epigrams criticized as slight or insubstantial, we should remember that this is an accepted limitation of the genre, not a remediable fault of the poet. Within the scope of the epigram Robert Herrick is a careful and consummate artist.[14]

* * *

Ulysses was her trial, her torture, and finally her triumph. It brought Shakespeare and Company a second celebrity, a living bard, who turned the shop into a literary shrine. It burdened our literature with a work of extraordinary versatility. It canonized Sylvia Beach. To those fitfully wondering whether to try and follow in her footsteps she was the object of envious glances and acclaim. What she had accomplished they had only dreamed of doing and, remarkably, she had done it despite a shaky budget and with little knowledge of what the effort would entail. She succeeded partly because she did not know what she could not or should not do. To contend, however, that success was practically guaranteed, given the prepublication publicity *Ulysses* received, is to suggest that the publisher was endowed with a degree of prescience she could not have had prior to February 1922. Even Joyce gloomily predicted dismal sales for his book. Sylvia Beach had what every publisher needs—intuition—and on that quality rested her lasting belief in Joyce and in the greatness of *Ulysses.*[15]

* * *

If the scientific world-view is really in decline, science fiction may yet be split between a popular fantasy-literature weaving a mythology out of disparate, "magical" elements of the scientific vision (a category which is, of course, as old as SF itself), and a minority of serious writers such as Lem and LeGuin struggling to expose the scientific outlook to psychological, epistemological, and ideological scrutiny. Gone, in other words, would be the large body of popular writing which, in the last fifty years, has simply endorsed and prop-

14. Robert W. Halli, Jr., "Robert Herrick's Epigrams on Commoners," *South Atlantic Bulletin,* 43 (1978), 40–41.

15. Hugh Ford, *Published in Paris: American and British Writers, Printers, and Publishers in Paris, 1920–1939* (New York, 1975), p. 33.

agated scientific values on the assumption that they embodied a coherent, challenging and imaginatively satisfying world-view. Such a development would probably mean the disappearance of SF as a separate genre. Yet, if there is a natural reluctance to write off SF in this way, still less is it feasible to write off the tradition of scientific thought. Science is still one of the most basic attributes of civilized humanity, however skeptical we may have become of nineteenth-century views of historical evolution and of nineteenth-century aspirations to galactic imperialism. The question of the future of some form of the scientific world-view is, very probably, the question of human survival itself. A new synthesis of scientific ideology, modified to meet men's changing perceptions and definitions of their real needs, would provide the best guarantee of a healthy and flourishing science fiction. In the future, as in the past, SF writers themselves could do much towards the emergence of such a synthesis. It may well be that this, rather than the cultivation of "style" and literary respectability, is their most urgent task.[16]

All the paragraphs between the opening and closing ones offer an equally healthy challenge to the scholar's shaping and stylistic powers. The construction and phrasing of a research paper demand as much care, in their own way, as do those of a work of imaginative literature. Not only must transitions be managed, relationships clarified, emphases developed, proportions adjusted, meanings expounded: the right tone must be achieved. The gray stylistic mien worn by the authors of so much of "the literature on the subject"—any subject—certainly gives substance to the old charge that the greatest success of scholarship has been its relieving literature of its connection with life. Nothing devitalizes a topic more effectively than the manner in which it is discussed, and how remote those grave files of journals on the library shelves seem from the dreams and impulses and triumphs of the human spirit! One is inescapably reminded of Yeats's lines in "The Scholars":

> Bald heads forgetful of their sins,
> Old, learned, respectable bald heads
> Edit and annotate the lines
> That young men, tossing on their beds,
> Rhymed out in love's despair
> To flatter beauty's ignorant ear.

16. Patrick Parrinder, "Science Fiction and the Scientific World-View," in *Science Fiction: A Critical Guide*, ed. Patrick Parrinder (London, 1979), p. 87.

Literature is a record of life, and (though we tend to overlook the fact today, in our preoccupation with "the human predicament" and similar funereal themes) it has its abundant portion of gaiety. In writing about it, we do not have to don suits of solemn black and assume a dejected 'haviour of the visage. We can talk about literature with the seriousness it deserves and yet not be grim or heavy-footed.

There is no harm, for instance, in disclosing that a human being has written your article. The notion that the first person singular should not be used in scholarly writing is nothing more than a superstition lingering from the days when literary researchers, being regarded as a breed of scientists, were expected to be as impersonal in their prose as in their procedure. Scientific writing to this day abhors the "I"; but in writing about literature no virtue resides in self-effacement *per se*, and if you think the first person singular is appropriate at a given place, use it without apology.

Some graduate students, in avoiding the Scylla of ponderosity, risk the Charybdis of excessive liveliness. I suppose this trait is simply a manifestation of subconscious rebellion against having renounced the world of undergraduate values, high among which is the ability to turn out a paper vibrating with clever phrases, for what is assumed to be the monastic austerity of Scholarship. But a manner that was admired as bright and bubbly in college has a way of becoming merely facetious when it is applied to the material of graduate study. Unless a student's development is arrested at the moment he takes his A.B., his nervous self-consciousness will soon disappear, and his writing as a graduate student will in due time achieve a tone suitable to its new purpose. Which is far from saying, however, that scholarly writing cannot accommodate humor. A touch of wit in a serious article is no more reprehensible than a *bon mot* in a lecture, yet it is a thousand times less common. Fortunately, there are a few scholars and critics who are unashamed to lighten their discourses. Everyone who has read Douglas Bush's books remembers with gratitude the unaffected wit that flickers here and there in those learned pages:

The sound and prosaic wisdom of the goddess [in Tennyson's "Oenone"] is so very Victorian that we become embarrassingly aware that she is undressed, apart from a spear, and it seems, to violate chronology and propriety, as if the Queen herself had started up in her bath and begun to address the Duke of Argyll.[17]

* * *

Mr. Eliot has even complained of Milton's obscurity. One may have, as I have, a great admiration for Mr. Eliot's writing in both verse and prose and still find a certain pleasure in visualizing the author of *The Waste Land* as he struggles with the meaning of *Paradise Lost.* [*And again:*] Milton is too big, too sternly strenuous, to allow us to feel at ease in his presence. . . . Like Dante, Milton is not what P. G. Wodehouse would call a "matey" person.[18]

Even a bibliographical article, under the right auspices, can delight as it informs:

A Modern Library Giant contains the complete poetic works of Blake and Donne, and will be useful to anyone who wants to have Blake and Donne bound up together.

[Ellis' *The Real Blake* is] a biography whose chief resemblance to the real Blake is in a certain facility for drawing without the model.[19]

A learned society should establish a special award for writers like these.[20]

But what about us less gifted mortals, who nevertheless are once in a while visited with humorous inspiration which we are tempted to preserve in our pages? The only possible answer is, Put it up to your conscience—and your taste. If, in the course of writing, an epigram or pun comes unbidden, it may, after a preliminary scrutiny, be allowed to stay— until our more sober judgment and our friends have a chance to review it.[21]

---

17. *Mythology and the Romantic Tradition in English Poetry* (Cambridge, Mass., 1937), pp. 205–6.

18. *The Renaissance and English Humanism* (Toronto, 1939), pp. 102–3.

19. Northrop Frye, "William Blake," in *The English Romantic Poets and Essayists,* ed. C. W. Houtchens and L. H. Houtchens (New York, 1957), pp. 4, 7.

20. For an example of the way a gifted scholarly stylist can couch a vital message in sophisticated and allusive wit, see Henri Peyre, "Facing the New Decade," *PMLA,* 76 (1961), 1–6.

21. A footnote is the proper locale for a subsidiary plea: Avoid cryptic titles. For too many years there has been a vogue among scholars and critics for picturesque, esoterically allusive, and studiedly uninformative titles. In column 166 of the *NCBEL,* Volume III, *The Broken Cistern*

Which brings me to a point on which I am admittedly a bit fanatical. To undergraduate and graduate students, I am aware that what I am about to say will sound like a ukase from Utopia. I know there are inexorable deadlines to be met; I know that academic terms rush by, and the concurrent requirements of two or three courses, with term papers and all the trimmings, drive students frantic. Nevertheless, I will say it, for the sake of that later day when the heat is off and what has been written in haste can be revised at leisure. Or, rather, I will let Dr. Johnson say it for me, in his "Life of Pope":

His publications were . . . never hasty. He is said to have sent nothing to the press till it had lain two years under his inspection: it is at least certain, that he ventured nothing without nice examination. He suffered the tumult of imagination to subside, and the novelties of invention to grow familiar. He knew that the mind is always enamoured of its own productions, and did not trust his first fondness. He consulted his friends, and listened with great willingness to criticism; and, what was of more importance, he consulted himself, and let nothing pass against his own judgement.

In this respect, at least, Pope was a wise man (and the wiser Johnson implies his own approval). No piece of scholarly writing can be the worse for mellowing; most books and articles, in fact, improve if they are allowed to age before bottling. A cardinal rule of scholarship, as of criticism, is to be wary of one's first enthusiasm. Indulge it, to be sure; let it run its

flows, nine entries later, into *The Sacred River*, and in the next column *The Visionary Company* is quickly metamorphosed into *The Lost Travellers*, who have a possibly significant proximity to *The Drunken Boat*. Most such titles, admittedly, are followed by subtitles that more or less explain what the book is about ("Studien und Interpretationen zur Dichtung der englischen Romantik"; "A Reading of English Romantic Poetry"; "A Romantic Theme with Variations"; "The Revolutionary Element in Romanticism"), but it would seem advisable to give this explanation, so far as possible, in the beginning; the subtitle should provide, not a key to the mystery, but a further explanation. There may be no grace in such titles as "Is Oxford the Original of Jefferson in William Faulkner's Novels?" or "The Dashes in Hemingway's *A Farewell to Arms*," but at least there is no concealment for the sake of a recondite reference. Whether for better or worse, bibliographers no longer enjoy the license granted to the contributors to *Poole's Index to Periodical Literature* a century ago: "In most instances the author's own title best expresses the subject of his paper; but if the author has given it an obscure or fanciful title, the indexer will give it a better one. . . ."

course in the composition of the first draft. But then let time do its slow work. Put the manuscript away for as long as you can—weeks, months, years. When you finally take it out again, you will have a new perspective. You will see where love-at-first-sight infatuation with your discovery or line of argument led you to exaggerate or confuse relationships, neglect contrary evidence, even draw wrong conclusions. But you will also see new implications in your material, and perhaps you will find yourself going to hitherto unthought-of sources to clarify and substantiate facts. "It is certain," Gamaliel Bradford wrote in his journal (February 7, 1920), "that even in investigating what seems to be the smallest and most limited subject there are always nooks and crannies that slip by one, facts of greater or less interest and importance that turn up afterwards and tend at least, or appear to tend, to modify one's judgment—too late." One of the reasons why manuscripts should be put aside for a reasonable time is to provide for that contingency.

Restraining the impulse to publish one's brainchild as soon as it is bathed and breeched has also this advantage: it encourages a second look at the style as well as the substance. The successive revisions I have spoken of above are best undertaken at fairly wide intervals, so that each time we return to the manuscript, our critical eye is as fresh as possible and the remedial measures more immediately apparent.

Of course there is no hard-and-fast rule that determines when one should stop working over his manuscript. There are many instances of learned authors seizing the (supposed) necessity for further revision to camouflage their unacknowledged fear of publication and consequent exposure to criticism. Each writer must decide for himself when his zeal for revision borders on the pathological, and lay down his correcting pencil forthwith. But on the whole I would say that there is more to be gained from considered and recurrent revision than from rushing into print. The illusion of spontaneity can be maintained as late as draft number six.

It is good to be one's own severest critic, but there are limits to the detachment with which one can view his own work. When you have done the best you can, ask people for whose judgment you have high respect to read your manuscript. Don't pick yes-men; turn, rather, to readers on whom you can depend to wield the blue pencil and ask the pointed question in utter candor, for they are the writer's best friends. Ask for, and receive in good and thankful spirit, the sternest criticism of which they are capable. Two or three such readers may represent a cross-section of the public that will eventually read your work in print, and they can alert you, before publication, to flaws that would otherwise be irrevocably preserved in type. (The same advice holds when you have written a paper intended to be read only by your teacher. If other people anticipate the professorial comment, and you act on their advice, you can spike his guns.)

Now a word about documentation. A superstition akin to the one about avoiding the first person singular holds that the scholarly quality of a paper is directly proportional to the number of footnotes, as if the heavy ballast at the bottom of each page insures against the balloon's soaring errantly into Cloud-Cuckoo-Land. No such thing. Footnotes, it is said, are for use, not ostentation.[22] They have two purposes. "Documentary" footnotes provide the reader with the sources of all the facts, as well as the opinions that are not original with the writer, so that if he is at all skeptical, he can check for himself. Moreover, they are an indispensable courtesy to later scholars who may wish to utilize some of the material and need clear directions as to where to find it. "Substantive" footnotes allow the writer a place to put incidental but relevant comment which would interrupt the flow of discourse in the text proper. The recent tendency has been toward absorbing some documentation into the text—a practice I have sometimes followed in this volume to illustrate the kinds of occasions on which it is appropriate. This is a legitimate and desirable way of reducing the number of footnotes, particularly those of the *ibid.* and *loc. cit.* variety—the kind Dickens called, in the third chapter of *Little*

---

22. Cf. the Roman emperor in Gibbon's *Decline and Fall of the Roman Empire* (Chapter 7): "Twenty-two acknowledged concubines, and a library of sixty-two thousand volumes, attested the variety of his inclinations; and from the productions which he left behind him, it appears that the former as well as the latter were designed for use rather than ostentation."

Dorrit, "hiccuping references." [23] Some readers dislike the practice, however, because it distracts their attention, just as superscript reference numerals do, from what is being said.

In our field, the standard guide on all matters of form, including footnotes, is the *MLA Handbook*, obtainable at small cost at campus bookstores. Its rules have been adopted by the English departments of most American colleges and universities and, sometimes with minor differences, by nearly all university presses and learned journals in the humanities. No matter what your intended audience is, master the *Handbook* so thoroughly that its prescriptions become second nature to you. On questions outside its scope, probably the most widely used guide is the University of Chicago Press's *Manual of Style*. These two works of scripture should be on every scholarly writer's desk, next to a good dictionary and H. W. Fowler's classic (and sometimes delightfully cranky) *Modern English Usage*. They, like footnotes, are for use; for it is remarkable how often we are content to play our typewriter by ear. If the manuscript is intended for an editor, be sure that it follows the rules of form laid down by the *MLA Handbook*.

Once we have verified all dubious spellings, corrected false idioms, ironed out faulty parallel constructions, and made sure that all documentation is in prescribed and consistent form, there remains the indispensable task of scanning the final copy for typographical errors. No matter how time presses, nor to whom the paper is addressed—a teacher or an editor of a journal—every line must be proofread. Courtesy and self-interest both require it, for a reader cannot be expected to do full justice to the argument of a paper if his attention is recurrently distracted, and his patience tried, by careless errors of typing.

Where shall the article be sent? You will save much time and postage if you carefully survey the market to single

---

23. A wonderful bird is the ibid.
    In appearance it's pale and insibid.
    It stands as a sage
    At the foot of the page
    To tell where the passage was cribbed.*

*In this case, from the *News Letter of the Institute of Early American History and Culture*, June, 1958.

out the journals and reviews that are most likely to welcome
a paper like yours. The most direct way is to look through
the current numbers on your library's shelves, but you may
also find useful one of the several current lists of periodicals
that publish articles in English and American literature. Sometimes informal report may help you decide where to send—or
not to send—your work; for example, some journals have so
large a backlog of accepted articles that it would seem wise to
send one's own newest essay to a journal that can publish it
sooner.

Accept all aid with gratitude, even if it damages your self-
esteem. I am thinking of that sinking feeling all scholars experience, now and again, when a cherished article bounces
from a journal, or a publisher rejects a book. If the manuscript
comes back with merely a printed slip, or what is obviously a
form letter from the editor, there is nothing to do but look up
Browning on welcoming each rebuff—and then, after having
cast a cold and critical eye over the neatly typed pages and
perhaps rewritten an inferior paragraph here and there, send
it out again. As often as not, however, the editor of the journal
or press sends along specific comment, which may embody
also the criticisms of consultants to whom the manuscript was
referred. For whatever comfort it may be, remember that
editors and their readers are not infallible. George Meredith,
who for many years read manuscripts for the firm of Chapman
and Hall, declined an imposingly long list of books that subsequently became famous. Sometimes readers are just plain
obtuse (though the writer may be at fault, for not making his
ideas sufficiently clear); sometimes they really don't know as
much about the subject as the writer does. Every editor of a
scholarly journal and every director of a university press can
testify how often a proffered manuscript can evoke bluntly
opposite reactions from consultants to whom it is sent for
their expert opinion. And most scholars have had an experience
similar to that confided to me by a well-known member of the
profession who once had an article returned to him from a
leading journal accompanied by a reader's comment: "This is
not an article. It's an example of how an article should not be
written. Mr. X knows how to use the language. But he has

nothing to say. The paper is a useless collection of unstructured information—useless because unstructured." The article was accepted and printed by the next journal to which it was submitted, and immediately after it appeared its author received a note from another scholar, also well known in the profession though not to him personally. "My congratulations upon a very fine study," she wrote. "I have assigned it to my graduate seminar as a paradigm of the just and the lively."

Discrepant though the reactions of critics often may be, most manuscripts are rejected with good cause, and the criticisms should be weighed with all the detachment at one's command. If the editor says the article is too long, probably it could be cut without grievous loss. If he says it does not make its case, probably it doesn't. If he notes that you have failed to take into account certain items of previously published scholarship that affect your argument—well, haven't you? In any event, apply to your colleagues, not for commiseration but for further criticism. Maybe it would be best to shelve the whole business for a while to gain additional perspective. But if you still have faith in what you have written (and never abandon faith too readily), let it resume its rounds.

Eventually, if the article or book really deserves to be published, it will be, for there are now enough periodicals and university presses to assure every scholar a hearing. Then comes that "one far-off divine event/ To which the whole [of scholarly] creation moves"—the arrival of galley proofs. Now (if you are like most writers) your doubts are resolved, your sagging morale receives a boost; for how authoritative, how convincing your hard-wrought sentences look in black type! Rejoice, and, apart from correcting whatever typographical errors there are, and verifying your quotations and references once again, make no changes. Corrections in proof are expensive, and it is standard practice to bill an author for any he makes which increase the printer's bill by more than 10 or 15 percent of the cost of original composition. Many authors, including the present one, are prone to detect in galley or even page proof deficiencies they failed to notice before, no matter how often they re-examined and revised their manuscript—ambiguities, awkward phraseology, false emphases, repetitions, overloaded paragraphs, outright errors. Somehow one's writing looks quite different when it appears in printer's type. But the price to be paid in "author's alteration" charges is steep, and only a Winston Churchill or, as we have seen, a William Faulkner could afford the luxury of re-writing a book in galleys.[24]

And now, after a suitable rest, to the next project—the one for which you've been accumulating notes over the past several years. Other topics, other materials, other methods of approach, but the four great requisites of good scholarly writing never change:

1. Accuracy of facts.
2. Soundness of reasoning.
3. Clear explanation of the topic's significance.
4. Unaffected, terse, LUCID prose.

24. Complicated and intractable though some histories of English and American literary texts may be, they are editorial child's play compared with those of Balzac, who re-wrote his books so many times in proof that an edition recording the development of the text is almost a practical impossibility. See Bernard Weinberg, "Editing Balzac: A Problem in Infinite Variation," in *Editing Nineteenth Century Texts,* ed. John M. Robson (Toronto, 1967), pp. 60–76.

CHAPTER NINE

The Scholar's Life

∿∿∿∿∿∿∿∿∿∿∿∿∿∿∿∿∿∿∿∿∿∿∿∿∿∿∿∿∿∿∿∿∿∿∿∿∿

> To say the best of this Profession, I can give no other
> testimony of them in general, than that of Pliny of Isæus;
> *he is yet a scholar, than which kind of men there is*
> *nothing so simple,* so sincere, none better; they are most
> part harmless, honest, *upright, innocent,* plain dealing men.
> —Robert Burton, *The Anatomy of Melancholy*,
> Partition 1, Section 2, Member 3, Subsection 15.

The scholar really never ceases being a scholar. He may firmly
lock his office door at the end of the day, but he never locks
or sequesters his intellect. Consciously or subconsciously he
continues to mull over the problems his restless curiosity about
books and history has set loose in his mind, and sometimes,
at the oddest moments—at 3 A.M. or while taking a shower—
a bright new idea may come to him from nowhere. In the midst
of alien affairs that necessarily command their minds as teachers, academic committee members, husbands and wives, parents,
participants in community activities and other good works,
scholars cannot turn off, even if they wished to, the flow of

questions and clues to the answers. The bookish excitement that has led them into the profession permeates their lives.[1]

This state of being, it has always seemed to me, is its own reward. We may not make much money (so the old chant goes), but we have a lot of fun. For despite the inescapable moments of doubt, cynicism, and even despair that assail the thoughtful members of any profession (a surgeon's patient dies, a nuclear physicist wonders whether his work is truly radiant with promise for humanity), our pleasures are many.

To be sure, few of us realize the dream we cherished all the way through college and graduate school—the delectable vision of being able, evening after evening, year after year, world without end amen, to savor at leisure all the books we merely read *about*, or flipped through on examination eve, in our student days. Once endowed with the Ph.D., we thought, we could relax and read Henry James with our feet on the fender. Nothing of the sort. Only the tweedy, pipe-smoking professors of legend, who did nothing but teach and read, their whole lives long, at some placid ivy-mantled college, could have approached that Utopian mode of life, and I doubt if even they read all they planned to. Nevertheless, no other profession offers so legitimate an excuse for reading great literature. And though the siren song of research may lead us to spend many hours in realms far removed from art, those very hours may themselves prove blessings, in that, if we learn our lesson correctly, they may sharpen our understanding and appreciation of the masterpieces to which we are devoted.

Hence, though time is always short, we have the lifelong company of books; and what is more, we have good human companionship. I suppose that literary scholars are no more gregarious than those in other lines of work. Nonetheless, our bond of common interest, of commitment to the humanistic ideal in general and in particular to literature as queen of the arts, is a peculiarly strong one. Love of books and a consuming interest in the intellectual and esthetic questions they pose make brothers of men with amazingly different

1. See Hardin Craig, "How to Be a Productive Scholar Without Any Time to Work," *American Scholar*, 35 (1965), 126–28.

backgrounds and tastes. In scholarship there is no prejudice born of national origin, creed, color, or social class; we live in the truest democracy of all, the democracy of the intellect. One of the unofficial but highly compelling functions of the year-end meetings of the Modern Language Association is to provide an occasion for the reunion of men and women who toiled together as graduate students, or later as colleagues in the same department; or who, one sabbatical spring, drank ale together at the Bull and Mouth pub, the lunchtime annex of the British Library. Leaving aside the occasional asperities and outright feuds that are inevitable in any group of mettled human beings, ours is a friendly profession, as anyone knows who has heard the animated chatter in the lobbies of the MLA's headquarters hotel.

We are no cloistered order. Though our closest professional associations outside the circle of fellow-scholars are, of course, with librarians and other bookmen-by-profession, our investigations often lead us to meet all sorts of men and women far removed from the library stacks. Some of us have had the good fortune to contract lasting friendships with people who have provided us with our documents or their personal memories of a great writer: people who have had initially to be approached with tact and deference, cultivated, discreetly flattered, indulged in their caprices and crotchets until the field was ours.[2]

Sometimes our quests have surprising and memorable conclusions. Several years ago, the upshot of protracted negotiations for photographs I needed for a book was a social visit to a certain English peer on his estate which he opened to the paying public several days a week as "the only Lion Preserve in the Midlands." ("Stay in your car," commanded a large sign at the entrance. "Survivors will be prosecuted.") I rode with

---

2. For shrewd, sound advice on how scholars should deal with collectors (and, by extension, owners of family archives), see Gordon N. Ray, "The Private Collector and the Literary Scholar," in Louis B. Wright and G. N. Ray, *The Private Collector and the Support of Scholarship* (Los Angeles, 1969), pp. 27–84. Another valuable guide is an MLA brochure (1974) by James Thorpe, *The Use of Manuscripts in Literary Research: Problems of Access and Literary Property Rights*. See also the entries for Buchanan, Holroyd, W. S. Lewis, and Plumb in the list of readings, pages 251–53.

him one cloudy Sunday afternoon as he happily drove his sleek miniature railway train, the locomotive powered by a Ford Cortina engine, across his well-tended acres; I sailed with him on his lake, aboard a tourist launch made in the reduced image of a Pacific cruise ship and also powered by Ford; I accompanied him in his Land Rover safari wagon as he visited his thirty lions lazing in supercilious ease atop their dens, converted from old British Railway boxcars; I inspected the added attractions, including his Lions Corner House snack bar (the pun will be appreciated by all who know London with its chain of Lyons Corner House restaurants) and the teashop set up in the former riding school. It was an experience that mingled strong elements of both Wodehouse and Waugh, and I wouldn't have missed it for the world.

In research, then, there are numerous perquisites: the constant company of books, the pleasures of travel, the unlooked-for adventure, the frequent encounter with delightful and helpful people. But we earn our perquisites with obligations. Like all professions, ours has its code of manners and ethics, the heart of which is the proposition that we are working together for the benefit of society, not for private aggrandizement. Scientists and technicians may have their patents, but in humane learning all knowledge is in the public domain. To be sure, there are legitimate property rights which must be respected.[3] Various libraries, moreover, have their own regulations about the use of unpublished documents in their possession. But there is no room in scholarship for the person who, having discovered or gained access to a body of documents or other as yet undistributed information, claims squatter's rights. Although no professional statute governs the matter, it is generally agreed that the possessor is entitled to exclusive rights to the use of his material only so long as he is actively working toward publication. That much can freely be conceded to him as the fortunate or ingenious discoverer. But if he simply sits on his claim indefinitely, meanwhile refusing to

---

3. Every trade publisher has his house policy regarding the amount of material that may be quoted without payment from books he controls. The American university presses, however, have adopted a uniform, and liberal, policy in respect to quotations from their books; see *PMLA*, 77 (September, 1962), iv–v.

let any other, more energetic, scholar mine it, he is contraven-
ing the very spirit of scholarship.

This plea is not as altruistic as it might seem. The same
treasury of wisdom which deplores a dog's growling over his
bone also urges one to cast his bread upon the waters, and the
Golden Rule is apropos here, too. Put bluntly, the idea is this:
He that cooperates, gets cooperated with. For every close-
fisted researcher, happily, there are a hundred others who
readily share what they have with whoever needs it. The long
lists of acknowledgments found in many books are proof
enough of most scholars' generosity in providing extra information and in reading other people's manuscripts with an expert
eye for errors of fact or interpretation. All of us, even the
most learned, repeatedly need the help not only of our fellow-
specialists but of colleagues in areas far removed from our own.
Thus, two principles emerge. First, let others know what you
are working on. Don't worry about boring them; if you are
genuinely excited, your excitement is bound to be contagious.
Time after time, as a result, you'll receive valuable tips: "Have
you seen this article in the new *Speculum?* I know you don't
usually expect anything related to your book to turn up there,
but . . ." or, "I was thinking over what you were talking about
the other day at lunch, and I seem to remember that in the Berg
Collection . . ." The second principle is corollary to the first:
Keep up with what other people are doing, not only in your
own field but in others as well. Maintain the same interest in
their research that you hope they have in yours. If you run
across something that might have escaped their attention, drop
them a note. If they already possess the information, no harm
done; if it's new to them, they will be grateful.[4]

Our profession has no room for intemperate criticism of
any kind, least of all in print. Differences of opinion there will
always be, and scholarly competence not being a gift distributed equally among all practitioners, lapses of judgment

4. For an interesting example of informal scholarly collaboration, "the
coöperative pursuit and recapture of an escaped Coleridge 'sonnet' of 72
lines," see David V. Erdman, "Lost Poem Found," *BNYPL*, 55 (1961),
249–68. Even though no copy of the London newspaper in which the
poem appeared is known to exist, the various clues contributed by five
researchers resulted in locating its printed text.

and imperfections of knowledge will sometimes call for comment. Otherwise literary study would stagnate, complacent in its intellectual lethargy and spotted with uncorrected errors. But the necessary process of debate and correction can, and should, be conducted with dignity and courtesy. Name-calling, personalities, aspersions on one's professional ability, and similar below-the-belt tactics are not to be condoned. Controversial points can be made, effectively and adequately, without betraying the ancient association of scholarship with civility.[5]

Thus our profession has ethical standards which, while unwritten, are as binding as the Hippocratic Oath and the Bar Association's canons. They are sustained by the desirability of fair play, self-respect, and professional morale. But these are obligations which relate primarily to ourselves, and an even more pressing one is to the society which—however reluctantly, insufficiently, and bemusedly—supports us in our mysterious pursuits. In the midst of a culture that is often said to be more determinedly materialistic and anti-intellectual than any other in history (though our scholarly insistence on seeing our age in historical perspective may persuade us to query the pervasive assumption), we sometimes are tempted to think of ourselves as parasites. In our more discouraged moods, we may share the belief, so prevalent in the world outside, that our achievements have an unreal quality, or, if they are real, at least they are futile: that they add nothing to the sum of human

5. A notorious display of bad manners is found in the editorial material of Randolph Hughes's edition of Swinburne's *Lesbia Brandon* (1952) and Hughes's letters to the *TLS* beginning with the issue of October 17, 1952, p. 677. Cecil Y. Lang's reply (*TLS*, October 31, 1952, p. 716) is a model of restraint. The chief occasion for the utterance of critical strictures on somebody else's work is, of course, a scholarly review. For a representative list, see Exercise x.3 (pages 297–98). The caustic wit A. E. Housman used against other editors of classical authors (see *A. E. Housman: Selcted Prose*, ed. John Carter [Cambridge, 1961]) can be relished by all of us, since we luckily are not among the number whose incompetence he excoriated. (Furthermore, much can be learned from Housman's exposition of the highest ideals of textual criticism.) But the furious tone of these prefaces, reviews, and "adversaria"—the Shropshire lad's *Dunciad*—would hardly be accpetable in present-day scholarly controversy. It is perhaps noteworthy that the sour polemics of Dr. and Mrs. F. R. Leavis (see, for example, their *Dickens: The Novelist* [1970]) were seldom returned in kind by their adversaries, sore though the temptation may have been.

wisdom or happiness. One can understand why the myth persists. "The world outside": it immediately recalls the hoary cliché of the ivory tower. Nobody in our profession has any reason to suspect that his habitat is that fabled, remote "Palace of Art" which the dutiful young Tennyson so regretfully abandoned. The noise of rush-hour traffic and jet planes, those ample symbols of a world that is too much with us, penetrates all too easily into our library studies.

Yet if we are unappreciated and undervalued, the fault is partly ours. We gladly learn, but outside the classroom we are curiously uninterested in teaching. Like many modern critics, scholars have developed the habit of talking only to each other, neglecting the broader audience of educated laymen. Perhaps the sustained indifference of the world has driven us to do so, but regardless of the provocation, we have much to answer for if we accept the notion that we are doomed to be forever talking to a virtually empty house. In the profession there is a pernicious snobbery which demotes the scholar who seeks a wider public to the status of "popularizer"—ugly word. It is true that many sins have been committed against scholarly ideals in the name of popularization. Not only the fastidious but the comparatively tolerant are too often repelled by the books and magazine articles that seek to reduce the substance of literary history, biography, and criticism to the assumed intellectual level of the populace. For this uninformed and frequently sensationalized journalism posing as learning, the correct word (another ugly one) is "vulgarization." Although to popularize may mean to vulgarize, it need not, and it should not. When scholars of distinction review books in the leading weeklies, they may write for the lay reader, but they do not condescend; they may simplify, but they do not misrepresent.

It is our responsibility to seize every opportunity (and to make such opportunities where they do not exist) to communicate to the lay audience the best that today is known and thought about literature. One can, without the slightest sacrifice of professional integrity, emulate Marchette Chute, who at her desk in the New York Public Library synthesized tons of learned articles and monographs into readable, and respected, lives of Chaucer, Shakespeare, and Jonson. And it is in this shockingly neglected activity of informing the wider public that scholars can find what may be their most tangible satisfaction.[5]

For teaching takes more than one form, and if we accept our obligation to share our constantly improving knowledge and perceptions with the non-specialists who populate our class-rooms, we have a similar responsibility to those outside. Few professional students of literature would deny that such an obligation exists, but among those who earn their bread in the classroom and eat their cake in the library, there is a persistent, though seldom fully articulated, uneasiness that teaching and scholarship cannot be accommodated in a single life. In one way, they are right, for teaching and its ancillary tasks consume much time and brain-power that we, in our vanity and impatience, are sure could be used to better advantage in research. But the conflict between scholarship and teaching is only superficial, and the bond much stronger. They are simply two phases of one high calling: as a scholar, one advances learning, and when he teaches—or publishes—he shares it with society. Learning without teaching is sterile, and teaching without learning is merely a way of passing time. The true scholar finds that the two are, in fact, inseparable; and his life necessarily has room for both.

Anti-Epigraphs

Suche faultes as have paste in Printyng, as ther in dede bee many, and everywhere aboundante, so of thy courtesie excuse us, whether they bee but letters, whole wordes, or otherwise, and as the sense shall leade thee, so amende what so thou findeste, or lackyng, or superfluous, assuryng thyself that it sometymes paste us in more perfecte wise than thou in these receivest them.

—T. Fortescue's translation of P. Mexia, *The Foreste* (1571), quoted by H. S. Bennett, *English Books & Readers 1558 to 1603* (Cambridge, 1965), pp. 283–84.

* * *

5. See Howard Mumford Jones, "The Social Responsibility of Scholar-ship," *PMLA*, 64 (1949), Supplement, Part 2, pp. 37–44, and R. J. Kauff-man, "The Academy: Its Covenant and Dream," *American Scholar*, 36 (1967), 381–92.

More errors have crept in than I could have wished. In some cases, in deference to some accepted authority, I have altered names and dates and other particulars which I had in my notes, and have found when too late that my original note was right and that my trusted guide was wrong. In other cases the mistakes are slips or oversights. In dealing with such a multitude of particulars, and with entries in many languages, it is difficult to avoid inaccuracy. The bibliography has been written on the margins and backs of a long series of proof sheets, so that occasionally some things have got out of joint and transcription has been at fault. What has been done I have done myself without assistance of any kind.

—David Murray, *Museums: Their History and Their Use* (Glasgow, 1904), I, xii.

* * *

. . . These kind friends—by researches through old newspapers and periodicals—unearthed correct dates for many of the earlier letters of E. D. to his brother John Dowden, which were either undated or bore dates which proved to be astray—often by several years. The erroneous figures were due to the fact that at a later period the Bishop of Edinburgh [John Dowden] wrote, from imperfect recollection, conjectural dates on the letters. In arranging the MS. for the printers we, the Editors, accepted unquestioned the dates thus written on these letters, and thereby determined their sequence.

With the correction of the errors in dates, came of course a disturbance of the order as previously arranged. But it was not possible to attempt a redistribution, the book being far advanced through the press when the discovery was made of what was amiss.

We can only ask the readers' indulgence, whenever they find themselves obliged to trace the sequence up and down through scattered pages.

A few other misplacements have occurred in consequence of our making, at the eleventh hour, an entire change in the structure of our book.

Yielding to the wise advice of our publisher, we adopted then the plan of chronological order, instead of that at first chosen—the grouping of all letters under the names respectively of each correspondent, regarding chronology only within each group.

In making this alteration, with the haste required, it chanced that some pages escaped their rightful sequence, and the mishap was not perceived until too late to remedy it.

These defects are obvious—and—regrettable.
> —Edward Dowden's widow and daughter, in *Letters of Edward Dowden* (London, 1914), Editors' Note.

* * *

I have not thought it necessary to put in asterisks on the few occasions when I have either omitted words or phrases in a paragraph [of quoted matter], or placed together sentences from different letters relating to the same subject.
> —Lady Anne Hill, *Trelawny's Strange Relations* (Stanford Dingley, 1956), Foreword.

For Further Reading

~~~~~~

THE JUSTIFICATION OF LITERARY SCHOLARSHIP
AND HUMANISTIC LEARNING

A selected list, chronologically arranged to trace the history of the
apologia from the heyday of "the new criticism" in the 1940's and
'50's to the briefer one of "the new left" in the late 1960's. To the
extent that many of these essays and lectures were occasional
pieces, designed to defend the citadel from whatever attack was
being mounted at the moment, they sometimes strike one as dated.
But the grounds upon which the relevance of research to criticism
and the importance of humane learning to society have been justified have remained essentially unchanged across the years.

Bush, Douglas. "Scholars, Critics, and Readers." *Virginia Quarterly
    Review*, 22 (1946), 242–50.
Tillyard, E. M. W. "Research in the Humanities." *Yale Review*, 38
    (1949), 689–97. (Expanded in his *Essays Literary & Educational*
    [London, 1962], pp. 192–203.)
Sherburn, George. "Words That Intimidate." *PMLA*, 65 (1950),
    3–12.
Trilling, Lionel. "The Sense of the Past." *The Liberal Imagination*
    (New York, 1950), pp. 181–97.

Woodhouse, A. S. P. "The Historical Criticism of Milton." *PMLA*, 66 (1951), 1033–44. (Cf. reply by Cleanth Brooks, "Milton and Critical Re-estimates," *ibid.*, pp. 1045–54.)

Pargellis, Stanley. "Double or Quits." *PMLA*, 67 (1952), 71–77.

Baugh, Albert C. "Justification by Works." *PMLA*, 68 (1953), 3–17.

Oates, Whitney J. "Philosophia Regina." *PMLA*, 73 (1958), 1–5.

Jones, Howard Mumford. *One Great Society*. New York, 1959.

Whalley, George. "Scholarship and Criticism." *UTQ*, 29 (1959), 33–45.

Bush, Douglas. "Literary Scholarship and Criticism." *Liberal Education*, 47 (1961), 207–28.

Nicolson, Marjorie Hope. "A Generous Education." *PMLA*, 79 (1964), 3–12.

Bishop, Morris. "Research and Reward." *PMLA*, 80 (1965), 3–8.

Black, Max, ed. *The Morality of Scholarship*. Ithaca, N.Y., 1967.

Daedalus, 99, No. 2 (Spring, 1970): Symposium on *Theory in Humanistic Studies*.

Hirsch, E. D., Jr. "Value and Knowledge in the Humanities." *In Search of Literary Theory*, ed. Morton W. Bloomfield. Ithaca, N.Y., 1972, pp. 57–72.

Leavis, F. R. *The Living Principle: "English" as a Discipline of Thought*. New York, 1975.

Brooks, Cleanth. "The Present State of Literary Scholarship." *South Atlantic Bulletin*, 44 (1979), 49–56.

The Humanities in American Life: Report of the Commission on the Humanities. Berkeley, 1980.

CULTIVATING AND APPLYING THE CRITICAL SPIRIT

Among the numerous treatises on the critical examination of evidence and allied matters are:

Barzun, Jacques, and Henry F. Graff. *The Modern Researcher*. 3rd ed., New York, 1977.
> Full of excellent practical advice. Part Two has useful chapters on the critical spirit in research; see especially Chapter 4 ("Finding the Facts") and Chapter 5 ("Verification").

Elton, G. R. *The Practice of History*. New York, 1967.
> A skillfully written description of the spirit of the true historian —a combination of hard thinking, skepticism, and imagination— and of the intellectual rewards of the craft.

Nevins, Allan. *The Gateway to History*. Boston, 1938.
  Designed for the general reader; full of good examples. There are a few misstatements.
A small selection of books, chapters, and articles which illustrate some of the points made in Chapter Two:

Adams, Percy G. *Travelers and Travel Liars, 1660–1800*. Berkeley and Los Angeles, 1962.
  On fraudulent travel narratives set in eighteenth-century America; a good demonstration of the methods used to expose literary fakery.
Adams, Ramon F. *Burs* [sic] *Under the Saddle: A Second Look at Books and Histories of the West*. Norman, Okla., 1964.
  A large bibliographical catalogue in which 424 books about the Old West are analyzed for their rich assay of misinformation and sheer invention.
Blanck, Jacob. "A Calendar of Bibliographical Difficulties." *PBSA*, 49 (1955), 1–18.
  On some of the anomalies and perplexities the author encountered in compiling his *Bibliography of American Literature;* replete with examples and written with a light touch.
Cross, Wilbur L. *The History of Henry Fielding*. 3 vols. New Haven, 1918.
  See III, 140–50: a dissection of the anecdotes (mostly unauthentic) contained in early biographies of Fielding. Additional materials in Frederic T. Blanchard, *Fielding the Novelist: A Study in Historical Criticism* (New Haven, 1926), *passim:* a noteworthy case history of biographical misinterpretation.
Fruman, Norman. *Coleridge, the Damaged Archangel*. New York, 1971.
  A devastating attack upon the poet as a compulsive and calculating plagiarist, in the form of a large-scale critical revaluation and interpretation of evidence, much of which was long available to scholars who failed to recognize its significance. Fruman possibly overstates his case against the received image of Coleridge as "the da Vinci of literature," but his analytic method should be studied by every aspiring scholar.
Furnas, J. C. *Voyage to Windward: The Life of Robert Louis Stevenson*. New York, 1951.
  Appendix (pp. 456–71) has much material on the growth of the Stevenson myth. See also G. Miallon, "La critique Stevensonienne du centenaire (13 Novembre 1950)," *Études anglaises*, 7 (1954), 165–84.

Levin, David. "The Hazing of Cotton Mather: The Creation of a Biographical Personality." *In Defense of Historical Literature* (New York, 1967), Chapter 2.
A case history of modern biographical interpretation and assertion which far exceeds the documentary facts. See also the next chapter, on Franklin's *Autobiography*.

Lounsbury, Thomas R. *Studies in Chaucer*. 3 vols. New York, 1892.
See Volume I, Chapters 1 and 2: a peppery, though perhaps a shade overindignant, narrative of the manifold myths and corruptions that flourished in Chaucer biography until a century ago.

Lovell, Ernest J., Jr. *His Very Self and Voice: Collected Conversations of Lord Byron*. New York, 1954.
The Introduction contains an excellent discussion of the credibility of witnesses, as illustrated from the scores of books and articles that contemporaries wrote about Byron.

Nowell-Smith, Simon. *The Legend of the Master*. London, 1948.
The Introduction is an absorbing account of the development of the "legend" of Henry James.

Schoenbaum, S. *Shakespeare's Lives*. Oxford, 1970.
A massive but highly readable narrative of the way in which many biographers, sane and insane, have elaborated the few grains of solid information about Shakespeare the man into imposing, usually fragile structures of speculation and mere myth.

Sutherland, James R. "The Progress of Error: Mrs. Centlivre and the Biographers." *RES*, 18 (1942), 167–82.
The title is sufficiently descriptive.

Viljoen, Helen Gill. *Ruskin's Scottish Heritage: A Prelude*. Urbana, Ill., 1956.
The Introduction, in addition to describing the destruction, withholding, and dispersal of Ruskin's papers, reveals the wholesale undependability of E. T. Cook and Alexander Wedderburn as Ruskin's editors and biographers.

Weber, Carl J. "The 'Discovery' of FitzGerald's *Rubáiyát*." *Library Chronicle of the University of Texas*, 7 (1963), 3–11.
Was it Rossetti or Swinburne whose discovery of a copy of the *Rubáiyát* in a bookseller's cheap box led to the poem's fame? Neither, as an examination of the old story and the invocation of other, neglected evidence demonstrates.

White, Newman I., Frederick L. Jones, and Kenneth N. Cameron. *An Examination of the Shelley Legend*. Philadelphia, 1951.
Reprints three long reviews of R. M. Smith et al., *The Shelley*

Legend (1945): a demonstration of the many ways in which evidence, assumptions, and conclusions are subjected to critical scrutiny.

Wilson, John Harold. *The Court Wits of the Restoration*. Princeton, 1948.

See especially "The Wits in Private Life" (pp. 25-46): a chapter rich in examples of how spicy facts have been embellished into scandalous fiction.

Winks, Robin W., ed. *The Historian as Detective: Essays on Evidence*. New York, 1968.

A lively anthology of excerpts from historical works and biographies illustrating the application of the rules of evidence, with a running accompaniment of references to detective stories involving the same points.

THE SEVERAL BRANCHES OF SCHOLARSHIP

General:

Beaurline, Lester A., ed. *A Mirror for Modern Scholars: Essays in Methods of Research in Literature*. New York, 1966.

A collection of exemplary and in some instances "classic" articles in the various fields of literary scholarship.

Daiches, David. *English Literature*. Englewood Cliffs, N.J., 1964.

A survey of the several major types of literary investigation and of trends in the early 1960's. The latter account is, of course, somewhat dated, but it describes the immediate antecedents of present-day interests and methods. See also Willard Thorp, "The Literary Scholar as Chameleon," in *Literary Views: Critical and Historical Essays,* ed. Carroll Camden (Chicago, 1964), pp. 159-73.

Morize, André. *Problems and Methods of Literary History*. Boston, 1922.

Still not obsolete. Contains valuable chapters on the preparation of an edition, source study, problems of authorship and attribution, reputation and influence, and the history of ideas and manners. The many examples are drawn almost exclusively from French literature.

New Literary History: A Journal of Theory and Interpretation (1969-   ).

Important high-level discussions of new trends in literary study.

Each issue is devoted to a single theme; e.g., periodization, literary and art history, ideology and literature.

Thorpe, James, ed. *The Aims and Methods of Scholarship in Modern Languages and Literatures*. 2nd ed. New York, 1970.
Discussions of basic problems and opportunities awaiting scholars in four fields: linguistics, textual criticism, literary history, and literary criticism.

—— *Relations of Literary Study: Essays on Interdisciplinary Contributions*. 2nd ed. New York, 1970.
Brief essays by several authorities on the literary relations of myth, biography, psychology, sociology, religion, and music.

Wellek, René, and Alvaro Ribeiro, eds. *Evidence in Literary Scholarship: Essays in Memory of James Marshall Osborn*. Oxford, 1979.
Twenty-three essays exemplifying a wide variety of present-day scholarly procedures. Wellek's introduction is an interesting account of the career of a wealthy former banker who devoted most of his life and fortune to scholarly research.

Zitner, Sheldon P., ed. *The Practice of Modern Literary Scholarship*. Glenview, Ill., 1966.
An anthology similar to Beaurline's, but with wider scope.

On analytical bibliography and the editing of texts:

Baird, John D., ed. *Editing Texts of the Romantic Period*. Toronto, 1972.
Essays on the editing of Shelley and of Coleridge's notebooks and marginalia, and on the annotation of Wordsworth.

Bentley, G. E., Jr., ed. *Editing Eighteenth Century Novels*. Toronto, 1975.
Discussions of editorial problems presented by Richardson's *Clarissa Harlowe* and by the new scholarly editions of Fielding, Smollett, and Sterne.

Bowers, Fredson. *Textual and Literary Criticism*. Cambridge, 1959.
Chapter I, to which the treatment of the subject in the present book is heavily indebted, is an eloquent argument for the importance of textual criticism in literary studies; Chapter II shows how critical examination of the manuscripts throws light on the growth and revision of poems.

Brack, O M Jr., and Warner Barnes, eds. *Bibliography and Textual Criticism: English and American Literature 1700 to the Present*. Chicago, 1969.
A collection of seventeen representative and influential articles illustrating various modern techniques. There is a useful bibliography.

Domville, Eric W., ed. *Editing British and American Literature, 1880–1920.* New York, 1976.
Essays on editing Hopkins, Robert Bridges, Henry James, Yeats, D. H. Lawrence, and Frank Norris.
Gaskell, Philip. *From Writer to Reader: Studies in Editorial Method.* Oxford, 1978.
Discussions of editorial difficulties presented by the progression of twelve authors' works from manuscript through various printed editions. The writers considered range from Milton to Tom Stoppard; the editorial principle growing out of the issues examined is that "the editor should not base his work on *any* predetermined role or theory."
Gottesman, Ronald, and Scott Bennett, eds. *Art and Error: Modern Textual Editing.* Bloomington, Ind., 1970.
Covers the same field as Brack and Barnes, but with an overlap of only three items.
Halpenny, Francess G., ed. *Editing Twentieth Century Texts.* Toronto, 1972.
Includes discussions of problems and practices involved in editing Faulkner, F. Scott Fitzgerald, and Virginia Woolf's *The Waves.*
Kenner, Hugh. "The Computerized *Ulysses.*" *Harper's Magazine,* 260 (April 1980), 89–95.
A lively description of the complexities of the book's textual history and the harnessing of Computer-Konstanz TR–440 to solve them.
Keynes, Geoffrey. "Religio Bibliographici." *The Library,* 5th series, 8 (1953), 63–76.
A leisurely, anecdotal apologia for an approach to bibliography somewhat more old-fashioned and (says Keynes) more humane than that of "the school of Professor Bowers."
Laird, J. T. *The Shaping of "Tess of the D'Urbervilles."* Oxford, 1975.
Documents, from the manuscript and the various printed editions, the extensive revisions of the novel produced over nearly a quarter-century. Disposes of many half-truths and outright errors, most of which resulted from Hardy's own misleading statements.
Lancashire, Anne, ed. *Editing Renaissance Dramatic Texts: English, Italian, and Spanish.* New York, 1976.
Essays describing the present state of textual scholarship on Renaissance dramatic works (including Shakespeare's) and suggesting areas of future research. Particularly important is the consideration of the work of earlier scholars, "the burden of the past."

MacKenzie, Norman H. "On Editing Gerard Manley Hopkins."
Queen's Quarterly, 78 (1971), 487–502.
  One of the best articles of its kind. Editing Hopkins' poems
  requires "the logic of a detective, the patience of a medieval
  monk, . . . the sensitivity of an artist," the laboratory at Scotland Yard, and a command of Victorian books on philology and
  the nature of lightning.

Manly, John M., and Edith Rickert. *The Text of the Canterbury
Tales*. 8 vols. Chicago, 1940.
  I, 1–28: a full description of the task of assembling and relating
  the many MSS of the *Canterbury Tales*.

Millgate, Jane, ed. *Editing Nineteenth Century Fiction*. New York,
1978.
  Textual problems in the novels of Dickens and Thackeray and the
  aesthetic effects of authorial excisions in works of Hawthorne,
  Twain, and Stephen Crane.

Potter, George R., and John Butt. *Editing Donne and Pope*. Los
Angeles, [1953].
  Two lectures which clearly discuss some of the decisions that
  must be made by editors of seventeenth- and eighteenth-century
  literary texts.

Rigg, A. G., ed. *Editing Medieval Texts: English, French, and Latin
Written in England*. New York, 1977.
  Discussion of special procedures required in editing Old and Mid-
  dle English, Anglo-Norman, and Medieval Latin texts.

Robson, John M., ed. *Editing Nineteenth Century Texts*. Toronto,
1967.
  See especially C. R. Sanders on editing the Carlyle letters and
  Robson on the collected edition of John Stuart Mill.

Schoeck, R. J., ed. *Editing Sixteenth Century Texts*. Toronto, 1966.
  Includes discussion of English dramatic texts, translations of Erasmus, and Tudor editions of Thomas More.

Smith, D. I. B., ed. *Editing Eighteenth-Century Texts*. Toronto,
1968.
  Informative talks on, among other topics, editing the letters and
  journals of Fanny Burney, textual problems in Blake, and the
  Yale Edition of Dr. Johnson's works.

——— *Editing Seventeenth Century Prose*. Toronto, 1972.
  On the editing of a wide variety of literary documents, including Lancelot Andrewes' sermons, Milton's *De Doctrina Chris-
  tiana*, Marvell's prose, and Jacobean and Restoration plays.

Stokes, Roy, ed. *Esdaile's Manual of Bibliography*. 4th ed. London,
1967.

A simplified alternative to Gaskell's *New Introduction to Bibliography*, which, however, is slightly more up to date.

Thorpe, James. *Principles of Textual Criticism*. San Marino, Calif., 1972.

A somewhat more moderate exposition of the uses of textual criticism than Bowers'. Especially noteworthy: the chapter on "The Aesthetics of Textual Criticism."

—— and Claude M. Simpson, Jr. *The Task of the Editor*. Los Angeles, 1969.

Simpson's lecture is a lively and informative description of some of the problems confronting the editor of Hawthorne's *American Notebooks*.

Wilson, F. P. *Shakespeare and the New Bibliography*. Revised by Helen Gardner. Oxford, 1970.

A readable and authoritative summary of the contributions "the new bibliography" has made toward the establishment of Shakespeare's text.

On questions of authorship:

Erdman, David V., and Ephim G. Fogel, eds. *Evidence for Authorship: Essays on Problems of Attribution*. Ithaca, N.Y., 1966.

A large collection of scholarly articles discussing and illustrating the usefulness and pitfalls of applying internal and external evidence to questions of authorship. The bibliography lists many more such treatments.

Schoenbaum, S. *Internal Evidence and Elizabethan Dramatic Authorship: An Essay in Literary History and Method*. Evanston, Ill., 1966.

A sensible, often witty account of what internal evidence can and cannot contribute to determining the true authorship of anonymous, multi-authored, and falsely attributed plays.

Vieth, David M. *Attribution in Restoration Poetry: A Study of Rochester's "Poems" of 1680*. New Haven, 1963.

Applies the various tools of evidence to "the many problems of the Rochester text and canon."

On source study:

Dent, R. W. *John Webster's Borrowing*. Berkeley and Los Angeles, 1960.

The Introduction, on the problems posed by the "most impressive borrower" of the Elizabethan age, contains many sound observations applicable to all source study.

Primeau, Ronald, ed. *Influx: Essays on Literary Influence*. Port Washington, N.Y., 1977.

Ten essays and a selected bibliography illustrating current thought on the nature of literary influence. Particularly stimulating sections consider intellectual history and tradition as essentially revisionist readings or misreadings, and the role of the reader as a shaper of his own influences.

Stallman, R. W. "The Scholar's Net: Literary Sources." *College English*, 17 (1955), 20–27.

A reply to the strictures of Kenneth Muir and F. W. Bateson in *Essays in Criticism*, 4 (1954), 432–40. For Bateson's rejoinder, see the same volume of *College English*, pp. 131–35.

On the history of ideas:

Crane, Ronald S. "Philosophy, Literature, and the History of Ideas." *The Idea of the Humanities* (Chicago, 1967), I, 173–87.

Lovejoy, Arthur O. *Essays in the History of Ideas*. Baltimore, 1948. See especially Essay I: "The Historiography of Ideas."

―――― "Reflections on the History of Ideas." *Journal of the History of Ideas*, 1 (1940), 3–23.

Mazzeo, Joseph Anthony. "Some Interpretations of the History of Ideas." *Ibid.*, 33 (1972), 379–94.

Nicolson, Marjorie. "The History of Literature and the History of Thought." *English Institute Annual 1939* (New York, 1940), pp. 56–89.

Robertson, D. W., Jr. "Historical Criticism." *English Institute Annual 1950* (New York, 1951), pp. 3–31.

FOR RELAXING READING

Some fairly recent books, or portions thereof, which in their various ways reflect the excitement, comedy, exasperation, and rewards of literary scholarship and book collecting—addenda, in effect, to the longer list of such writings contained in the Bibliographical Notes to *The Scholar Adventurers*. Several additional items bear on the personal and pre-professional concerns of graduate students.

Alpers, Antony. "Biography—The 'Scarlet Experiment.'" *TLS*, March 28, 1980, pp. 369–70.

Episodes incidental to the revision and expansion of the author's biography of Katherine Mansfield.

Arnheim, Rudolf, et al. *Poets at Work*. New York, 1948.

The Introduction, by Charles D. Abbott, narrates some episodes associated with the building of the collection of modern poets' MSS at the Lockwood Memorial Library, SUNY at Buffalo.

Baring-Gould, William S., ed. *The Annotated Sherlock Holmes.* 2 vols. New York, 1967.

". . . a beautifully presented, and never tedious, exercise in parody of scholasticism. No man who is incapable of seeing the ludicrousness of the excess should be allowed to edit, or write for, a 'serious' literary journal." (*The Year's Work in English Studies,* 49 [1968], 320.)

Bevington, Helen. *A Book and a Love Affair.* New York, 1968.

On being the wife of a graduate student in English at Columbia University, especially during the Great Depression. (The author has also published several volumes of light verse with literary subjects.)

Buchanan, David. *The Treasure of Auchinleck: The Story of the Boswell Papers.* New York, 1974.

An engaging and authoritative narrative beginning with Boswell's ambiguous will and including such matters as the momentous consequences of an erroneous footnote, the five-year conspiracy of silence on the materials at Fettercairn House, three decades of legal maneuverings, in-fighting among scholars and publishers, and finally the arrival of the whole collection at Yale.

Clifford, James L. *From Puzzles to Portraits: Problems of a Literary Biographer.* Chapel Hill, N.C., 1970.

Part One, "Finding the Evidence," abounds in anecdotes of the author's search for material on Mrs. Thrale and Dr. Johnson; Part Two, "Putting the Pieces Together," discusses questions of biographical evidence and its presentation. See also Clifford's "Some Problems of Johnson's Obscure Middle Years" in *Johnson, Boswell, and Their Circle: Essays Presented to Lawrence Fitzroy Powell in Honour of His Eighty-Fourth Birthday* (Oxford, 1965), pp. 99–110.

Coburn, Kathleen. *In Pursuit of Coleridge.* Oxford, 1978.

Charmingly details the author's lifelong search for Coleridge material, particularly marginalia and notebooks.

Foxon, David F. *Thomas J. Wise and the Pre-Restoration Drama: A Study in Theft and Sophistication.* London, 1959. (Supplement to the Bibliographical Society's Publications, No. 19.)

Startling evidence of the scope of Wise's criminal activities, this time as a pillager of books in the British Museum.

Holroyd, Michael. "Speaking of Books: Eminent Biographer." *New York Times Book Review,* April 7, 1968.

The author's adventures in gathering material for his two-volume life of Lytton Strachey.

Lane, Margaret. "The Ghost of Beatrix Potter" and "Beatrix Potter: the Missing Years." *Purely for Pleasure* (New York, 1967), pp. 279–99.

Two formidable obstacles to the writing of biography: an uncooperative subject and then her equally obstructive widower. (For the story of how an engineer cracked Beatrix Potter's cipher, see Leslie Linder's edition of *The Journal of Beatrix Potter 1881–1897* [London, 1966].)

Lewis, Roy Harley. *Antiquarian Books: An Insider's Account.* London, 1978.

Broad survey of the field of antiquarian book collecting, written largely "to interest and to amuse." Relates a variety of incidents which portray the "dealer in his various roles of detective, scholar, agent, psychologist, and fortune-teller."

Lewis, Wilmarth S. *Collector's Progress.* New York, 1951.

The earlier phase of Lewis' indefatigable quest for anything and everything relating to Horace Walpole. More is told in Lewis' autobiography, *One Man's Education* (New York, 1967). See also Israel Shenker, "Can he be the real Walpole or is he Wilmarth Lewis?" *Smithsonian Magazine*, 10 (May 1979), 102–108.

Lodge, David. *The British Museum Is Falling Down.* New York, 1967.

A moderately bawdy comic novel, with authentic Reading Room atmosphere; the anti-hero and his cronies are trying, not very hard, to write their dissertations.

Matthews, William. *British Diaries.* Berkeley and Los Angeles, 1950. See the Preface: a genial review of the pleasures of bibliographical research.

Munby, A. N. L. *Portrait of an Obsession: The Life of Sir Thomas Phillipps, the World's Greatest Book Collector,* adapted by Nicolas Barker. London, 1967.

Phillipps was a megalomaniac of appalling character and behavior. The book is based on Munby's more detailed *Phillipps Studies* (5 vols., Cambridge, 1951–60).

Murray, K. M. Elizabeth. *Caught in the Web of Words: James A. H. Murray and the Oxford English Dictionary.* New Haven, 1977.

Based on family and business correspondence, an account, by Murray's granddaughter, of his heroic thirty-eight-year struggle to produce the *OED*.

"O'Toole, Simon." *Confessions of an American Scholar.* Minneapolis, [1970].

A bilious autobiography which confirms the clichés cherished by generations of graduate students. Readable and plausibly "factual," but to be treated with the reserve appropriate to exposés based on generalizations from individual cases.

Plumb, J. H. "Speaking of Books: Trials of a Biographer." *New York Times Book Review*, March 13, 1966.

A Cambridge historian in pursuit of the papers of eighteenth-century statesmen copes with the eccentricities of elderly peers and the chill of their mansions.

Powell, Lawrence Clark. *Bookman's Progress: The Selected Writings of Lawrence Clark Powell*, ed. William Targ. Los Angeles, 1968.

A "sampler" of Powell's voluminous writings on favorite books and other subjects. Henry Miller called him, in awe, "a librarian who reads books"; as first dean of the UCLA Library School, he implemented his long-standing conviction that the first requisite for librarians is devotion to books rather than technical expertise.

Reid, B. L. *The Man from New York: John Quinn and His Friends.* New York, 1968.

Prize-winning biography of a New York lawyer who collected the MSS and first editions of numerous modern writers, among them Eliot and Joyce, and who often subsidized them as well.

Robbins, Rossell Hope. "Mirth in Manuscripts." *Essays and Studies* (English Association), n.s. 21 (1968), 1–28.

The pleasure and profit to be had from studying medieval manuscripts, including the acquisition of many kinds of curious information.

Rollins, Hyder E., and Stephen M. Parrish. *Keats and the Bostonians.* Cambridge, Mass., 1951.

The story of Tantalus re-enacted in twentieth-century Boston: the redoubtable Amy Lowell at the sadistic mercy of a Keats collector who told her what he had but refused to let her see his prizes.

Sadleir, Michael. *XIX Century Fiction: A Bibliographical Record Based on His Own Collection.* 2 vols. Cambridge, 1951.

"Passages from the Autobiography of a Bibliomaniac" (I, xi–xxvi): the frustrations and triumphs of a collector of popular Victorian literature. The collection described in these volumes is now at UCLA.

Symons, Julian. *Bland Beginning.* New York, 1949.

A detective story suggested by the career of T. J. Wise.

Wolf, Edwin, 2nd, with John F. Fleming. *Rosenbach: A Biography.* Cleveland and New York, 1960.

An ample, unexpurgated narrative of the life and transactions of America's most famous rare-book dealer, a shrewd, tireless, profane, hard-drinking, and not ungenerous Philadelphian who had a Ph.D. in English literature.

Wyatt, Will. *The Secret of the Sierra Madre: The Man Who Was B. Traven.* Garden City, N.Y., 1980.

The producer of a BBC television documentary on the mysterious "B. Traven," author of several novels on the exploitation of workers in exotic locales, describes how his searches in the archives of two continents and interviews with witnesses from Mexico to Poland led to the probable identification of the man and a reconstruction of his restless, rootless life.

Young, Philip. "Author and Critic: A Rather Long Story." *Ernest Hemingway: A Reconsideration* (University Park, Pa., 1966), pp. 1–28.

A lively, sometimes farcical tale of how Young and his publishers had to contend with Hemingway's opposition to the publication of this book, of whose thesis he disapproved.

Exercises

~~~~~~

The exercises in the following pages are intended to encourage acquaintance with the printed materials of research and to afford practical experience in collecting material, weighing evidence, reaching conclusions, and writing scholarly notes and articles. Some of the questions can be answered briefly; others can serve as subjects for term papers. Some require original investigation in primary sources, but the majority utilize, in various ways, the published results of scholarly study.

I. The Tools of the Trade

The following short-answer questions are designed to illustrate the scope and usefulness of the chief bibliographies and reference works used by literary investigators, and to provide practice in one important and constantly recurring phase of research, the establishing of small individual facts. The books containing the answers are listed in the most up-to-date bibliographical manuals for the study of English and American literature. In each instance, the answer should be accompanied by a statement of the means by which it was found, including missteps.

1. How many books did James Branch Cabell publish in this country during his lifetime? Were any of them translated into foreign languages?

2. You are interested in a minor but prolific nineteenth-century English writer for whom the entry in the *NCBEL* is decidedly inadequate. Where can you find larger lists of his books?

3. Where can one find an annual bibliography of "books, parts of books, dissertations, and articles dealing with the analysis of style"?

4. Compile a preliminary bibliography for a paper on the variety and general availability of magazines for and by women in the Restoration and eighteenth century.

5. Prepare a list of bibliographies published in the past ten years on black writers in America.

6. One way to measure the progress of some modern authors' reputations is to determine how often selections from their works have appeared in anthologies. Choose a writer in whom you are especially interested and make a list of such reprintings in, say, the past ten or twenty years.

7. Other than the information available in Harold Williams' edition of Swift's poetry, what can you discover about the Reverend Patrick Delany?

8. What well-known authors wrote under the following names?
Some-body; A Graduate of Oxford; Johnstone Smith; John Sinjohn; Derry, Derry Down; A Person of Honour; Signor Corolini

9. Make a list of articles published in the past five years dealing with the influence of French poetry (including individual poets) on English poetry, 1860–1900.

10. Identify the bibliography published in 1979 about which the following claim has been made: "This book will now be the starting point for every critic, scholar, and student who sets out to write on a work of Old English literature or on the Anglo-Saxon period in general, and for every teacher preparing a course in Old English literature."

11. What important books were published and what noteworthy public events occurred in the year of Milton's birth?

12. After it appeared in 1928, Herbert R. Mayes' *Alger: A Biography Without a Hero* was relied upon—by subsequent biographers as well as by such standard authorities as the *Dictionary of American Biography*—as a source of authentic information on the life of that popular nineteenth-century American author of rags-to-riches stories. It is now totally discredited. What, according to the author when he admitted his "fraud" in the early 1970's, was his purpose in writing it?

13. Look up synopses of a novel you know well in three standard reference sources. Are they inaccurate in any significant respect? How do they differ in emphasis? Is there any evidence of derivativeness?

14. In 1979, Samuel Beckett's *Happy Days* was performed simultaneously in London and New York. What important differences in interpretation existed between these two versions as noted by the reviewers? Did either version have Beckett's sanction?

15. Without consulting any biographies, describe the events of George Bernard Shaw's brief visit to the United States in 1933.

16. In 1847-50 a series of sensational murders in England provoked much public discussion. Make a list of at least a half-dozen periodical articles published at that time which dealt with the supposed crime wave and its social implications.

17. What is the name of a series of fifty-one reprinted autobiographies of American women? Who published it? What is its announced scope?

18. Where is the nearest complete file of *Cobbett's Political Register* (1802-36)?

19. Make a reasonably full list of newly published scientific books that would have been of interest to a member of the Royal Society in 1693.

20. Quote the entry for Hooker's *Laws of Ecclesiastical Polity* in the Stationers' Register, find its *STC* number, and, without reference to the *NUC*, locate a copy of the first edition (1593) in America.

21. Locate three or four articles which discuss rhetorical features characteristic of the critical essay.

22. Who was the only American playwright to win the Nobel Prize?

23. Have any books or articles appeared in the past ten years which have some bearing on the number and status of black servants in eighteenth-century England?

24. In the winter of 1849-50, Margaret Fuller (Ossoli), the New England critic and feminist, was working on a history of the Roman revolution which had occurred the preceding year. What happened to it?

25. What have the following in common?: laisse, virelai, sirventes, mal mariée, ensenhamen.

26. Where on the east coast of the United States is a good collection of Henry James first editions and manuscripts?

27. The British Library owns a copy of a Bulgarian abridgment (1897) of *David Copperfield*. What is its pressmark (call number)?

28. Describe, from a secondary source, the contents of Thomas Foxcroft's *Lessons of Caution to Young Sinners* (Boston, 1733). What is the library closest to your campus that possesses a copy of this book?

29. How many books were published, 1840–1900, on the archaeological excavations at Babylon, Nineveh, and Tyre?

30. How many editions of Virginia Woolf's *To the Lighthouse* were published in England down to 1960?

31. Mark Twain's *Roughing It* contains the popular long-winded anecdote "The Story of the Old Ram." What version of this story did Twain use on his lecture tours, and why?

32. In how many European countries were editions or translations of Byron's *Childe Harold* published down to 1850?

33. What are the five latest books on the contemporary American stage?

34. How many dissertations on Melville (perhaps in conjunction with other figures) have been accepted at American universities in the past five years?

35. Using at least three sources, compile a list of all books and articles published on Blake in 1979. Why is it necessary to refer to more than one source?

36. From what reference source can you get a lead to lists of books with Devonshire settings or by Devonshire authors?

37. Name "the more important texts and the standard modern works" dealing with rogues and vagabonds in the Elizabethan era.

38. What major British novelist died the same day that President John F. Kennedy was assassinated?

39. What bibliographical information exists on the first editions of books by Don Marquis, creator of Archie and Mehitabel?

40. Compile a preliminary bibliography of recent theoretical books and articles which examine the ways readers apprehend and respond to literary works.

41. In a letter written by a young Victorian girl you find a reference to a mechanical chamber organ called the Apollonicon. Write a footnote explaining what it was and where she probably saw and heard it.

42. Approximately how many versions are known of the medieval

"Debate Between the Body and the Soul"? How many manuscripts are there of what is said to be "the best-known Middle English piece," "Als I lay in a winteris nyt/ in a droukening bifore the day"? Where are they, and have they all been printed?

43. Your study of the popular reception of the novels of Raymond Chandler and Dashiell Hammett necessitates consideration of motion picture adaptations of their stories. How can you identify these films and find sufficient details about them for your needs?

44. Does the Guildhall Library in London possess a complete file of the *Mirror of Literature* (1822–47)?

45. Copy, from an authoritative modern source, the exact wording on the title page of *Every Man in His Humour* (1601).

46. Make a list of the explications so far offered of specific passages in Marvell's "The Garden."

47. At what London theaters and on what dates were Wilkie Collins' dramatizations of his novels *No Name, Armadale, The Woman in White,* and *The Moonstone* first performed?

48. To whom did Gertrude Stein refer in her famous remark, "You are all a lost generation"? In what circumstances was it uttered?

49. After reading the commentary published in an annual reference source, make a synopsis of the chief topics and issues of Chaucer scholarship in the past five years.

50. How many pre-1700 editions of Bunyan's *Grace Abounding* are known to exist?

51. How many stories by the science fiction writer Robert Silverberg have been anthologized in English language publications?

52. What are the present retail prices of the complete *NCBEL,* Baugh's *Literary History of England,* the *Concise DNB,* and the compact edition of the *Oxford English Dictionary?*

53. According to one present-day authority, what are the relative values of the biographies of Keats by Sidney Colvin, Amy Lowell, Walter J. Bate, Aileen Ward, and Robert Gittings?

54. You have found a hitherto unknown letter by Thoreau which internal evidence proves was written between 1849 and 1856. It is dated simply "Friday, May 5." What was the year?

55. Compile a list, including publishers and prices, of Margaret Atwood's works published in Canada and still in print.

56. What bibliographical aids exist for a study of the English poet Ted Hughes?

57. What is the distinction between the heresy of Molinism (Miguel de Molinos, 1627–96) and the Molinism associated with Luis de Molina (1535–1600)?

58. In what year and under what circumstances was Henry Miller's *Tropic of Cancer* permitted publication in the United States for the first time?

59. Twelve presentation copies of Mrs. Henry Wood's Victorian best-seller, *East Lynne*, were specially bound. What was the color of that binding? How was Michael Sadleir's imaginative reconstruction of the circumstances behind the choice of binding proved to be a mistake?

60. Find a descriptive and evaluative review of the criticism pertaining to Edwin Arlington Robinson published down to 1967.

61. What is the relative value of the several twentieth-century editions of the *Encyclopaedia Britannica*, and which current encyclopedias have the best reputation for accuracy?

62. Is the manuscript of James Jones's *From Here to Eternity* available for scholarly scrutiny?

63. Sometime in the 1960's a book was published in England under the title of *Search Your Soul, Eustace*. What was its American title, and what was it about?

64. The *Oxford English Dictionary* erroneously credits John Wilson Croker with the first use of the word *Conservative* as a designation for a political party (*Quarterly Review*, 1830). Has it been determined who really should have the credit?

65. You are examining a rare book which you have reason to believe was part of the library of Richard Heber (1773–1833). What identifying mark should you look for?

66. Since 1965, the appearance of previously unpublished fiction, autobiography, and letters by Bloomsbury figures has increased interest in that group. Cite at least ten recent book-length studies relating to the Bloomsbury group.

67. *Songes and Sonettes*, by Sir Thomas Wyatt, the Earl of Surrey, and others (1557), is familiarly known as "Tottel's Miscellany" because it was printed by Richard Tottel. Name four other books he printed in the same year. What was his London address?

68. What was the first full-length critical study of Langston Hughes?

69. You have written a seminar paper on Mrs. Gaskell's novel *North and South* which your instructor thinks may well be publishable. Your

citations, however, are to the Penguin edition which the class used, and scholarly practice requires that, whenever possible, a published paper cite the most reliable text. What text of the novel is best?

70. A medieval alchemical poem begins, "Here ys an erbe men call lunayrie." How many manuscript versions are known? Where are these manuscripts? Where can one find a printed text?

71. Where is the manuscript of Thomas Shadwell's play, *The Humorists?* What company first performed it? When?

72. A 1950 dissertation by Lars Åhnebrink was entitled *The Beginnings of Naturalism in American Fiction.* At what university was it accepted, and has it been published?

73. What was the association between T. S. Eliot and the *Boston Daily Evening Transcript?*

74. Books with the following titles have been written about a major English poet: *Some Graver Subject, From Shadowy Types to Truth, The Celestial Cycle, The Club of Hercules, The Harmonious Vision, Heroic Knowledge.* Who is the poet? What is the source of each title? Is each title truly appropriate to the subject of the book?

75. The manuscripts, proofs, first editions, and other primary materials relating to James Joyce are widely scattered. Where can one find a comprehensive list ("census") of Joyce collections? Is it necessary for scholars to travel to the various libraries to consult the original documents?

76. What were the nineteenth-century British and American antecedents of the modern paperback?

77. In 1770 there was printed at New York a broadside entitled *The Dying Speech of the Effigy of a Wretched Importer . . .* Whom did the effigy represent, and what was the occasion of its being burned? Where can one find a copy of the broadside?

78. Make a list of the materials published in the past three years on the mythic and folklore elements in *Beowulf.*

79. Summarize the details of the discovery of Byron and Shelley manuscripts in a locked chest deposited in a London bank in 1820 by the Reverend Scrope Berdmore Davies and not opened until 1976. List the contents of this now famous chest.

80. How was Act III, Scene i, of *Hamlet* altered for the Olivier film?

81. What is the collation of the first edition of Jack London's *The Call of the Wild?* What is the evidence for its date of publication?

82. In the text (page 73) mention was made of the manuscript of

Donne's verse letter to Lady Carey. After its rediscovery it was sold at auction. Who sold it, who bought it, what price did it bring, and has it reappeared on the market since?

83. After examining the six or eight latest issues of the *TLS*, make a list of a half-dozen distinct and important services its various editorial features supply to literary scholars.

84. At what university library can one find the James A. Healy collection of Irish literature?

85. You are studying the significance of metaphors relating to time in the work of a modern novelist and need to broaden your philosophical orientation. Find a source that discusses the various conceptions of time entertained by modern philosophers as well as by such figures as St. Augustine, St. Thomas Aquinas, Proust, and Sartre.

86. How many different productions of Dryden's *All for Love* appeared in London theaters in the eighteenth century?

87. English travelers to America in the 1840's, including Dickens, praised the working and living conditions in the textile factories at Lowell, Massachusetts. Among the amenities was a magazine, the *Lowell Offering*, written, edited, and published by the factory girls. Has any book been published about this periodical?

88. In what kind of literary work, and from what period, might an allusion to each of the following be found?

the Gorham case, the Quorn, Robert the Devil, Mohocks, Grace Darling, Anacharsis Clootz, Babu, Martin Marprelate

89. What public figures made statements to the English press on the occasion of the death of C. P. Snow in 1980?

90. Prepare a checklist of articles considering realism in American film.

91. On May 15 (25), 1696, in a letter preserved among the manuscripts at Longleat, seat of the Marquis of Bath, Sir William Trumbull paid a handsome compliment to his correspondent, the poet Matthew Prior. What was it? (And why, incidentally, is the double date given?)

92. How many of the novels of Edna Ferber are currently in print?

93. The Pierpont Morgan Library owns a manuscript of Lydgate's *Siege and Destruction of Troy*. What work is bound with it, how many leaves does the volume contain, and how many miniatures and drawings are present?

94. Limiting yourself to one source, identify the single work in which

each of the following words appears: *inaccessibleness, decays* (noun), *misappear, miswrite, divineness, dwarfishly*.

95. You need to refresh your memory concerning the essential nature of Freud's theories of sexuality, the unconscious, repression, and regression. Where can you find succinct summaries of these topics, along with a selected bibliography?

96. What single source provides a complete list of the publications of the Cambridge University Press 1700–1750?

97. It is well known that Longfellow derived some of the materials for *Hiawatha* from the ethnological writings of Henry R. Schoolcraft. Why is it highly unlikely, however, that he used Schoolcraft's *Cyclopedia Indianensis: or a General Description of the Indian Tribes of North and South America* (New York, 1842)?

98. In reviews which compare Stanley Kubrick's film of *Barry Lyndon* with Thackeray's novel, are any of the differences between the versions regarded merely as necessary results of the differences between print and film?

99. In 1969 the University of Illinois–Chicago Circle Library acquired Franklin J. Meine's collection of material on various aspects of American social history. Would it be of any value to a student of nineteenth-century American humor?

100. Compile a list of at least five articles in the past decade discussing the place of science fiction in American literature.

101. Identify:
   Le Diable Boiteux, Julius Caesar Scaliger, gongorism, Skidbladner, epicedium, Jean Crapaud, Dismas, Flavius Josephus

102. The British Museum acquired the first autograph draft of Carlyle's *Past and Present* in 1928. Of how many leaves does it consist, who presented it, and what is its number among the Additional Manuscripts?

103. What clues led investigators to discover a dozen early stories by George Gissing buried in the files of Chicago newspapers? Where were two additional ones found in 1980, and what was the clue this time?

104. In 1980 an English television comedian, Terry Jones *(Monty Python's Flying Circus)*, published a book which radically challenged the customary view of Chaucer's Knight. What was his argument, upon what kinds of evidence was it based, and how was the book received by Chaucer scholars?

105. With the aid of the appropriate reference tools, explain the Bib-

lical allusions in this passage (*Paradise Lost*, VI, 750–59):

> ...forth rush'd with whirl-wind sound
> The Chariot of Paternal Deity,
> Flashing thick flames, Wheel within Wheel, undrawn,
> Itself instinct with Spirit, but convoy'd
> By Four Cherubic shapes, four Faces each
> Had wondrous, as with Stars thir bodies all
> And Wings were set with Eyes, with Eyes the Wheels
> Of Beryl, and careering Fires between;
> Over thir heads a crystal Firmament,
> Whereon a Sapphire Throne, inlaid with pure
> Amber, and colors of the show'ry Arch.

106. Here is a list of words, found in sixteenth- and seventeenth-century English poems, whose meanings in those contexts are no longer current. Assuming that each suggested synonym fits the context, what reason is there to believe that it represents a current meaning of the italicized word at the date shown?

disease (Howard, 1557): "discomfort"
read (Spenser, 1589): "advised"
freakes (Spenser, 1590): "unpredictable tricks"
inward touch (Sidney, 1591): "true imagination"
engaged (Shakespeare, 1598): "held as hostage"
triumphs (Marlowe, 1604): "parades"
adulteries (Jonson, 1609): "adulterations"
determinate (Shakespeare, 1609): "expired"
tells (Jonson, 1616): "counts"
slack (Crashaw, 1633): "backward"
sped (Herbert, 1633): "supplied, satisfied"
approve (Donne, 1633): "put to proof, find by experience"
bestead (Milton, 1645): "help, avail"
pale (Milton, 1645): "enclosure"
quaintest (Vaughan, 1650): "most elaborate"
perspective (Vaughan, 1655): "telescope"
close (Marvell, 1681): "unite"
dishonest (Dryden, 1681): "disgraceful"

107. What does each of the following words, used by American writers, mean, and when and where was it apparently first used?

smallage (Hawthorne, 1835)
a *face* of country (Emerson, 1836)
unhandselled (Emerson, 1837)
a *Norway mile* (Poe, 1841)
a *virgin-zone* (Hawthorne, 1844)
scoriac (Poe, 1847)

Bose (Thoreau, 1854)
crook-necks (Lowell, 1867)
pungle (Twain, 1884)
Jonah's toss (Melville, 1888)
crawfished (Twain, 1895)
Vega-cura (Dreiser, 1900)
Snow Bird (Fitzgerald, 1931)

II. Bibliographical Listing and Identification

1. Two older guides to the printed works of English Renaissance authors are Lowndes's *Bibliographer's Manual of English Literature* (new ed., 1857–64) and the various volumes of "collections and notes" by W. Carew Hazlitt (1867–1903; most of these are conveniently indexed by G. J. Gray, 1893). Choose a relatively minor sixteenth- or seventeenth-century author, and using the most authoritative modern bibliographical tools, including the *STC* and Wing, establish how trustworthy and complete Lowndes's and Hazlitt's information is.

2. A similar older guide is Allibone's *Critical Dictionary of English Literature and British and American Authors* (1858–71, 1891). Select a nineteenth-century English or American author in whom you are interested, and as in the preceding exercise, determine what value, if any, Allibone has to a scholar wishing to do intensive work on that author.

3. How up to date, thorough, and accurate are the existing bibliographical guides to the writings by and about the following authors?

Sean O'Casey, Hart Crane, Katherine Anne Porter, Dylan Thomas, Wallace Stevens, Theodore Dreiser, Sherwood Anderson, Robert Frost, W. H. Auden, Robert Lowell, William Carlos Williams, John Berryman, Saul Bellow, Louis Golding, Marianne Moore, Randall Jarrell, Thomas Wolfe, Edith Wharton, Richard Wright, Iris Murdoch, Carson McCullers, Joyce Carol Oates

4. Of how many printed items does the canon of Cotton Mather consist?

5. What is the current name of the periodical begun as the *Kate Chopin Newsletter?*

6. In some anthologized versions of Joel Chandler Harris' "The Wonderful Tar-Baby Story" only half of the complete episode involving Br'er Rabbit and his sticky adversary is printed. What are the title and content of the second part of the tale? Where were both

parts first published? Why, do you think, have anthology editors often ignored this second part?

7. In his important Introduction to the *Portable Faulkner,* written in 1945, Malcolm Cowley helped initiate serious consideration of Faulkner's fiction. How many of the novelist's works were then in print?

8. Describe the means by which one can compile a full bibliography of the publications of a present-day literary scholar.

9. In Wordsworth's library were nearly 300 books belonging to Coleridge. Find a list of these titles.

10. (a)* The library of the poet Edmund Waller, to which his descendants added after his death in 1687, was sold in 1832. The sale catalogue includes the following items. Establish the correct title and date of each and identify by *STC* or Wing number. Are there any which the poet could not have known?

> Bacon's Natural History, and The Sovereign's Prerogative
> Palmerin of England, 2 Parts
> Josephus's Works, by L'Estrange, 3 vols.
> Turner's Military Essays, and Knox's History of the Island of Ceylon
> Memoirs of the Sieur de Pontis, and Bentivoglio's History of the Wars in Flanders
> Weever's Funeral Monuments, and Richardson's State of Europe
> Spriggs's Anglia Rediviva, and Wotton's State of Christendom
> Swinburne's Travels through Spain—Buck's Life of Richard III. and Wilson's History of King James
> General Ludlow's Memoirs, 3 vols.—Perrault's Characters of Illustrious Men, 2 vols.—Life of Robert Earl of Leicester, and Hayward's Lives of the Three Norman Kings

(b) Try to locate a copy of each of the following works represented in Swift's library, sold in 1745:

> [Berkeley, Geo. Bishop] His Discourse address'd to Magistrates. Dub. 1738
> A new Miscellany of original Poems. [London] 1701
> Buchanan Rerum Scotiarum Historia. Elzev. Amst. 1643
> Fontenelles Noveaux Dialogues des Morts. Par. 1683
> Wilkes on the Existence of God. Belf. 1730

* Materials for parts a–d of this exercise are drawn from A. N. L. Munby's series of facsimile *Sale Catalogues of Libraries of Eminent Persons* (London, 1971-75).

Doctor Gibb's Translation of David's Psalms in Verse; with
  Doctor Swift's Jests upon it. Lond. 1701
The Barrier-Treaty vindicated. Lond. 1712
Vossius, de Sybillinis [n. d.]
Ludlow's Memoirs 3d. vol. Switz 1699
(c) Give the full and correct title of each of these works, included in the sale of Laurence Sterne's library in 1768. Can you
find a contemporary notice (in book trade sources, periodicals,
etc.) of the publication of each work?

  Caxton's Game and Play of the Chesse. ["This Book," wrote
    the bookseller offering the collection, "is allowed by all the
    Typographical Antiquaries to have been the first Specimen
    of the Art among us." True?]
  Tarsis and Zelie, a famous Romance. 1685
  Koehoorn's new Method of Fortification, with Cuts. 1705
  Cleopatra, or Love's Master-piece, a Romance. [n.d.]
  Fuller's Pisgah-Sight of Palestine, with Cuts. 1662
  Chaucer's Works, "a very old Copy, black Letter, wants Title,
    imprinted at London by Kele." [n.d.]
  Fraser's History of Kuli Khan, Emperor of Persia. 1742
  Marriott's Female Conduct. 1759
  Young's Centaur not fabulous. 1755
  King's Art of Love, in Imitation of Ovid de Arte Amandi.
    [n.d.]
  Trapp on the Trinity. 1731
  Young on Opium. 1753
  Cadiere's Case, wherein Father Girard is accused of seducing
    her.—Father Girard's Defence, 3 parts. 1732
(d) Identify the following books owned by the self-taught poet
Robert Bloomfield (1766–1823). Can you also identify Blackets,
Freeman, Flowerdew, Hitchcock, and Evans?

  Loder's History of Framlingham
  Mason's English Garden
  Kentish Poets. 2 vols.
  Guthrie's Grammar
  Antiquarian Cabinet. 4 vols.
  The Remains of Joseph Blackets
  Dayes' Essays on Painting. 8vo
  Freeman's Regulbium (presented by the Author)
  Flowerdew's Poems (presented by the Author)
  Poems, by David Hitchcock (the self-taught American Poet)
    sent by the Author to Mr. Bloomfield

Evans' Seasons (presented by the Author)
Memoirs of the Peers of England
North Georgia Gazette

(e) The following items are drawn from a list made by Richard Woodhouse of books owned by John Keats. Printing the list in his *Keats* (1917), Sidney Colvin remarked, ". . . it would be an attractive bibliographical exercise . . . to identify particular editions." How far can this be done? Are any of Keats's copies known to exist today?

Aikin's History of the year   12mo
Davies' Celtic Researches   8vo
Lady Russell's Letters   12mo   2 vols.
Erasmus' Moriae Encomium   36mo
Ariosto da Boschino   18mo   2 vols.
Coleridge, Lamb and Lloyd   8vo
Auctores Mythographi Latini   4to
Lemprière's Class. Dict.   8vo
Z. Jackson's Illus. of Shakespeare   8vo
Bailey's Dictionary   8vo
Fencing familiarized   8vo
Conducteur à Paris   12mo
Mickle's Lusiad   18mo

(f) In the passages in his *Autobiography* describing the reading he accomplished as a youth, Benjamin Franklin mentions the following:

"Dr. Mather's . . . Essays to do Good"
"a Book, written by one Tryon, recommending a Vegetable Diet."
The New England Courant
——Using Evans, Sabin, Brigham, and whatever other standard guides to early American printing may be needed, identify these items, give fuller bibliographical information, and locate copies in American libraries.

Defoe's *Essays on Projects*
"Cocker's Book of Arithmetick"
"an odd Volume of the Spectator"
"Locke on Human Understanding"
"Xenophon's Memorable Things of Socrates"
——Were there American editions of these works at the time mentioned (ca. 1720–25)? In lack of American editions, what English edition may Franklin have known?

Franklin also mentions a "Dr. Brown" who "wickedly undertook some Years after to travesty the Bible in doggrel Verse as Cotton had done Virgil." Identify Brown's and Cotton's books by title and date of publication.

III. The Detection and Correction of Error; Conflict of Authorities

1. In the *TLS* for April 20, 1973, a reviewer listed some of the mistakes in Felix Felton's book on Thomas Love Peacock:

> Thomas Taylor, the Platonist, is described as of Norwich, which seems to summon up the ghost of William Taylor; Shelley and Harriet depart for Tanyrallt with a mysterious and hitherto unknown Helen Tinsley, presumably Miss Hitchener, the Brown Demon; the Bentley's Standard Novels volume which contains the first collection of Peacock's novels is not No LXII but No LVII. Far more serious, one of the best of Peacock's shorter poems, "I dug, beneath the cypress shade", is irretrievably ruined by the inclusion (twice) of the word "they" when it ought to be "thy".

In like manner, correct all the errors alleged by the same reviewer in the passage just preceding the one quoted:

> Shelley and Hogg were sent down from Cambridge; Mary Wollstonecraft had an affair with Ismay; Fair Rosamund was a martyred nun; Thomas Avory was a novelist, the author, presumably, of "John Bancle"; Rabelais was responsible for a character called Frère Jean Entanmeures; Blake's "Island in the Moon" caricatures statesmen; Meredith wrote a novel called *The Angry Marriage*.

2. Choose a certain number of pages in J. W. Saunders' *The Profession of English Letters* (1964) and verify each factual statement in a dependable source. How many errors can you find?

3. Winifred Gérin has acquired a considerable reputation for her biographies of the Brontë sisters, especially for her study of Charlotte (*Charlotte Brontë: The Evolution of Genius* [Oxford, 1967]). At least two critics, however, have questioned her reliability as a scholar. (See Tom Winnifrith, *The Brontës and Their Background: Romance and Reality* [London, 1973], pp. 5–6, 221, and Valentine Cunningham, *Everywhere Spoken Against: Dissent in the Victorian Novel* [Oxford, 1975], p. 291.) Compare the charges of Winnifrith and Cunningham with the evidence cited for praise (and blame) in the popular and scholarly reviews, and formulate your own assessment of Gérin's accomplishment in *Charlotte Brontë*.

4. In a review of James Baldwin's *Another Country*, Trevor Blount

noted an important inconsistency in the opening scene of Chapter 4. What is the inconsistency and what interruption in tone and mood is the result?

5. Describe the controversy over the acknowledgment of sources in John Gardner's *The Life and Times of Chaucer* (New York, 1977). What was Gardner's response?

6. The son of the prolific novelist Mary Elizabeth Braddon (*Lady Audley's Secret*, etc.), writing late in life, said that "all records" of her early career as an actress had disappeared. Her stage name, he thought, was "Mary Seaton." Describe how a recent biographer's correction of this error enabled him to reconstruct Miss Braddon's acting career. What were the main sources of his information?

7. Find five or six reviews of William Styron's *The Confessions of Nat Turner* and as many interviews as you can with Styron and others on the subject of this book. Then summarize in a short paper the controversy that surrounded Styron and his novel.

8. *Hanta Yo*, a novel by Ruth Beebe Hill depicting Sioux Indian life on the plains in the period from roughly 1750 to 1835, became in 1980 a center of controversy and litigation. Explain the major points of the dispute. Were any of the charges, defenses, or explanations made on artistic grounds?

9. How many mistakes can you find in this sentence? "Another succession was that of Lord Macaulay (historian, essayist, politician, editor of the *Edinburgh Review*), Sir George Otto Trevelyan (Macaulay's brother-in-law, cabinet minister, popular historian), and George Macaulay Trevelyan (Macaulay's nephew, the heir of his library, a great and popular historian)." (Aldon D. Bell, *London in the Age of Dickens* [Norman, Okla., 1967], p. 137.)

10. Correct the following entries appearing in the *NCBEL*, Volume III (the numbers in parentheses refer to columns, not pages):

> Hartmann, J. E. The mess of Gareth and Lynette. Harvard Lib
>   Bull 13 1959   (431)
> DeVane, W. C. A Browning handbook. Ithaca 1935, New York
>   1955 (rev). The standard handbook.   (440)
> [three successive entries:]
> Wallace, S. A. Browning in London society. MLN 66 1951.
> —— Curious annals: new documents on Browning's murder
>   case. SP 49 1952.
> —— New documents relating to Browning's Roman murder
>   story. Toronto 1956.   (456)
> Tanzy, C. E. Browning, Emerson and Bishop Blougram's apol-
>   ogy. MP 58 1960.   (458)

Cazamian, L. L'influence de la science 1860–90. Strasbourg
   1923.   (659)
Rogers, W. H. Portraits of romantic poets in contemporary
   minor fiction. Western Research Univ Bull 34 1931.   (661)
Haycroft, H. Murder for pleasure: the life and times of the
   detective story. 1942.   (662)
Hart, F. R. Manuscripts of Wilkie Collins. Princeton Univ Lib
   Chron 18 1957.   (928)
(Can you explain how the compiler of this section came to
make the last error?)

11. Morris Croll's *Style, Rhetoric, and Rhythm* (1966) is a collection of the author's essays which were earlier printed in journals.
In his introduction the editor, J. Max Patrick, enumerates the sins
of omission and commission which disfigured the essays in their
original form and required wholesale checking and amendment
when gathered for this volume. Select one of the essays and make a
list of the scholarly lapses found in its original version.

12. The annotation of literary texts in modern classroom editions is
sometimes defective. Here is a selection of errors found in the
notes to various editions of Carlyle's *Past and Present* (1843) and
to anthologized excerpts from that book. What is the correct explanation?

(a) "Yes, in the *Ugolino Hunger-tower* stern things happen;
best-loved little Gaddo fallen dead on *his Father's* knees!" (I.i;
the allusion is to Dante's *Inferno*, XXXIII.)
   Annotator A: "Count Ugolino who with his two sons and two
   grandsons was starved in prison."
   Annotator B: "He died, with four sons, in prison, starved to
   death."
   Annotator C: "He was imprisoned with two sons and two
   nephews . . ."
   Annotator D: ". . . the story of Ugolino and his two
   sons . . ."
(b) ". . . in killing Kings, in passing Reform Bills, in French
Revolutions, *Manchester Insurrections*, is found no remedy."
(III.i)
   At least four annotators identify this as the Peterloo Massacre
   (1819).
(c) ". . . for him and his there is no continuance appointed,
save only in Gehenna and *the Pool*." (III.ii)
   "The Thames River for several miles below London Bridge."
(d) ". . . the Anti-church of Hume and *Paine* . . ." (III.vi)

"David Hume, Scottish rationalist philosopher, and Thomas Paine, atheist, symbolized the anti-Christian tendencies of the eighteenth century."

(e) ". . . *Owen's Labour-bank* . . ." (III.xii)

Annotator A: "Planned by Robert Owen . . . but not achieved."

Annotator B: "An enterprise proposed by the Chartists in 1847."

(f) "In the case of *the late Bribery Committee* . . ." (IV.ii)

One annotator identifies as a committee of Parliament appointed in 1835 to investigate charges of electoral corruption.

(g) ". . . mad Chartisms, *impracticable Sacred-Months*, and Manchester Insurrections . . ." (IV.iv)

"An allusion to the revolutionary calendar adopted in France in 1793."

13. (a) The following book titles and author's names are sometimes printed in one form, sometimes in another. Even the most reputable reference books occasionally differ. In some cases, only one form is correct; establish which it is. In the other instances, where more than one is correct, explain why.

Shakespeare/Shakespere/Shakspere
Raleigh/Ralegh
Humphrey Clinker/Humphry Clinker
Mrs. Humphry Ward/Mrs. Humphrey Ward
The Sign of Four/The Sign of the Four
Henry Crabb/Crabbe Robinson
Edmond/Edmund Malone
[Jane] Clare/Claire Clairmont
Finnegan's Wake/Finnegans Wake
A Pilgrim's Progress/*The* Pilgrim's Progress/Pilgrim's Progress
Waverly/Waverley

(b) What is the correct pronunciation of each of the following names? How do you know? (Do not depend on dictionaries; go to reliable biographies or similar sources.)

Samuel Pepys
Sir John Vanbrugh
Abraham Cowley
William Cowper
Lewis Theobald
Lord Auchinleck
Robert Southey
Elia

Boz
Benjamin Jowett
Sir Walter Besant
John Addington Symonds
Arthur Symons
Sartoris

14. (a) How many different birth dates can you find in contemporary sources such as obituaries, and in modern reference works, for the following figures? Which, if any, is the correct one in each case?

Eliza Cook (*NCBEL:* 1812; Allibone: 1817; *DNB:* 1818)

Bret Harte ("frequently given as 1836 or 1839")

Willa Cather (1873, 1875, 1876)

A. B. Grosart, editor of literary texts (in his case, fourteen sources cite five different years)

(b) How convincingly, and on what kind of evidence, did Albert E. Johnson (*Modern Drama,* 11 [1968], 157-63) solve the long-vexed question of when the famous actor and playwright Dion Boucicault was born?

(c) No record is known of the birth of the early American poet Edward Taylor. Upon what kinds of evidence have various scholars suggested dates between 1642 and 1646?

(d) The *NCBEL,* III, col. 746, says that the Gothic novelist Charles Robert Maturin was born in 1782, as do other standard authorities such as the *Oxford Companion to English Literature* and the *DNB.* Benét's *Readers' Encyclopedia,* on the other hand, gives 1787. What is the evidence for the true date, and why was the compiler of the bibliography of Maturin in the *NCBEL* especially culpable in allowing the 1782 date to stand?

15. Consulting at random a statistically significant number of dictionaries, encyclopedias, and other reference works, one would probably discover that they split down the middle on the question of whether the term *incunabula* applies to books printed before 1500 or before 1501. Canvass your own list of "authorities" on this matter, and then try to determine which definition is accepted by the best *scholarly* authorities.

IV. The Critical Examination of Evidence

1. What authority is there for each of the following stories? Which have been proved to be untrue or inaccurate?

(a) Chaucer met Petrarch while in Italy.

(b) Shakespeare left Stratford because his poaching proclivities were getting him into constant trouble, especially with Sir Thomas Lucy.

(c) John Donne was a rake in his youth.

(d) Thomas Gray moved from Peterhouse to Pembroke College because a false alarm of fire, raised by prankish undergraduates, had forced him to use the rope ladder he had stored in his room.

(e) Boswell took stenographic notes of Dr. Johnson's conversation in the great man's very presence.

(f) Wordsworth made a secret trip to France in 1793.

(g) The Blakes had an amiable habit of sitting nude in their summerhouse.

(h) Coleridge composed "Kubla Khan" while in a dream state induced by opium; the poem is unfinished because he was interrupted by a man from Porlock who came to collect a tailor's bill.

(i) Dickens' unflattering treatment of the United States in *American Notes* and *Martin Chuzzlewit* was due in part to his having lost money in a Cairo, Illinois, land and canal speculation.

(j) Thomas Hardy had an illegitimate child by Tryphena Sparks.

(k) The disabling disease from which George Meredith suffered in his last years was locomotor ataxia.

(l) Matthew Arnold died of a heart attack as the result of running to catch a tramcar in Liverpool.

(m) Nora Joyce refused to read her husband's books because she found them "filthy" and their author a "dirty-minded" man.

(n) John O'Hara's practice was never to rewrite or revise; hence the manuscripts he sent to his publishers were, in effect, first drafts.

(o) Jack Kerouac composed at least one of his novels on rolls of toilet paper.

2. The "Highland Mary" episode in Burns's life has been the subject of controversy for well over a century. By consulting all available sources, make three lists: (a) of the soundly attested *facts* concerning "Highland Mary"; (b) of the legends that grew up around her; and (c) of the hypotheses to which the facts and legends in turn gave rise. How much, actually, do we know about her?

3. The following books contain psychological interpretations of various writers and literary works. How solid and extensive is the factual evidence upon which the argument rests, and how convincing is the argument itself?

Betty Miller, *Robert Browning: A Portrait* (1952)

Phyllis Greenacre, *Swift and Carroll: A Psychoanalytic Study of Two Lives* (1955)

George L. Watson, *A. E. Housman: A Divided Life* (1957)

Peter Green, *Kenneth Grahame* (1959)

Katharine Wilson, *The Nightingale and the Hawk: A Psychological Study of Keats's Ode* (1964)

Frederick C. Crews, *The Sins of the Fathers: Hawthorne's Psychological Themes* (1966)

Beverly Fields, *Reality's Dark Dream: Dejection in Coleridge* (1967)

Geoffrey Yarlott, *Coleridge and the Abyssinian Maid* (1967)

Bernard C. Meyer, *Joseph Conrad: A Psychoanalytic Biography* (1967)

Richard J. Onorato, *The Character of the Poet: Wordsworth and "The Prelude"* (1971)

Christine Gallant, *Blake and the Assimilation of Chaos* (1978)

(Many articles suitable for this exercise can be found in the files of *American Imago*, the *American Journal of Psychiatry*, the *Psychoanalytic Review*, and *Literature and Psychology*. Authors like Stephen Crane have been repeatedly subjected to Freudian or Jungian interpretation; for such treatments, see the appropriate current "guides to research" and author bibliographies.)

4. In 1914 A. F. Leach asserted, on the basis of a contemporary manuscript, that "the production of plays by schoolmasters . . . was equally prevalent in the fourteenth as it had been in the twelfth and was to be in the sixteenth century." The assumption went unchallenged for forty years, until Roger Sherman Loomis finally demolished it (*MLN*, 69 [1954], 31–34). What was the flaw in the argument, and what moral did Loomis draw from the story?

5. What evidence would you require to be persuaded that the following statements are not exaggerated?

(a) ". . . the sale of books in general has increased prodigiously within the last twenty years. According to the best estimation I have been able to make, I suppose that more than four times the number of books are sold now than were sold twenty years since. The poorer sort of farmers, and even the poor country people in general, who before that period spent their winter evenings in relating stories of witches, ghosts, hobgoblins, &c. now shorten the nights by hearing their sons and daughters read tales, romances, &c. and on entering their houses, you may see Tom Jones, Roderick Random, and other entertaining books stuck up on their bacon racks, &c. and if *John* goes to town with a load of hay, he is charged to be sure not to forget to bring home 'Peregrine Pickle's adventures;' and when *Dolly* is sent to market to sell her eggs she is commissioned to purchase 'The history of Pamela Andrews.' In short all ranks and degrees now READ." (James Lackington, *Memoirs of the First Forty-Five Years of the Life of James Lackington* . . . [London, ca. 1791], pp. 254– 55.)

(b) "The mere news that Oscar Wilde had been arrested and taken to Holloway startled London and gave the signal for a strange exodus. Every train to Dover was crowded; every steamer to Calais thronged with members of the aristocratic and leisured classes, who seemed to prefer Paris, or even Nice out of the season, to a city like London, where the police might act with such unexpected vigour. . . . Never was Paris so crowded with members of the English governing classes; here was to be seen a famous ex-Minister; there the fine face of the president of a Royal society; at one table in the Café de la Paix, a millionaire recently ennobled, and celebrated for his exquisite taste in art; opposite to him a famous general. It was even said that a cele- brated English actor took a return ticket for three or four days to Paris, just to be in the fashion." (Frank Harris, *Oscar Wilde: His Life and Confessions* [New York, 1916], I, 250–51.)

6. The identity of Sir Thomas Malory remains a matter for dispute. Look up the reviews of William Matthews' *The Ill-Framed Knight* (1967) and the separate discussions which have appeared since the book was published, and analyze the chief points in question.

7. Two books by A. L. Rowse, *William Shakespeare: A Biography* (1963) and *Shakespeare the Man* (1973), stirred up fierce contro- versy. Read as many reviews as you can find, including those in such places as the intellectual weeklies and the Sunday book supple- ments, and then sum up what the chief issues were between Rowse and his critics, in terms of the kinds of evidence Rowse used and the reasoning that lay behind his conclusions.

8. (a) In biographies written in more devout times than ours, death- bed scenes often tempted biographers to alter or even fabricate evi- dence for the sake of the edifying lessons readers could derive from them. B. R. Jerman's investigation of the death and burial of Robert

Browning (*UTQ*, 35 [1965], 47–74) uncovers many distortions and fabrications in the "first-hand" accounts of those commentators who were perhaps over-concerned with the wholesome moral to be learned from the death of this so-called "optimistic" poet. In a brief essay, summarize Jerman's method of investigation, and, using those procedures as a guide, describe the specific steps one should take to substantiate accounts of the last days of famous persons.

(b) However, a distinction might be made between "public" and "private" deaths. Robert G. Walker has argued recently that "the deaths of Rochester, Addison, Hume, and Paine . . . are all public deaths . . . in the sense that these men deliberately shaped the final days of their lives just as they would shape the conclusion of a work of art to convey a particular polemical message, in full knowledge that their end would be reported not only to their peers but also to the public at large" ("Public Death in the Eighteenth Century," *Research Studies* [Washington State University], 48 [1980], 11–24). In a manner similar to that followed in (a), describe the arguments and the methods of investigation Walker uses to support the idea of a consciously manipulated death in the cases of Rochester, Addison, Hume, and Paine.

(c) Using the kind of evidence and reasoning employed by Jerman and Walker, try to decide whether another classic instance, Lockhart's description of Sir Walter Scott's last moments, is believable. What considerations weigh in favor of its being more or less a myth?

9. Between 1959 and 1979, at least sixteen articles and parts of books on Hemingway dealt with the alleged confusion in two lines of dialogue between the two waiters in his famous short story, "A Clean, Well-Lighted Place," published in 1933. In 1965, the publisher's decision to alter the questioned lines aroused sharp controversy. In 1975, when certain Hemingway manuscripts became available for the first time, a pencil manuscript of this story was discovered which seems to have resolved the debate. What was the resolution? Summarize the evidence discovered.

10. One of the most famous ideological-personal confrontations in modern history was that between Thomas Henry Huxley and Bishop Samuel Wilberforce at the 1860 meeting of the British Association in Oxford. As Gertrude Himmelfarb writes (*Darwin and the Darwinian Revolution* [New York, 1959], p. 292), "Since there was no full and objective contemporary account of the event, we are at the mercy of the 'lives and letters' later published by eyewitnesses," as well as of summarized press accounts. Study as

many versions of the encounter as you can find to determine how wide and numerous are the discrepancies in the sources that historians and biographers must depend on. A partial list is in Owen Chadwick, *The Victorian Church*, Part II (New York, 1970), p. 11.

11. In the reading list in the original edition of this book appeared the following entry:

Super, R. H. "A Grain of Truth about Wordsworth and Browning, Landor and Swinburne." *MLN*, LXVII (1952), 419–21.
   Disposes of two well-known anecdotes told by Edmund Gosse— of Wordsworth's drinking Browning's health at a famous dinner, and of Landor's cholerically pressing Swinburne to accept the gift of an alleged Correggio.

A dozen years after the latter story was "disposed of," the discreditation was itself discredited. How has Gosse been proved to be right, after all?

12. According to the received story, "on reading of Nell's death [in *The Old Curiosity Shop*], most of Dickens's readers wept." Why does this legend represent the danger of generalizing from a few conspicuous instances? (See the Pilgrim edition of *The Letters of Charles Dickens*, ed. Madeline House and Graham Storey, II [Oxford, 1969], ix–xii.)

13. Examine the following arguments to determine the nature and reliability of the evidence adduced, and the cogency of the reasoning by which the conclusion is reached.
   (a) Tennyson's love affair with Rosa Baring generated psychological stresses which can be recognized in *Maud* and other poems. (Ralph W. Rader, *Tennyson's "Maud": the Biographical Genesis* [1963].)
   (b) Olivia Clemens was not, as has been assumed, "a woman who wasted a fair portion of her married life dictating literal propriety to a recalcitrant husband and making his prose less salty than it might otherwise have been." (Sydney J. Krause, "Olivia Clemens's 'Editing' Reviewed," *AL*, 39 [1967], 325–51.)
   (c) The supposedly Zoroastrian imagery in *Prometheus Unbound* (I, 191–221) was actually derived from the Teutonic-Celtic figure of the *doppelgänger*. (Margaret Loftus Ranald and Ralph Arthur Ranald, "Shelley's Magus Zoroaster and the Image of the Doppelgänger," *MLN*, 76 [1961], 7–12. N.B.: Pay particular attention to the use made of Scott's footnotes.)
   (d) The lack of unity in Poe's "Narrative of Arthur Gordon Pym" is explained by the circumstances of its composition. (J. V. Ridgely and Iola S. Haverstick, "Chartless Voyage: The

Many Narratives of Arthur Gordon Pym," *Texas Studies in Literature and Language*, 8 [1966], 63–80.)

(e) The peculiarities of spelling in Milton's printed poems are attributable to his amanuenses or compositors; they do not reflect his own practice. (John T. Shawcross, "One Aspect of Milton's Spelling: Idle Final 'E,' " *PMLA*, 78 [1963], 501–10.)

(f) Bryant's "Thanatopsis" was composed in 1815 rather than in 1811, the traditional date. (William Cullen Bryant II, "The Genesis of 'Thanatopsis,' " *New England Quarterly*, 21 [1948], 163–84.)

(g) There is no basis for the familiar story that Shakespeare and Ben Jonson had wit combats at the Mermaid Tavern. (S. Schoenbaum, *Shakespeare's Lives* [Oxford, 1970], pp. 294–96.)

(h) Pepys's diary as we have it is the result of his thorough re-writing and polishing of the original notes. (*The Diary of Samuel Pepys*, ed. Latham and Matthews, I, xcvii–cvi.)

14. After examining each of the books cited, explain in concrete terms the basis of the judgments delivered in Frank Jordan, ed., *The English Romantic Poets* (3rd ed., New York, 1972), pp. 287, 316, 364:

(a) Ethel C. Mayne's *Life and Letters of Lady Byron* (1929): it is characterized by "bias and inaccuracies."

(b) G. Wilson Knight's *Byron and Shakespeare* (1966): its "great flaw . . . lies in its mad or immoral treatment of evidence."

(c) Eustace Chesser's *Shelley and Zastrozzi: Self Revelations of a Neurotic* (1965): "completely worthless."

V. Biographical Research

1. From the lists of "minor" writers in the various genres given in *NCBEL*, Volumes II and III, select one upon whom little if any recent biographical work has been done. (You will want to check this further by referring to the appropriate serial bibliography covering scholarship published since the cut-off date of the *NCBEL* entry.) The existence of book-length lives or biographical articles dating from before, say, 1910 is no bar to the selection of a given figure, because these older treatments usually are more or less unreliable and require constant verification.

Having decided upon a promising figure, write as full a biographical account as the available materials permit, beginning with the *DNB* article (if he or she has merited one) but spreading a wide net to include articles and obituaries in newspapers and periodicals, contemporary memoirs and letters, official documents, and every other primary source of information. Present the results of your research in a thoroughly documented, tautly organized, and readable paper, such as you might offer to the editor of a learned journal.

The same exercise may involve a minor American author. There are ample lists in such reference works as Burke and Howe's *American Authors and Books* and Herzberg's *Reader's Encyclopedia of American Literature.*

2. The article on Thomas Powell in the *Dictionary of American Biography* is remarkable for what it does not say about its subject. What aspect of his character and career does the author discreetly omit?

3. Select one of the literary figures about whom John Aubrey left memoranda in his *Brief Lives*, and determine how many of Aubrey's statements are capable of independent verification. Where such checking is possible, how trustworthy does Aubrey turn out to be?

4. Among the minor seventeenth- and early eighteenth-century poets whom Dr. Johnson mentions in his *Lives of the Poets* are George Stepney, William Walsh, Edmund Neale (known as Smith), William King, Samuel Garth, John Hughes, Elijah Fenton, Thomas Yalden, James Hammond, William Somerville, and William Broome. Rewrite the biographical portion of Dr. Johnson's treatment of one of these men, correcting his facts wherever necessary and supplementing them wherever possible.

VI. *Textual Criticism and Editing; Bibliographical Analysis; Publishing History*

1. Scholars should never quote from popular reprint editions of literary works, however convenient they may be, if a more authoritative text can be had. Substantiate this axiom by comparing the text of, say, an Everyman, Modern Library, or Signet edition of an older work with a scholarly one.

2. Summarize the particular problems (available manuscripts, printed editions, dubious ascriptions, etc.) involved in determining the text, and in some cases the canon, of Dekker, Ben Jonson, Donne, Tourneur, Crashaw, Herrick, Defoe, Matthew Arnold, Yeats, or Auden. (Be sure that you take into account the latest published information and discussion.)

3. What kind of textual scholarship remained to be performed on Thoreau's *Walden* after the publication of the Princeton critical edition of that work in 1971?

4. A study you are making of the English popular novel in the 1830's and 1840's requires that you focus particular attention on the publishing house of Richard Bentley & Son. Where are the firm's archives, and how can you gain access to them?

5. William Faulkner revised his Nobel Prize acceptance speech for publication. What were the changes he made and how do you account for them?

6. During the nineteenth century, Harper and Brothers published in America such major British novelists as Dickens, the Brontës, Thackeray, and Hardy. What specific books of each author did the firm publish, and how much was paid to the author for each work?

7. John Barth's novel *The Floating Opera* was first published in the United States in 1956. In 1968 it was revised and published in England for the first time. Why was publication in England delayed and how extensive were the revisions?

8. To commemorate the 250th anniversary of the first edition of *Gulliver's Travels* an edition described as the "true 'original'" version was published. On what text was this later edition based? Where is that text to be found?

9. W. W. Greg's parallel-text edition of Marlowe's *Dr. Faustus* has been called "one of the major triumphs of modern literary scholarship." What is the apparent relationship between the two printed texts (1604 and 1616)? On the basis of what evidence, and by what reasoning, did Greg arrive at his conclusions? What is the value of this edition to literary students?

10. What is the relation of the so-called "old *Arcadia*" (first discovered in two manuscripts in 1907) to the printed texts of Sidney's romance (1590 and 1593)? Is there an edition which embodies the readings of all the manuscripts (several more have subsequently turned up) and of the dozen editions printed down to 1674?

11. In 1929 Peter Alexander (*Shakespeare's Henry VI and Richard III*) argued that the plays known as *The First Part of the Contention betwixt the two famous Houses of Yorke and Lancaster* (1594) and *The true Tragedie of Richard Duke of Yorke* (1595) are "bad quartos" of the plays we know as Shakespeare's *Henry VI*, parts 2 and 3. Summarize the reasoning by which Alexander reached this conclusion. So far as you can determine, is his view now generally accepted?

12. Compare the standards and practices adopted by three modern editions of Milton: the Columbia (prose and poetry, 1931–38),

Helen Darbishire's (poetry, 1952–55), and the Yale (prose, 1953–   ).
Where there are variations in editorial principles or methods, which
do you think are the most defensible?

13. Look up the principal reviews of Helen Gardner's edition of
Donne's poems (1965), especially Mark Roberts' in *Essays in Criticism*, 16 (1966), 309–29, William Empson's in *Critical Quarterly*, 8
(1966), 255–80, and *TLS*, April 6, 1967. What criteria do these
critics use in evaluating an edition of a poet's works? (Incidentally,
is the *TLS* reviewer justified in saying that Empson's article is in
"brilliant bad taste"?)

14. Lawrence J. Zillman has published two editions of Shelley's
Prometheus Unbound (1959, 1968). By consulting the reviews of
both editions, compile a list of the major issues raised by Zillman's
two different methodologies.

15. The "definitive" edition of Browning's poems being issued by the
Ohio University Press has had a number of major adverse reviews.
After studying these, explain the principles of textual editing that
have been at issue. What is the latest information on the progress of
this edition?

16. After consulting the introductions to modern scholarly editions
of the following works or personal documents, or books and articles
devoted to the topic, describe the special problems offered by the
sources of the text of each work. How have their latest editors dealt
with these difficulties? Which works are still in need of definitive
editing?

> *Piers Plowman; Sir Gawain and the Green Knight; The Faerie
> Queene; Religio Medici; Hudibras; MacFlecknoe;* Evelyn's diary;
> Pope's letters; *A Sentimental Journey;* Boswell's journals; Frank-
> lin's *Autobiography; Don Juan; Dr. Grimshawe's Secret; Walden;
> Leaves of Grass; The Mysterious Stranger; The Education of
> Henry Adams; The Importance of Being Earnest; Winesburg,
> Ohio; The Red Badge of Courage*

17. Select any one of the literary works listed in the preceding
question and summarize, with appropriate illustrations, the light
which a knowledge of its textual history throws upon its meaning
and art.

18. Describe the importance to literary study of each of the following documents or collections of documents. Are they all adequately edited? Where is each located?

Henslowe's diary
The Auchinleck Manuscript

The Arundel Harington Manuscript of Tudor poetry
The Revels Accounts
The Term Catalogues
The Lovelace Papers
Crabb Robinson's diary
The Brontë juvenilia
The Esdaile Notebook
The Crewe MS of "Kubla Khan"
The Mark Twain papers formerly owned by his daughter
Woodhouse's interleaved and annotated copy of Keats's *Poems*
    (1817)
Macaulay's diary
The first draft of Yeats's *Autobiography*
The manuscript of *Great Expectations*
George Eliot's "quarry for *Middlemarch*"
The manuscripts of Tennyson's *In Memoriam*

19. As a study in contrasts, compare Fanny Burney's editorial prac-
tices, as described by Joyce Hemlow (*The History of Fanny
Burney* [1958], Chapter XVII) and Roger Lonsdale (*Dr. Charles
Burney: A Literary Biography* [1965], Chapter XI), with the
practices now being followed by Miss Hemlow in editing Fanny's
own papers. See her "Letters and Journals of Fanny Burney:
Establishing the Text" (*Editing Eighteenth-Century Texts*, ed.
D. I. B. Smith [Toronto, 1968], pp. 25-43).

20. Describe the significance of the revisions Izaak Walton made in
successive editions of his *Lives*.

21. What relevance has the textual history of "The Bear" to an
understanding of it as an example of Faulkner's art?

22. (a) When they collect their periodical essays and reviews into
volumes, writers often make significant revisions. Compare the
first-published and revised texts of one or more of the following
articles, and suggest the author's probable reasons for making
the changes you note:
    In T. S. Eliot's *Selected Essays:* "Hamlet (and His Problems)";
      "The Function of Criticism"; "Arnold and Pater"
    In Lionel Trilling's *The Liberal Imagination:* "Tacitus Now";
      "Kipling"; "Freud and Literature"
    In Edmund Wilson's *The Shores of Light:* "T. S. Eliot and the
      Church of England"; "Citizen of the Union"; "Thornton
      Wilder"; "A Great Magician"; "Poe at Home and Abroad";
      "The Pleasures of Literature"; "The Literary Worker's Polo-
      nius"

(b) Most of the contents of the following collections were originally printed in periodicals. Select one or more essays, and determine whether or not they were revised for book publication. If they were, what was the extent and significance of the changes?

> William Butler Yeats, *Ideas of Good and Evil; Essays 1931 to 1936*
>
> Norman Douglas, *Old Calabria; Experiments*
>
> Aldous Huxley, *On the Margin; Essays New and Old; Do What You Will; Themes and Variations; Collected Essays*
>
> Virginia Woolf, *Collected Essays*
>
> Horace Gregory, *Spirit of Time and Place*
>
> Malcolm Cowley, *A Second Flowering: Works and Days of the Lost Generation*
>
> Richard Hoggart, *Speaking to Each Other*
>
> Benjamin De Mott, *Supergrow: Essays and Reports on Imagination in America*
>
> Tom Wolfe, *Mauve Gloves and Madmen, Clutter and Vine*

(c) The critic Francis Jeffrey made hundreds of significant changes in the text of his *Edinburgh Review* articles when preparing them for his four-volume *Contributions to the "Edinburgh Review"* (1844). For a sampling of these, see Ronald B. Hatch, " 'This Will Never Do,' " *RES*, n.s. 21 (1970), 56–62. Try the same procedure with some other nineteenth-century critic who often wrote for periodicals, such as Macaulay, George Henry Lewes, Leslie Stephen, John Morley, Augustine Birrell, Edward Dowden, or George Saintsbury.

23. Handling it with the utmost care, examine a book printed in England before 1700. Write a full and accurate transcription of its title page, describe its physical makeup (i.e., collate it), and identify it by *STC* or Wing number. Use the form employed by Greg in his *Bibliography of the English Printed Drama*, with whatever curtailments or modifications are directed.

24. (a) Locate a copy of a first edition of a book by an American author who died after 1930, or who is not, in any event, represented in Jacob Blanck's *Bibliography of American Literature*. Examine it carefully, and describe it according to the formula used by Blanck.

(b) Locate a copy of a first edition of any book listed in Blanck and compare it, detail by detail, with Blanck's description, identifying, if necessary, the printing, issue, or state to which it belongs.

25. Printed below are five extracts from the printed texts of documents written by or to prominent literary men. Assuming that you

are preparing a definitive edition of the private papers of one of these authors, annotate every allusion that you think a future user of your edition will need to have explained. Assume further that none of the allusions has been annotated in connection with previous letters in the series.

(a) Southey to his wife, Brixton, May 9, 1799 (Charles Cuthbert Southey, *Life and Correspondence of the Late Robert Southey* [London, 1850], II, 16–17):

> G. Dyer is foraging for my Almanac, and promises pieces from Mrs. Opie, Mr. Mott of Cambridge, and Miss Christall. I then went to Arch's, a pleasant place for half an hour's book news: you know he purchased the edition of the Lyrical Ballads; he told me he believed he should lose by them, as they sold very heavily. . . . My books sell very well. Other book news have I none, except, indeed, that John Thelwall is writing an epic poem, and Samuel Rogers is also writing an epic poem; George Dyer, also, hath similar thoughts. . . . William Taylor has written to me from Norwich, and sent me Bodmer's Noah, the book that I wanted to poke through and learn German by. He tempts me to write upon the subject, and take my seat with Milton and Klopstock; and in my to-day's walk so many noble thoughts for such a poem presented themselves, that I am half tempted, and have the Deluge floating in my brain with the Dom Daniel and the rest of my unborn family. . . . Horne Tooke's letter to the Income Commissioners has amused me very much: he had stated his under sixty pounds a year; they said they were not satisfied; and his reply begins by saying he has much more reason to be dissatisfied with the smallness of his income than they have.

(b) Henry Brevoort to Washington Irving, Edinburgh, March 1, 1813 (*Letters of Henry Brevoort to Washington Irving*, ed. George S. Hellman [New York, 1918], pp. 74–78):

> Kemble is now performing here; I have seen him in nearly all his great parts & can truly say with Cato "I am satisfied." . . . His acquaintance is sought by men of the highest rank and by men of the highest genius.—I dined in company with him at Walter Scotts the day before yesterday.—The party consisted of Mr Henry Mackenzie, Mr Jeffrey &c., and as the conversation turned upon dramatic poetry and upon the art of acting it was kept up for several hours with very extraordinary ability. . . . He is an intimate friend of Talma and resided in the house of that great actor whilst in Paris; he bears willing testimony to his transcendent merit beyond all his french competitors; indeed Talma stands unrivaled upon the french stage. . . . He was also well acquainted with Clairon, of whom he got many anecdotes of Garrick, particularly the one of the Spittlefields Weaver & the child that dropped from his arms into the Streets.—I ought to have told you that Scott is also a dramatist; Mr Erskine has in his possession a manuscript Tragedy written many years ago, which is distinguished by many marks of his fine genius.

Kemble told me that he was perfectly satisfied with Mr Coopers
offers, and felt desirous of seeing America, but that the War prevented his emigration. . . . I really think we should all like Kemble
both on & off the Stage—he occasionally pays too much court to
the bottle, but his transgressions are not frequent nor are they
followed by such disgusting consequences, as we have witnessed in
the case of poor George Fred: Cook Esqr.—

(c) Richard Harding Davis to his family, Managua, Nicaragua,
February 13, 1895 (*Adventures and Letters of Richard Harding
Davis*, ed. Charles Belmont Davis [New York, 1917], p. 152):

I had a great deal to tell you, but we have just received copies of
the Panama *Star* and have read of the trolley riots in Brooklyn, a
crisis in France, War in the Balkans, a revolution in Honolulu and
another in Colombia. The result is that we feel we are not in it and
we are all kicking and growling and abusing our luck. How Claiborne
and Russell will delight over us and in telling how the militia fired
on the strikers and how Troop A fought nobly. Never mind our
turn will come someday and we may see something yet. We have
had the deuce of a time since we left Tegucigalpa. Now we are in
a land where there are bull hide beds and canvas cots instead of
hammocks and ice and railroads and direct communication with
steamship lines. Hereafter all will be merely a matter of waiting until the boat sails or the train starts and the uncertainties of mules
and cat boats are at an end.

(d) F. Scott Fitzgerald to Maxwell Perkins, Paris, January 21, 1930
(*Dear Scott/Dear Max: The Fitzgerald-Perkins Correspondence*,
ed. John Kuehl and Jackson R. Bryer [New York, 1971], p. 161):

(3) Thank you for the documents in the Callaghan case. I'd rather
not discuss it except to say that I don't like him and that I wrote
him a formal letter of apology. I never thought he started the rumor
& never said nor implied such a thing to Ernest.
(4) Delighted with the success of Ernest's book. I took the responsibility of telling him that McAlmon was at his old dirty work
around New York. McAlmon, by the way, didn't have anything to
do with founding *Transition*. He published Ernest's first book over
here & some books of his own & did found some little magazine but
of no importance.
(5) Thank you for getting *Gatsby* for me in foreign languages.
(6) Sorry about John Biggs but it will probably do him good in
the end. *The Stranger in Soul Country* had something & the *Seven
Days Whipping* was respectable but colorless. *Demigods* was simply
oratorical twirp. How is his play going?
(7) Tom Boyd seems far away. I'll tell you one awful thing tho.
Lawrence Stallings was in the West with King Vidor at a *huge* salary to write an equivalent of *What Price Glory*. King Vidor told
me that Stallings in despair of showing Vidor what the war was
about gave him a copy of *Through the Wheat*. And that's how
Vidor so he told me made the big scenes of the *Big Parade*. Tom
Boyd's profits were a few thousand—Stallings were a few hundred
thousands. Please don't connect my name with this story but it is
the truth and it seems to me rather horrible.

(e) Henry Miller to Lawrence Durrell, Paris, December, 1936 (*Lawrence Durrell & Henry Miller: A Private Correspondence*, ed. George Wickes [New York, 1963], pp. 35–36):

> Why not make the contributors to the review pay for the printing and mailing, etc.? Say about 250 francs apiece—about $12.50. No avant-garde magazine can hope to make money. Not today. . . . The first thing to do would be to write the potential contributors and see if they were willing. I have a few people in mind who I would think would respond, with good contributions and with money. To wit:
> Fraenkel, Lowenfels, Saroyan, Laughlin, Anaïs Nin, James Stern, Van Heeckeren—possibly Hilaire Hiler and Mayo for drawings. Stern is a young Irish writer, who wrote a book of excellent short stories on Africa. Van Heeckeren might give us something about China—he is an adventurer. Mayo is a Greek painter whose drawings are almost made to illustrate my books. Hiler is a painter and a good friend of mine, now in Hollywood. There may be others—I think of these at random. The point is that the magazine, or anthology, or whatever you wish, should be fairly inexpensive. One could use both English and French, I imagine. Perlès could then come in with some of his marvellous passages from the *Quatuor*. You have your friends. Zarian sounds interesting. Make him write that letter, by all means! I would give you something from *Capricorn*, something beyond either *Tropic* or *Black Spring*, or something from *Hamlet*, or a long short story called "Max," which I am sure you would like. Or "The Universe of Death," from the Lawrence book. Anyway, there would be no dearth of material.

VII. Questions of Authorship

1. Who was the actual author of the standard life of Thomas Hardy (*The Early Life of Thomas Hardy* and *The Later Years of Thomas Hardy*)?

2. A scholar has recently discovered that the novel *A Year at Hartlebury, or the Election* (1834) was written by Benjamin Disraeli and his sister Sarah under the pseudonyms of "Cherry" and "Fair Star." What is the subject of the book? How has its authorship been established? (Disraeli did not possess a copy in his personal library.)

3. Three hitherto unknown literary documents of Henry Fielding—two autograph poems and a pseudonymous letter to the editor of *Common Sense* (dated April Fool's Day, 1738, and published May 13, 1738)—have recently been identified. Locate published discussion of these finds and summarize how their authorship was determined and what significance is claimed for them by their discoverers. Describe the pieces.

4. Several years ago a manuscript of an unknown play allegedly by Jane Austen was discovered. The play was called *Sir Charles Grandi-*

son, or the Happy Man, a Comedy and was freely adapted from Richardson's novel. Give the details of this find. Has the authorship been firmly established?

5. Edward L. Saslow has written two articles raising questions about works generally attributed to Dryden: "Dryden's Authorship of the *Defense of the Royal Papers*," *SEL*, 17 (1977), 387–95, and "Dryden as Historiographer Royal, and the Authorship of *His Majesties Declaration Defended*," *MP*, 75 (1978), 261–72. Choose one or the other of these articles, summarize Saslow's argument, and present your assessment of his evidence and the effectiveness of his presentation.

6. In 1972 a hitherto unknown Renaissance play was discovered and attributed to Thomas Heywood. Where was the manuscript found and on what basis was the attribution made?

7. Generously sample the pages of Volume III of the *Wellesley Index to Victorian Periodicals, 1824–1900* and make a list of the various kinds of internal and external evidence used by the editors to establish authorship. Which kinds are usually the most reliable, and which result in only tentative attributions?

8. In 1946 the Bodleian Library acquired a copy of Marvell's *Miscellaneous Poems* (1681) with extensive manuscript additions. What authority has this volume, and what effect have its contents had upon our knowledge of the Marvell canon?

9. Who wrote the review of Coleridge's *Christabel* published in the London *Times*, May 20, 1816? What is the evidence for this ascription?

10. Following is a list of works whose authorship is, or until lately has been, in doubt. Summarize the arguments found in the existing discussions of each problem, and decide what the most acceptable answer is, so far as the available evidence permits one to judge.

  (a) The "anonymous" life of Milton
  (b) The play of *Sir Thomas More*
  (c) The glosses (by "E.K.") in Spenser's *Shepherd's Calendar*
  (d) The poems signed "Anomos" in Francis Davison's *Poetical Rhapsody* (1602)

11. In the *Knickerbocker Magazine*, 12 (1838), 349–66, James Fenimore Cooper wrote a lengthy attack on Lockhart's life of Scott. In it he clearly implied—while stoutly denying any such suspicion—that Lockhart had been the author of a scathing review of Cooper's recent book on England ("so ill-written—ill-informed—ill-bred—ill-tempered, and so ill-mannered a production it has never yet been our fortune to meet"). In what British periodical did that review appear, and was Lockhart actually the author?

12. In the appendix of his ground-breaking little book, *New Essays by Oliver Goldsmith* (1927), Ronald S. Crane listed a number of essays and other contributions to periodicals which he suspected to be by Goldsmith but in lack of sufficient evidence declined to attribute to him. Of these possible ascriptions, how many have subsequently been strengthened or rejected?

13. "The first American novel," *The Power of Sympathy* (1789), was long attributed to Sarah Wentworth Apthorp Morgan. What evidence is there that the author was, instead, William Hill Brown?

14. Did the "*Gawain* poet" write the saint's legend of St. Erkenwald?

15. Describe the grounds upon which R. W. Chambers (*Thomas More* [London, 1935], p. 82) was "compelled to deprive [William Grocyn] of one half of his extant works."

16. Using the most recent books on the subject, principally F. E. Halliday's *The Cult of Shakespeare* (1957), R. C. Churchill's *Shakespeare and His Betters* (1958), Walter Hart Blumenthal's *Paging Mr. Shakespeare* (1961), and H. N. Gibson's *The Shakespeare Claimants* (1962), summarize and evaluate the arguments by which various people have tried to prove that "Shakespeare's" plays were written by authors other than Shakespeare. A not irrelevant incidental question is: Are these books entirely dependable in their facts and fair in their interpretations of others' positions?

17. On what grounds have the following poems been attributed to their respective "authors"? How sound is each attribution?
    (a) "A Fragment of an Epic Poem": Charles Churchill?
    (b) "Epilogue Intended to have been spoken by the Lady Henr. Mar. Wentworth when *Calisto* was acted at Court": Dryden?
    (c) "Jack Frenchman's Lamentation": Swift?
    (d) Metrical paraphrases of the first seven Psalms (the first beginning: "Blest is the man that never would/ in councels of th' ungodly share"): Herbert?
    (e) "The Sparke": Carew?
    (f) "Autumn. an Ode": Dr. Johnson?

18. In the first edition of "Tottel's Miscellany," ninety-seven poems are attributed to Wyatt, forty to Surrey, forty to Nicholas Grimald, and the remainder to "uncertain authors." Since the appearance of Hyder Rollins' edition of this great Tudor anthology (1928–29), how many further identifications or reassignments have been made, and on what grounds?

19. To what extent, if at all, does the disputed authorship of "A Letter of Advice to a Young Poet" undermine the argument of John Holloway in "The Well-Filled Dish: An Analysis of Swift's

Satire" (*Hudson Review*, 9 [1956], 20–37)? What is the present state of scholarly opinion on this perennial problem of attribution?

VIII. Problems of Source and Influence

1. By an analysis of internal and (if possible) external evidence, estimate the debt of Thomas Love Peacock's *The Four Ages of Poetry* to Sidney's *Defense of Poesie*. Is it likely that Peacock consciously modeled his essay, at least in part, on Sidney's?

2. From such sources as the *MLA International Bibliography*, the annual *American Literary Scholarship*, and the quarterly bibliography in *American Literature*, select a half-dozen recent articles dealing with the purported use made of sources by Poe, Melville, Hawthorne, Longfellow, Stephen Crane, or Thomas Wolfe. After critically reading each article, decide how sound each argument is.

3. In *Sidney's Poetry* (1965) David Kalstone discusses Sidney's debt, in *Arcadia*, to the Italian pastoral tradition, especially the *Arcadia* of Sannazaro. How good a case does he make for this indebtedness?

4. In what ways did Macaulay, in his essay on Sir William Temple, draw upon Monk's *Life of Bentley*, Boyle's *Dr. Bentley's Dissertation on the Epistles of Phalaris*, and Bentley's *Dissertation* itself?

5. Donald Davie's *The Heyday of Sir Walter Scott* (1961) studies Scott's influence on several nineteenth-century authors. How impressive, and of what kinds, is the factual evidence Davie presents?

6. How persuasive are the following books and articles on sources and influences?

(a) Thora Balslev, *Keats and Wordsworth: A Comparative Study* (1962).

(b) Werner Beyer, *The Enchanted Forest* (1963).

(c) Albert Goldman, *The Mine and the Mint: Sources for the Writings of Thomas De Quincey* (1965).

(d) K. L. Goodwin, *The Influence of Ezra Pound* (1966).

(e) David L. Frost, *The School of Shakespeare: The Influence of Shakespeare on English Drama 1600–42* (1968).

(f) L. G. Salingar, "*The Revenger's Tragedy:* Some Possible Sources," *MLR*, 60 (1965), 3–12.

(g) Alfred S. Reid, "Hawthorne's Humanism: 'The Birthmark' and Sir Kenelm Digby," *AL*, 38 (1966), 337–51.

(h) John Shroeder, "Miles Coverdale as Actaeon, as Faunus, and as October: With Some Consequences," *Papers on Language and Literature*, 2 (1966), 126–39.

(i) John Hazel Smith, "The Genesis of the Strozza Subplot in

George Chapman's *The Gentleman Usher,*" *PMLA,* 83 (1968), 1448–53.

(j) Thomas B. Gilmore, Jr., "Swift's *Modest Proposal:* A Possible Source," *PQ,* 47 (1968), 590–92.

(k) Harry Stone, "The Genesis of a Novel: *Great Expectations,*" *Charles Dickens 1812–1870,* ed. E. W. F. Tomlin (New York, 1969), pp. 109–31.

(l) Hershel Parker, "Dead Letters and Melville's Bartleby," *Resources for American Literary Study,* 4 (1974), 90–99.

(m) Sara DeSaussure Davis, "Feminist Sources in *The Bostonians,*" *AL,* 50 (1979), 570–87.

7. (a) Make a list of the literary works that have so far been proposed as sources for characters, episodes, etc. in Conrad's fiction. (A further exercise would be to judge the certainty and critical significance of a selected group of these source ascriptions.)

(b) Jerry Allen (*The Sea Years of Joseph Conrad* [1965]) and Norman Sherry (*Conrad's Eastern World* and *Conrad's Western World* [1966, 1971]) have ransacked a vast range of non-literary sources, from shipping records and files of Southeast Asian newspapers to old-timers' photograph albums and the records of London dynamitings, to reveal the real-life incidents and characters that were grist to Conrad's mill. How good a case do Allen and Sherry make for the critical significance of their discoveries?

8. Examine the following book-length studies of English romantic poets' reputation and influence in the Victorian period:

Samuel C. Chew, *Byron in England* (1924), Sylva Norman, *Flight of the Skylark* (1954), Katherine M. Peek, *Wordsworth in England* (1943), George H. Ford, *Keats and the Victorians* (1944), Ronald A. Duerksen, *Shelleyan Ideas in Victorian Literature* (1966), and Deborah Dorfman, *Blake in the Nineteenth Century* (1969)

What is the special emphasis of each? Can any be said to cover the whole subject? How many functions does an influence-and-reputation study have? Is it desirable that all these purposes be fulfilled in a single work?

9. Burton's *Anatomy of Melancholy* "exerted an influence upon the early seventeenth century comparable to the work of Freud today" (Thomas Marc Parrott and Robert Hamilton Ball, *A Short View of Elizabethan Drama* [New York, 1943], p. 242). Describe, as specifically as possible, how you would proceed to substantiate or disprove this statement.

10. Anne Bradstreet revealed a sophisticated seventeenth-century knowledge of medicine in "Of the Foure Humours in Mans Constitution" (*The Tenth Muse*, 1650). What was the probable source of this knowledge?

11. Scholars are generally agreed that Émile Zola strongly influenced Frank Norris' style and choice of subject matter. Most of the evidence for this conclusion comes from Norris' novels and journalism. What other evidence exists? How persuasive is it?

12. Identify five articles detailing Thomas Pynchon's use in *Gravity's Rainbow* of popular movies, songs, comic book characters, or radio melodramas from the 1930's and 1940's.

13. In his "Dorothea's Husbands: Some Biographical Speculations" (*TLS*, February 16, 1973, pp. 165–68), Richard Ellmann suggested a number of men whose character traits may have served George Eliot in her delineation of the character of Edward Casaubon in *Middlemarch*. In doing so, Ellmann stirred a lively reaction in the correspondence columns of the *TLS* which lasted for some months. Summarize the major issues in these exchanges and determine which arguments seem most ably supported.

IX. The Historical Background of Literature

1. Collect authentic information sufficient for a substantial explanatory footnote on one of the following topics:

(a) Rules of conduct for cultivated young ladies in Jane Austen's time

(b) Periodicals published by American utopian communities

(c) The social makeup of the congregation who listened to Donne's sermons

(d) Shipboard conditions in the American merchant marine at the time of *Two Years Before the Mast*

(e) The interior arrangement and furniture of medieval inns

(f) Means of household illumination in Dickens' England

(g) The response of the people to the elimination of eleven days from the calendar in 1752

(h) The nature of the medical training Smollett and Goldsmith received

(i) The attitude toward astronomical portents in the Elizabethan age

(j) The social status of actors in Shakespeare's time

(k) Dinner menus and table habits in Dr. Johnson's time

(l) Nocturnal amusements in Pepys's London

(m) The introduction of movable scenery on the London stage

(n) The buying power of the dollar in 1850

(o) Patronage in Washington politics during the Reconstruction period 1865–1877 (*The Gilded Age*)

(p) Russian expatriates in Berlin at the time of the Weimar Republic (for information clarifying action in one of Nabokov's works)

2. Find a contemporary source, preferably a first-hand account or personal reaction (such as a diary entry, passage in a letter, or a newspaper or magazine story) describing each of the following events which are mentioned in English and American literature:

The bad weather in the summer of 1594 (*A Midsummer Night's Dream*, II.i)

The stage war involving the children's companies (*Hamlet*, II.ii)

Fears of the end of the world (Dryden's *Annus Mirabilis*)

The Great Plague (Defoe's *Journal of the Plague Year*)

The execution of the Rev. Dr. William Dodd (Boswell's *Life of Johnson*)

The Gordon riots (Dickens' *Barnaby Rudge*)

"The Dark Day of New England" [May 19, 1780] (Whittier's "Abraham Davenport")

The Convention of Cintra (Wordsworth's tract)

The Luddite riots (Charlotte Brontë's *Shirley*)

Sir Samuel Romilly's suicide (Byron's *Don Juan*, I, xv)

The Peterloo Massacre (Shelley's "The Mask of Anarchy")

The dedication of the Concord monument (Emerson's "Concord Hymn")

Layard's discovery of the great bulls at Nimrud (Rossetti's "The Burden of Nineveh")

Adulteration of food in the 1850's (Tennyson's *Maud*)

The laying of the transatlantic cable (Whitman's "Passage to India")

The funeral of the Duke of Wellington (Tennyson's "Ode on the Death of the Duke of Wellington")

The wreck of the *Deutschland* (Hopkins' poem)

The "Easter Rising" in Ireland (Yeats's "Easter 1916")

The murder of Stanford White by Harry K. Thaw (Doctorow's *Ragtime*)

Barnstorming (Faulkner's *Pylon*)

Marathon dancing (Horace McCoy's *They Shoot Horses, Don't They?*)

The bombing of Dresden (Vonnegut's *Slaughterhouse-Five*)

The march on the Pentagon (Mailer's *The Armies of the Night*)

3. In an essay in a collection, *Dickens and the Twentieth Century*, ed. John Gross and Gabriel Pearson (1962), John Holloway asserted that Dickens' picture of utilitarian education in *Hard Times* was untrue to the facts. Upon what grounds is his thesis contested by Robin Gilmour (*VS*, 11 [1967], 207–24) and K. J. Fielding (*Imagined Worlds*, ed. Maynard Mack and Ian Gregor [London, 1968], pp. 183–203)?

4. Select a literary event which occurred in your locality (e.g., an important writer lived there briefly but vividly, Dickens toured through it, Emerson or Matthew Arnold lectured in the old Opera House), and using as many files as are accessible, report on contemporary newspaper coverage of this subject.

5. Using newspaper and magazine files as your primary source, write a comparative survey of the London and New York (or Boston, Philadelphia, or Cincinnati) theater during a given season in the nineteenth century.

6. You are preparing an edition of H. L. Mencken's *Prejudices* for the use of readers in 1990. The abundance of topical allusions in Mencken requires much annotation. Select one or more of the following essays, and write an explanatory note for every allusion that you think will puzzle a future reader. Add the source of your information in the proper scholarly form.

First series: "Professor Veblen," "The American Magazine"
Second series: "The Sahara of the Bozart"
Third series: "The Forward-Looker," "Education," "The Dismal Science"
Fourth series: "The American Tradition," "Reflections on Human Monogamy," "Totentanz," "Meditations in the Methodist Desert," "The American Novel"
Fifth series: "In Memoriam: W.J.B.," "The Father of Service," the individual parts of "The Fringes of Lovely Letters"
Sixth series: "Journalism in America," "God Help the South!", the individual parts of "Souvenirs of a Book Reviewer," "Invitation to the Dance," "Appendix from Moronia"

If directed, write a short introduction to the essay you have annotated, explaining the background of social, cultural, or literary circumstance which occasioned it.

7. The following sentences come from Emerson's essay "The Poet" (1844):

> Readers of poetry see the factory-village and the railway, and fancy that the poetry of the landscape is broken up by these; for these

works of art are not yet consecrated in their reading; but the poet sees them fall within the great Order not less than the beehive or the spider's geometrical web. Nature adopts them very fast into her vital circles, and the gliding train cars she loves like her own. (*The Complete Works of Ralph Waldo Emerson,* Centenary Edition [Cambridge, Mass., 1903], III, 19.)

In order to annotate these sentences, ascertain the extensiveness of the railway system in the United States in the early 1840's. What first-hand knowledge of the railroad could Emerson have had at that time?

8. For an essay, find out all you can about the "Wanton Wife," a favorite subject of printed broadsides in Renaissance England.

9. How many plays were produced at the Globe Theater? How long did the theater survive?

10. Select an important work of English literature published between 1725 and 1925, or of American literature published between 1825 and 1925, for which the exact date of publication can be ascertained. (For instance, the first two cantos of *Childe Harold* were published on March 10, 1812.) By every means that occurs to you, assemble materials directly bearing on the English *or* American literary scene at that moment. You are allowed a leeway of one week in each direction; for example, if you should select *Childe Harold,* anything occurring between March 3 and 17, 1812, would be admissible.

Write an essay entitled "The Day ———— Was Published." Your purpose is to give the reader, who may be assumed to be well educated but not a specialist, an authoritative, panoramic, and meaningful account of the whole immediate literary (and relevant historical) background. Primary emphasis should be upon the immediate topicality of the book—the various ways in which its subject-matter (ideas, social setting, etc.) is illuminated by the events and attitudes then in the news: the elements in the contemporary scene that made it "timely."

The following are among the topics you might investigate:

(a) The principal non-literary events of the day (political, economic, military, social, etc.)—the sort of things newspapers were reporting and people were worrying over or rejoicing about, from governmental crises to new fashions in women's clothing. (b) What readers of various classes were reading and discussing (bestsellers, magazine articles, literary gossip, etc.): the "literary news" of the hour.

(c) What the author of the book was doing and saying, and what was the nature of his private life.

(d) What each of the important living authors was doing and saying. (Include prospectively important writers, even if at this moment they are still in diapers or in school, as well as writers whose eminence has by this time faded. Account for the whereabouts and activities of as many figures as you can. If no documentary evidence is available for the specific two-week period, cautious inference is permissible; e.g., if a certain poet of the next generation is known to have been in boarding school during the year in question, you are entitled, in the absence of contrary information, to place him there during the period with which you are concerned.)

Practice the technique of skillful condensation. Make every fact count; pack as much as you can into a limited space. Keep your survey continuously interesting. And *document* every statement you make.

X. *The Quality of Essays and Reviews*

1. In "A Mirror for the Lamp" (*PMLA*, 73 [1958], No. 5, Part 2, pp. 45–71) Maynard Mack and other experts printed an interesting list of what they considered the most "outstanding and influential" articles published in *PMLA* over fifty years. Their reasons for their selections provide a good cross-section of opinion on what a successful scholarly paper should be like.

(a) Bearing these criteria in mind, examine the following articles, published in *PMLA* and subsequently awarded the William Riley Parker Prize for articles of distinction appearing in that journal, to determine whether they did in fact deserve such recognition.

David J. De Laura, "Arnold and Carlyle," 79 (1964), 104–29.

Elisabeth W. Schneider, "*The Wreck of the Deutschland: A New Reading*," 81 (1966), 110–22.

Donald Rackin, "Alice's Journey to the End of Night," 81 (1966), 313–26.

Stanley B. Greenfield, "Grammar and Meaning in Poetry," 82 (1967), 377–87.

Rudolf B. Gottfried, "Our New Poet: Archetypal Criticism and *The Faerie Queene*," 83 (1968), 1362–77.

E. D. Lowry, "The Lively Art of *Manhattan Transfer*," 84 (1969), 1628–38.

R. A. Yoder, "Toward the 'Titmouse Dimension': The Development of Emerson's Poetic Style," 87 (1972), 255–70.

Elisabeth W. Schneider, "Prufrock and After: The Theme of Change," 87 (1972), 1103–19.

George T. Wright, "The Lyric Present: Simple Present Verbs in English Poems," 89 (1974), 563–79.

Walter J. Ong, "The Writer's Audience is Always a Fiction," 90 (1975), 9–21.

R. G. Peterson, "Critical Calculations: Measure and Symmetry in Literature," 91 (1976), 367–75.

Evelyn J. Hinz, "Hierogamy versus Wedlock: Types of Marriage Plots and Their Relationship to Genres of Prose Fiction," 91 (1976), 900–13.

(b) Using the same standards, rate the articles appearing in the current issue of one of the leading scholarly journals. Are any of them of award-winning caliber? Should any of them not have been printed?

2. Select a major work published since 1970 of bibliography, biography, or criticism, or an edition of correspondence, or an edition of a literary work. Acquaint yourself thoroughly with the book. Then locate, read, and take notes on at least eight scholarly reviews of it, and write a paper entitled "————: A Review of Reviews," in which you describe and evaluate the various critics' estimates of the book. What various conceptions of the nature and purpose of a scholarly review are represented in the notices you read? What do *you* think constitutes an ideal scholarly review?

3. The following is a representative list of reviews which, because of their controversial subject-matter, made special demands upon their respective authors' fund of scholarly decorum. How effectively, in each case, does the reviewer reconcile the sometimes conflicting duties of forthright criticism and professional courtesy? Does the tone of any of them strike you as being inadmissible in scholarly discourse?

Morse Peckham, "Recent Studies in Nineteenth-Century English Literature," *SEL*, 3 (1963), 595–611. (Contrast Jonas Barish, "Recent Studies in the Elizabethan and Jacobean Drama," *ibid.*, 6 [1966], 357–79.)

William E. Fredeman, review of Lona Mosk Packer's *Christina Rossetti*, *VS*, 8 (1964), 71–77.

James Rieger, review of K. N. Cameron's edition of *The Esdaile Notebook*, *Essays in Criticism*, 14 (1964), 401–9.

Douglas Bush, "Calculus Racked Him," *SEL*, 6 (1966), 1–6.

Brewster Ghiselin, "The Burden of Proof," *Sewanee Review*, 74 (1966), 527–40.

Robert W. Dent, " 'Quality of Insight' in Elizabethan and

Jacobean Tragedy," *MP*, 63 (1966), 252–56.

U. C. Knoepflmacher, "Mr. Haight's George Eliot: 'Wahrheit und Dichtung,'" *VS*, 12 (1969), 422–30.

J. M. Osborn, review of Peter Quennell's *Alexander Pope, PQ*, 48 (1969), 380–82.

Three reviews of Kathleen Raine's *Blake and Tradition:*
by Morton D. Paley, *ELN*, 7 (1970), 304–10;
by G. E. Bentley, Jr., *UTQ*, 9 (1960), 88–93;
by Jean H. Hagstrum, *MP*, 68 (1970), 76–82.

Donald T. Torchiana, review of Denis Donoghue's *Jonathan Swift: A Critical Introduction*, *PQ*, 49 (1970), 383–85.

George H. Ford, "Leavises, Levi's, and Some Dickensian Priorities," *Nineteenth-Century Fiction*, 26 (1971), 95–113.

Fredson Bowers, "McKerrow Revisited," *PBSA*, 67 (1973), 109–24.

4. Read Grant T. Webster, "A Potter's Field of Critical Rhetoric," *College English*, 27 (1966), 320–22, then examine a dozen or so reviews in current issues of scholarly periodicals. How many of Webster's "ploys" do you find there? How many can you add to Webster's list?

5. In 1979, a new annual called simply *Review* began publication. Each volume contains a large variety of critical reviews. Briefly describe the range of different types and techniques of scholarly criticism they exemplify.

Index